AF513328

RELEVANCE OF AMBEDKAR TODAY

RELEVANCE OF AMBEDKAR TODAY

Editor

Sudhir Singh

PENTAGON PRESS

Relevance of Ambedkar Today
Editor: Sudhir Singh

ISBN 978-81-8274-947-4

First Published in 2017

Copyright © RESERVED

All rights reserved. No part of this publication may be reproduced, stored in a retrieval system, or transmitted in any form or by any means, electronic, mechanical, photocopying, recording or otherwise, without the prior written permission of the Publisher.

Disclaimer: The views and opinions expressed in the book are the individual assertion of the Authors. The Publisher does not take any responsibility for the same in any manner whatsoever. The same shall solely be the responsibility of the Authors.

Published by
PENTAGON PRESS
206, Peacock Lane, Shahpur Jat
New Delhi-110049
Phones: 011-64706243, 26491568
Telefax: 011-26490600
email: rajan@pentagonpress.in
website: www.pentagonpress.in

Aegean Offset Printer, Greater Noida, UP.

Contents

Preface

India is a divine land where great souls mark their presence at regular intervals to ensure justice. Justice has been the hallmark of Indian civilisation much before the idea of justice was conceived by its modern harbingers who hail from the Western world. We have a series of this stream of great people. And needless to say, Ambedkar was one of the most important among them. One of the cardinal weaknesses of modern democracy has been inequality among the masses. There is hardly any democracy in contemporary world where such inequalities do not prevail. However, democracy has evolved as a significant structural mechanism to reduce inequalities.

Ambedkar was one of the most visionary leaders of our freedom struggle. Despite his barrage of differences with Gandhi, he had great respect for him. Both had different ideas and opinions when it came to the ways with which to construct a strong country, but their goals were the same. When India got independence, Gandhi was instrumental in getting Ambedkar nominated as the chairman of the drafting committee to shape the constitution of the country. Ambedkar proved true as perceived by the founders of the country, and framed an excellent constitution. This was highlighted by T.T. Krishnamachari who was himself a Member of the Drafting Committee when, in one of his speeches in the Constituent Assembly, he said:

> "The House is perhaps aware that of the seven members nominated by you, one had resigned from the House and was replaced. One died, and was not replaced. One was away in America and his place was not filled up, and another person was engaged in State affairs, and there was a void to that extent. One or two people were far away from Delhi and perhaps reasons of

> health did not permit them to attend. So it happened ultimately that the burden of drafting this Constitution fell on Dr. Ambedkar, and I have no doubt that we are grateful to him for having achieved this task in a manner which is undoubtedly commendable.'"[1]

He had not only understood this problem in a comprehensive manner but had ensured its solution through constitutional mechanism. It was Ambedkar who provided new dimensions to the concept of justice. We regard him as the 'Champion of Social justice'. Ambedkar had a liberal concept of justice. Like Gandhi, for Ambedkar, justice is simply another name for liberty, equality and fraternity. In this sense, the core value of Ambedkar's concept of justice is human equality, equal distribution of the welfare concept of the state and discrimination-free society. Thus, the spirit of social justice, according to Ambedkar, gives a significant place to mutual sympathy and respect.

Whatever he achieved, that would have been possible for his strength of character which manifested his individual charisma. As a statesman, scholar and crusader of the downtrodden, Ambedkar has left an incredible impression on Indian history. He has been an inspiring force for all across the globe who wish to fight against any kind of discrimination. His contribution to uplift the downtrodden made him a cult figure among the have-nots across the globe.

Due to parochial interests, Ambedkar has been confined mainly as the harbinger of reservation. Conveniently, people have forgotten that there is hardly any relevant arena where Ambedkar had not given due attention to ensure national interests. For Ambedkar, dignity to all deprived sectors of the society will ensure real notion of social justice. Ambedkar was a great Champion of women and human rights as well. He was one of the maiden leaders during the formation of the constitution who gave specific rights to women to safeguard their basic dignity. Today, even after two decades of 21st century, women are suffering multiple discriminations. Unlike others, Ambedkar never shed crocodile tears for women but gave them actual legal protection to fight against discrimination. Likewise, as the earliest law minister, he laid the foundation of modern labour rights. Today, despite our sustainable growth which has overtaken China in financial year 2015-

2016, our rural sector is far behind in this path of sustainable development. It is also a reality that without bringing this sector into the mainstream of development, we could not ensure all-round development. Ambedkar was concerned about this situation and as an economist, gave solid solutions. It has been rightly stated by Dr. Krishna Gopal, joint general secretary of RSS, in his interview that appeared in the Economic Times (22 June 2015):

> "Dr Ambedkar had flagged the challenges of small land holdings in rural India and suggested remedies. He believed that industrialisation of India was the soundest remedy for rural agricultural problems of India. Even today, 60 per cent of population is rural-agricultural, but its contribution to the GDP is below 15 per cent. There is a need for reforms for this 60 per cent population. Their dependence on farming needs to be changed. It can be done through industrialisation. Small holdings are not viable. A way needs to be found out."

It is important to mention here that Ambedkar was in favour of common civil code, which is provided within the ambit of Article 44 of our Constitution. Ambedkar was of the opinion that it will ensure justice to all without any discrimination. On the question of Uniform Civil Code, answering various members, Dr. Ambedkar said that there was already in the country a uniform code of laws covering almost every aspect of human relationship. To support his contention, he quoted a number of laws which operated throughout the territory of India. According to him, the only area where the civil law had not been able to evade so far was marriage and succession. He, therefore, found nothing wrong in incorporating certain portions of the Hindu law. He formulated civil code applicable to all citizens. These provisions, in his view, would be incorporated not because they were within the Hindu law but because they were found to be the most suitable. Expressing concern towards the sentiments of the Muslim community in this particular matter, he declared in the Assembly: I quite realise their feelings in the matter, but I think they have read rather too much, which merely proposes that the State shall endeavour to secure a civil code for the citizens of the country.[2]

But unfortunately, due to pseudo secularism, it has not been implemented till date. India's first Prime Minister Pandit Jawaharlal

Nehru assured the Parliament that it will be implemented within 10 years. Today, even after 69 years of our independence, it has not been implemented despite many directives of the Supreme Court. All declared harbingers of women's rights are silent even today, and do not demand common civil code due to vote bank politics; Ambedkar did it just after independence. He was working tirelessly for women's rights because he believed that without developing women at par with man, India could not become a strong country. His passionate voice for the women's cause is remarkable in the backdrop of the global status of women today. For the first time, a woman has become Mayor of Rome (Italy) in 2016. After 240 years of existence, America witnessed a woman (Hillary Clinton) candidate for Presidency in 2016. Because of solid foundational work done by Ambedkar, many women have occupied top positions in our country, which is not the case in European or North American countries, who claimed to be the nursery of democracy. Ambedkar gave equal rights to women irrespective of any categorisation.

He was also a great harbinger of nationalism. This is an aspect which has been left by majority of scholars who have done work on him till date due to their parochial political ideologies. Ambedkar had exclusive knowledge of foreign policy. In June 2016, former foreign secretary Rasgotra gave an account of Himalayan blunders committed by first PM Nehru, including permanent membership at the UN, Kashmir and (Tibet) China front. It is significant to mention here that Nehru was arrogantly claiming his command over realm of foreign policy. In contrast, Patel and Ambedkar never claimed themselves as knowledgeable about contours of foreign policy but both had an excellent knowledge and will power to promote our national interests through foreign policy. It is pertinent to mention here that time, particularly after independence, was quite sensitive for the formulations of our foreign policy. If Nehru would have been given heed to sagacious Kautilayan advice of Patel and Ambedkar, the standing of India today at the global table of governance would have been much different. India could have been a member of UN Security Council in 1960s itself, for which our diplomacy is doing Bharatnatyam today; but despite that goal of becoming UN Security Council permanent member seems to a remote possibility at least for immediate future. Beside that, Ambedkar gave special direction for the all-round development of the country.

He had an excellent economic policy. He insisted on the importance of education and termed it as a tool for the removal of ignorance.

Democratic socialism is the key note of his political thought and constitutionalism is the only way to achieve it.

India accorded recognition to China after its independence. Dr. Ambedkar wished that India should have accorded this recognition to Tibet instead of China, and there would have been no Sino-Indian border conflict today. He was then the Member of Rajya Sabha, and he said the following to Prime Minister Pandit Jawaharlal Nehru in front of a full house:

> "Our Prime Minister is depending on the Panchsheel which has been adopted by Comrade Mao, and the Panchsheel in which one of the clauses is the No-Aggression Treaty on Tibet. I am indeed surprised that our Hon'ble Prime Minister is taking this 'Panchsheel' seriously. Hon'ble Members of the House, you must know that Panchsheel is one of the significant parts of the Buddha Dharma. If Shri Mao had even an iota of faith in Panchsheel, he would have treated the Buddhists in his country in a different manner. Panchsheel has no place in politics. The truth inherent in Panchsheel is that morality is forever changing.
>
> There is nothing called morality. You can abide by your promises in accordance with today's morality and by the same propriety, you may violate your own promise simply because tomorrow's morality will have different demands... in my opinion our, Prime Minister will realise the truth in my words when the situation matures further... I don't really know what is going to happen. By letting China take control over Lhasa (Tibetan Capital), the Prime Minister has in a way helped the Chinese to bring their armies on the Indian borders. Any victor who annexes Kashmir can directly reach Pathankot, and I know it for sure that he can reach the Prime Minister's House also."

In the NSG membership, we have witnessed China's all-round opposition. In this issue, China has exposed herself as the in-built enemy of India. This has happened in 2016 and Ambedkar had predicated this kind of irresponsible Chinese behaviour in 1954 itself. This vindicates the level of pragmatism of Ambedkar even in the realm of foreign policy. Due to certain ideological commitments, many established pundits of foreign policy only mentioned greatness of Pandit Nehru about his innovation in the realm of foreign policy, but they have conveniently forgotten Kautilayan pragmatism of Ambedkar. It will be tough task for any innovative researcher to find any foreign policy opinion of Ambedkar, but almost all books written since independence till 2000 will easily find lucrative interpretations of Pandit Nehru's meticulous knowledge about world affairs. After knowing the gamut of foreign policy advices given by Ambedkar to Nehru, one will firmly believe about the Himalayan blunders committed by Pandit Nehru in the realm of foreign policy.

Ambedkar was a great nationalist. He sacrificed his life for the strengthening of the country. Ambedkar had given his thoughts for every walks of our national life. Dr. Ambedkar gave expression to his firm faith in a united India (he was participating in the debate on the historic Objectives Resolution moved by Jawaharlal Nehru).

"I have got not the slightest doubt in my mind as to the future evolution and the ultimate shape of the social, political and economic structure of this great country. I know today we are divided politically, socially and economically. We are a group of warring camps and I may go even to the extent of confessing that I am probably one of the leaders of such a camp. But Sir, with all this, I am quite convinced that given the time and circumstances, nothing in the world will prevent this country from becoming one: with all our castes and creeds, I have not the slightest hesitation that we shall in some form be a united people."[3]

Ambedkar was concerned to sustain the progress of the country, for which unity and integrity had to be the bedrock. As a true nationalist, he had no hesitation in condemning all those he perceived as acting against the core interests of the country. His (Dr. Ambedkar) concluding speech just before the formal acceptance of the newly-prepared draft of the Constitution on November 26, 1949, in itself is a historic document for its comprehension and futuristic vision. In the contemporary context, it is relevant to recall how he had expressed his apprehensions, particularly about those who would try their best to sabotage what 'We the people' were giving to ourselves on January 26, 1950.

The communists and 'those who think alike' and consistently shout hoarse as being the sole protectors of the weaker sections, never hesitate to sabotage democratic functioning and, to achieve their sinister designs, are ready to sacrifice national interests:

> "The condemnation of the Constitution largely comes from two quarters—the Communist Party and the Socialist Party. Why do they condemn the Constitution? Is it because it really is a bad Constitution? I venture to say no. The Communist Party wants a Constitution based upon the principle of the Dictatorship of the Proletariat. They condemn the Constitution because it is based upon parliamentary democracy. The socialists want two things. The first thing they want is that if they come in power, the Constitution must give them the freedom to nationalise or socialise all private property without payment of compensation. The second thing that the socialists want is that the Fundamental Rights mentioned in the Constitution must be absolute and without any limitations so that if their party fails to come into power, they would have the unfettered freedom not merely to criticise, but also to overthrow the State."[4]

Dr. Ambedkar was concerned for the unity and integrity of the country. According to him, "My mind is so full of the future of our country that I feel I ought to take this occasion to give expression to some of my reflections thereon. On January 26, 1950, India will be an independent country *(cheers)*. What would happen to her independence? Will she maintain her independence or will she lose it again? This is the first thought that comes to my mind. It is not that India was never an independent country. The point is that she once lost the independence she had. Will she lose it a second time? It is this thought which makes me most anxious for the future. What perturbs me greatly is the fact that not only has India once before lost her independence, but she lost it by the infidelity and treachery of some of her own people.

In the invasion of Sind by Mohammed-bin-Qasim, the military commanders of King Dahar accepted bribes from the agents of Mohammed-bin-Qasim and refused to fight on the side of their king. It was Jaichand who invited Mohammed Gori to invade India and fight against Prithviraj and promised him the help of himself and the Solanki kings. When Shivaji was fighting for the liberation of Hindus, the other Maratha noblemen and the Rajput Kings were fighting the battle on the side of Mughal emperors. When the British were trying to destroy the Sikh rulers, Gulab Singh, the principal commander of the Sikhs, sat silent and did not help to save the Sikh kingdom."[5]

Unfortunately, Ambedkar was analysed with the prism of parochial politics till the dominance of the single party got dismantled in the 1990s. The propellers of this line has only highlighted that Ambedkar talks a lot and gave it formal constitutional validity to affirmative measures in order to ensure social justice. Right from our Vedic literature till John Rawls, we have witnessed the notion of social justice. Much before this Western discourse of social justice, Lord Buddha also gave an earliest shape to the notion of social justice. I am intended to highlight that India is a divine land from where in every era, voice for social justice and human rights were given. Ambedkar was one of the important continuity within this sagacious heritage of India.

In the mainstream academics, Ambedkar still posseses a marginalised space. This prevailing discourse is changing very fastly though Prime Minister Narendra Modi-led NDA government has commemorated his 125th anniversary with a new zeal in 2016. This de jure acceptance of Ambedkar as a nation builder along with Gandhi, Sardar Patel, Subhash Bose and Pandit Nehru compelled academic world to think differently as well.

Since independence till 1990, Ambedkar was perceived as an icon of one particular segment of the society. Both Vajpayee and Modi government have not only thrown this image into the dustbin but in addition, perceived him as a great nation builder, and honestly accepted the prevailing socio-economic deficit in our society and vowed to fill the gap. PM Modi has stressed that without bringing deprived sectors into the mainstream, India could not achieve its desired goal of sustainable development.

India has maintained the growth rate of over 6 per cent since last two decades, and for the first time in history overtaken China in terms of annual growth of economy in FY of 2015-2016. According to the gamut of global economic pundits, India is all set to sustain this growth saga in next decades and by 2050, will be among the top three global economics.

After nearly a century as the world's preeminent economic power, the United States is projected to relinquish this title to China in 2032.

Rapid annual growth of 5.6 per cent and a strengthening currency—the Renminbi's real exchange rate against the dollar is predicted to appreciate by more than 1 per cent per year—will drive China's US dollar GDP up from $3.3 trillion in 2009 to $46.3 trillion in 2050—20 per cent larger than that of the United States in real dollar terms and 90 per cent larger in PPP terms.[6]

The world in 2050 will also be profoundly different in human terms. Rapid growth in the emerging economies will pull hundreds of millions of people out of absolute poverty, leaving only a small fraction of the G20 population behind. Absolute poverty will, however, remain a significant, though much smaller, phenomenon in Africa.

In 2005, the World Bank estimated that over 1.3 billion people—over one quarter of the world's population—lived in extreme poverty, consuming less than $1.25 a day in PPP terms. Nearly twice this number, or half the world's population, lived on less than $2.00 a day. By 2050, no country in the G20 will have more than 5 per cent of the population living in extreme poverty; significant portions of society will still be living on less than $2.00 a day though.[7]

Poverty rates are expected to decline significantly in Indonesia, Brazil, Mexico and Turkey, but growth in China and India—nations that were home to 48 per cent of the world's population living on $1.25 a day in 2005—will be the driving force behind this shift. Over the past 25 years, over 600 million people emerged from poverty in China (excluding China, global poverty has actually increased since 1981); from 2005 to 2050, China and India will be responsible for lifting 600 million more people from the most extreme forms of poverty.[8]

India is predicted to have the most rapid growth—5.9 per cent annually—of all G20 countries; the modest current size of India's economy will prevent it from surpassing either China or the United States in real US dollar terms though. India's PPP GDP, however, will be nearly 90 per cent as large as that of the United States. A growing population—India is expected to become the world's most populous nation in 2031—will push US dollar GDP to $15.4 trillion in 2050, over fourteen times its current level.[9]

Despite these positive formulations, one of the serious challenges in this process will be sustainable widening income deficit between haves and have-nots. Ambedkar outlined solutions of this problem.

He was a great nation builder, and he gave ideas to resolve all relevant problems...and these structural suggestions are more relevant than his lifetime.

This book is intended to asses Ambedkar's idea with the new prism. Till recently, Ambedkar was deliberately perceived as a sectarian leader. The crystal reality is that he was a towering nation builder and his ideas are taking care of every walk of our national life. He suggested structured mechanism for the resolution of all important national problems. We believe that if we will adhere with Ambedkar's mechanism of resolution of our national problems, India will not only sustain its desired growth rate despite a gamut of prevailing global odds, but also become an important global power.

This book is, therefore, an attempt to take all these ideas of Ambedkar into consideration and is structurally intended to highlight these crucial aspects for consideration for all those who are concerned. We are hopeful that this book will provide a new holistic academic debate about Ambedkar, and will be fruitful for readers and policy formulators alike.

Sudhir Singh

END NOTES

1. *Constitutional Assembly Debate*, 17 December 1946, p. 100 .
2. *Constitutional Assembly Debate,* 17 December 1946, p. 100.
3. *Text of the Speech of Dr. B.R. Ambedkar Delivered in the Constituent Assembly on* 17 *December* 1946 *on the Resolution regarding Aims and Objects.*
4. Prof. J.S Rajput Article, *The Pioneer,* New Delhi, 13 March 2016.
5. Ibid.
6. Uri Dadush and Benntt Stancil' The World Order in 2050, *Carnegie Endowment for International Peace*, Washington, April 2010, p.16.
7. Martin Ravallion and Shaohua Chen have pioneered poverty analysis and also developed PovcalNet—a leading source of poverty data, including various methods for estimating future poverty levels. Ravallion's and Chen's projections typically rely on computing poverty elasticities relative to household income growth. This method is more data intensive than the method employed in the text, and is also more appropriate for short to medium term projections. See, for example, Martin Ravallion and Shaohua Chen, "What Can New Survey Data Tell Us about Recent Changes in Distribution and Poverty?", *World Bank Economic Review,* vol. 11, no. 2, (1997), pp. 357-82, and Martin Ravallion, "Can high-inequality developing countries escape absolute poverty?", *Economic Letters* 56 (1997) pp. 51-57.
8. Op. cit., No. 6, p.17.
9. Op. cit., No. 6, p.17.

List of Contributors

Dr. Alok Kumar Gupta is Associate Professor, Central University of South Bihar, Gaya, Bihar.

Prof. Anuradha Mukherjee is Professor, Department of International Studies, Jadavpur University, West Bengal.

Ms. Binita Batsa is Research Scholar, Jawaharlal Nehru University, New Delhi.

Dr. Chandra Mohan Uppadhyaya is Associate Professor, Department of Political Science, Kishan Degree College, Bahraich, Uttar Pradesh.

Mr. Daniel Debbarma is Assistant Professor, Department of Education, Govt. Degree College, Dharamnagar, Tripura.

Dr. Deepak Yadav is Assistant Professor, Department of Political Science, Kalindi College, University of Delhi, New Delhi.

Prof. J.S Rajput, former Director, NCERT and Member of New Education Policy, MHRD, Govt. of India.

Dr. Kaushiki Dasgupta is Assistant Professor, Department of History, Gour Banga University, West Bengal.

Dr. Krishna Gopal was Librarian, Jawaharlal Nehru University, New Delhi.

Dr. Mridusmita Baruah is Assistant Professor, Department of English, Dyal Singh College (Evening), University of Delhi, New Delhi.

Ms. Nitumoni Kakati is Research Scholar, Indira Gandhi National Open University, New Delhi.

Dr. Pratyaa Dutta is Assistant Professor, Department of Political Science, Vidyasagar Evening College, University of Calcutta, Kolkata.

Dr. Ruchika Singh is Assistant Professor, Department of History, I.P. College, University of Delhi, New Delhi.

Dr. Shweta Singh is Assistant Professor, Department of History, Dyal Singh College, University of Delhi, New Delhi.

Prof. S.N. Choudhury is Director, Rajiv Gandhi Centre for Contemporary Studies, Baraktullah University, Bhopal.

Prof. Swaraj Basu is Director, School of Social Sciences, Indira Gandhi National Open University, New Delhi.

Shri Sudhir Gupta is Member of Parliament (Lok-Sabha) from Mandsore, Madhya Pradesh.

Dr.S. Prabhakar is Joint Director, Lok-Sabha, New Delhi.

Dr. Suresh R is Associate Professor, Department of Political Science, Kerala University, Kerala.

Prof. Tridib Chakraborty is Professor, Department of International Studies, Jadavpur University, West Bengal.

1

Architect of the Indian Constitution: Role of B.R. Ambedkar

Alok Kumar Gupta

United Nations observed Bhim Rao 'Babasaheb' Ambedkar's 125th birth anniversary in April 2016, and showcased the universal appeal of the principal architect of India's Constitution, who fought caste injustice and stood for social reforms. It is indeed a matter of great pleasure for every Indian that one of their leaders attained a stature that has been celebrated by a multilateral international institution. This is more so when political parties across India have been fighting for appropriation and misappropriation of the leaders of yesteryears irrespective of the political ideology and party they were affiliated to and served during their lifetime. As far as Ambedkar is concerned, indeed, from being an icon solely of Dalit parties, his legacy is enjoying a revival with political parties across India's ideological spectrum. Therefore, it is of great significance that with inequalities a rising concern and cause for political turmoil in Western countries, Ambedkar's appeal has reached Western shores as well.[1] This makes it increasingly relevance that role and contributions of Ambedkar must be developed and discussed in proper perspective.

Ambedkar's own country too celebrated his birth anniversary with much fanfare, but largely as a political symbol to gain political mileage. While Prime Minister belonging to ruling party went to Mhow in

Madhya Pradesh, the birth place of Ambedkar and observed it as 'Social Harmony Day'; the opposition Congress party organised a big rally in Nagpur, the headquarters of Rashtriya Swayam Sangh (RSS).[2] He was portrayed by both the parties as a champion of social engineering. The fact remains that Ambedkar believed that caste hierarchies are an intrinsic part of Hinduism and that is why he converted to Buddhism. Ambedkar also resisted that appropriation of the caste hierarchies by contemporary leftists as well. Therefore, he may be regarded as a critique of Hinduism and the caste hierarchies within. He disagreed with Mahatma Gandhi's philosophy of self-governing villages as India's foundation, viewing them instead as dens of inequality. He opposed insertion of the terms 'socialist' and 'secular' in the preamble to the Constitution. He also opposed Article 370 and was an ardent supporter of the Uniform Civil Code.[3] However, owing to his seminal role in the framing of the Indian Constitution, Dr. B.R. Ambedkar is regarded as the 'Father of the Indian Constitution' and that the Constitution is his brainchild. He was the chief architect of the Indian Constitution as well as an astute constitutionalist. This paper is an endeavour to discuss the role of Ambedkar as an Architect of Indian Constitution and the controversies that have been raised so far.

Ambedkar: A Brief Profile

Dr. Ambedkar is popularly known all over India as the chief architect of the Indian Constitution. However, his efforts to eradicate social evils were remarkable and that is why he is also called the 'messiah' of the Dalits and downtrodden in India. He was a crusader against Untouchability and the caste system. The prevailing discrimination within Hinduism on the basis of caste hierarchy prompted him to eventually embrace Buddhism in 1956. He contributed immensely towards the philosophy of Indian Constitution; constitutional jurisprudence; and also defined the will, goal and the vision of India. He rightly pointed to the British Government, "Let the consent of the people and not the accident of logic is the touchstone of your new Constitution." His role in its making and adoption can be appreciated fully by considering, in an objective way, the nature of the political society he provided for free India, and secondly the legal and constitutional restraints upon authority in the form of Fundamental Rights. He gave free India its legal framework, and to the people, the basis of their freedom. He was a firm believer in political and social democracy. He said, "The third thing we must do is not be content with mere political democracy. We must note that our political democracy cannot last unless there lies at the base of it social democracy. What does social democracy mean? It means a way of life which recognises liberty, equality and fraternity as the principles of life."[4] Ambedkar advocated his economic doctrine of "state socialism" in the Draft Constitution. He proposed state ownership of agriculture with a collectivised method of cultivation and a modified form of state socialism in the field of industry. But due to strong opposition in the Constituent Assembly, he could not incorporate his scheme of state socialism under the fundamental rights as a part of the Constitution.[5] As a matter of fact he was an economist and his various scholarly works and speeches indicate his deep understanding of the problems faced by the Indian society. He was appointed as the nation's first Law Minister and posthumously awarded the Bharat Ratna in 1990.[6] His contribution was significant, substantial and spectacular and is deeply rooted in his strivings for ensuring justice—social, economic and political—for one and all. Ambedkar thus was a true crusader against the different forms of social discrimination and always fought for the same.

The Indian Constitution: Ambedkar's Legacy

One may read a clear message into the statue of Ambedkar with the Book of Constitution at the entrance gate of Indian Parliament that Indian Constitution was the handiwork of Dr. Ambedkar. The message is writ large not only to the people of India but also to the outside world. However, his contributions in the making of Constitution have always been a matter of debate since this honour has been bestowed upon him by the posterity. The common-sense approach to it makes it obvious that such a herculean task cannot be the handiwork of one person or even a few. As an individual a personality like Ambedkar could have been instrumental in giving a broader direction to the task or may have contributed towards making a part of it which might have been related to his vision and philosophy. Therefore, such advocacies and expositions of giving the entire credit to one person, for whatever reason, belittles the contributions made by the jurists and various other stalwarts who were members of the Constituent Assembly. This also belies the history of drafting the Constitution. Therefore, the author makes an endeavour to enumerate the cross-section of opinion before concluding the entire credit to Ambedkar so far as Constitution-Making is concerned.

Whatever be the controversy, the fact remains that Columbia University at its Special convocation on June 5, 1952 conferred the LLD degree (*Honouris Causa*) on Dr. Ambedkar in recognition of his drafting the Constitution of India. The Citation read, "The degree is being conferred in recognition of the work done by him in connection with the drafting of India's Constitution."[7] The University hailed him as "one of India's leading citizens, a great social reformer and valiant upholder of human rights.

The Making of Indian Constitution: Role of Ambedkar

The Constitution of India as it emerged from the Constituent Assembly is said to be chiefly the handiwork of an astute constitutionalist Dr. B.R. Ambedkar. His role in its making however requires to be discussed in an objective manner. Ambedkar claims that the attitudes of many of the Assembly members were not positive towards him. There are reasons for that, firstly he was a non-congress man and secondly he was not a staunch follower of Gandhi. There were other members who were jurists, scholars, statesmen, social activists and political leaders in the Assembly but he was given this stupendous task of piloting the Draft Constitution.[8] Therefore, the apprehensions of Ambedkar about attitudes of others do not count much as the task assigned to him was of a very high order.

It was during the 1990s that India witnessed a wave of Ambedkarisation. Many politicians started describing Ambedkar as the 'Father' or 'The Maker' of Indian Constitution. On the other hand, experts on Constitutional law expressed reservation to such expressions, because both the Constituent Assembly and its Drafting Committee headed by Dr. Ambedkar were the formal centres of work. The real place of work was the Congress Working Committee, which took all the important decisions there. The prominent role was played by leaders like Nehru, Patel, Rajendra Prasad or Constitutional jurists like Alladi Krishna Swami Ayaar, K.M. Munshi and others. It was frankly admitted by Mahavir Tyagi, one of the members of Drafting

Committee, and Dr. Ambedkar himself that their hands were tied and they were only carrying out the wishes of the majority.[9] Ambedkar had recognition as an intellectual having his own philosophy and interpretations, but he lacked leadership qualities and mass appeal. Therefore, it may be possible that the philosophy behind the Constitution was envisioned by the Congress Working Committee and the details were to be worked out by Drafting Committee. However, this again has been contradicted by many as discussed later in the chapter.

Ambedkar as the Chief Architect of the Indian Constitution: How and Why?

History of Constituent Assembly and India's struggle for independence is replete with admirers, staunch supporters, critiques and worst critique of Ambedker. Such a debate is quite usual about any past or present political icon, as there happens to be 'politics of political icon' as well. This becomes more obvious when the given political icon happens to be a representative of a particular community based on caste, class, religion or any other primordial loyalty; and he is regarded as hero or messiah by the members of that particular community. Such political icon leads to a rivalry and competition among the existing political parties as each of them compete to project him or her as their revered leader. The reason behind such a competition is the political vote bank. Massaging the image of such political icon brings the vote of that particular community to that political party which is comparatively more successful in its endeavour towards luring the community through different strategy.

Ambedkar has been one of the leading representatives of Dalit community in India and worked for the cause of upliftment of the downtrodden classes and castes of India. Hence, every political party in India tries to project as its own leader to woe the votes of Dalit community in its own favour. This becomes more obvious whenever there is an impending election either at the national level or in some states of India. However, irrespective of what political parties are involved into; the journalists and academicians try to bring the truth to the people as political parties in their endeavour to serve their selfish interests may falsify the contributions of such political leaders either way. Therefore, it makes it imperative to discover the truth about the real contributions of Dr. Ambedkar towards constitution making, even though this is quite a complex task as many of the information may have been distorted by now. Yet an endeavour to decipher the contributions of Ambedkar in making of the constitution is essential to mitigate the confusion and put the things in right perspective.

Dr. B. Pattabhi Sitaramayya, the veteran Congress historian, referred to the 'steam-roller intellect' that Dr. Ambedkar brought to bear upon the magnificent and tremendous task of framing the Constitution, irresistible, indomitable, unconquerable, levelling down tall palms and short poppies, whatever he felt right he stood by, regardless of consequences."[10] Almost in the same tone, appreciating the great services rendered by Ambedkar, the chief architect of the Indian Constitution, T.T. Krishnamachari, one of the members of the Constituent Assembly, said in the Assembly, "...the House is perhaps, aware that of the seven members nominated by you, one had resigned from the House, and was not replaced. One died and was not replaced. One was away in America and his place was not filled up and another person was engaged in State Affairs and there was void to that extent. One or two people were far away from Delhi and, perhaps, for reasons of health did not attend. So it happened ultimately that the burden of drafting the Constitution fell on Ambedkar and I have no doubt that we are grateful to him for having achieved this task in a manner which is undoubtedly commendable."[11]

There is hardly any doubt that Ambedkar has made immense contribution to the philosophy of Indian Constitution and to the constitutional jurisprudence; and this is universally accepted also. However, what is irksome is that this has led to the belief that Ambedkar was the sole guiding force of the Constitution. He was the chief architect of the Constitution to define the will, goal and the vision of India. He is regarded as the father of the Constitution to define the will, and the Constitution is his brainchild. Therefore, whatever principles have been incorporated in the constitution, Ambedkar is regarded as a source of it.[12] Therefore, this has been deliberated at length in the later section of this paper. Prime Minister J.L. Nehru, while paying tribute to Ambedkar in the Lok Sabha said that Dr. Ambedkar had played the most important part in the framing of India's constitution.

He has identified two facts to this effect: (i) Dr. Ambedkar played a very constructive role in the making of the Constitution even before his election to the Drafting Committee, and (ii) No one took greater trouble and care over the Constitution making than Dr. Ambedkar.[13]

Dr. M.V Paylee, the well-known Constitutional historian and author, made the remark about Dr. Ambedkar, "In the Constituent Assembly none else was so forceful and persuasive in arguments, clear and lucid in expression, quick and arresting in debate. And yet, he had always the generosity to concede the credit to a critic who made a valid point and to frankly acknowledge it. Ambedkar's contribution to the Constitution is undoubtedly of the highest order. Indeed, he deserves to be called the father or the Chief Architect of the Constitution of India."[14]

Ambedkar was one of the chosen among other equally available members of the Constituent Assembly simply because of the treasure, the treasure of his intelligence, the treasure of his keen knowledge of the subject, the treasure of his interests in constitutionalism, and the treasure of his professionalism of being an advocate. It was in 1946 when he became the Chairman of the Drafting Committee, Ambedkar emphasised and took initiative and deliberatively introduced the principle of reservation for Dalits in Parliament, educational institutions and in government jobs. The work done by Dr. Ambedkar in various sub-committees of the Assembly was considered very useful and convinced the Congress bosses beyond doubt that the legislation and solidification of freedom would not be easy without the services of Dr. Ambedkar. The Congress which had earlier opposed tooth and nail his entry into the Assembly came forward and sponsored his candidature. In his letter dated 30th June 1947 Dr. Rajendra Prasad, President of the Constituent Assembly requested Mr. B.G. Kher, the then Prime Minister of Bombay to elect Dr. Ambedkar immediately. Accordingly, Dr. Ambedkar was re-elected in July 1947 from Bombay as a member of the Constituent Assembly and on 29th August 1947 the Assembly unanimously elected him as Chairman of the Drafting Committee which assigned him the task of framing the Constitution.[15] Once elected he forgot his personal anxiety and joined hands with the Congress in general and Pandit Nehru in particular as both were ready to sink their differences and agreed to work together for the betterment of the newly born nation. However, it must not be mistaken that he had greed for the position he was offered by the Congress, rather he was bold and firm with his demands and whenever he got chances he criticised the government also.

Dr. Rajendra Prasad, the President of the Constituent Assembly, and later the first President of Independent India, said, "Sitting in the Chair and watching the proceedings from day to day, I have realised as nobody else could have, with what zeal and devotion the members of the Drafting Committee and especially its Chairman, Dr. Ambedkar, in spite of his indifferent health, have worked. We could never make a decision which was or could be ever so right as when we put him on the Drafting Committee and made him its Chairman. He has not only justified his selection but has added lustre to the work which he has done."[16] Dr. Nani Palkhivala, one of India's leading lawyers of modern India went to the extent of saying, "The highest tribute we can pay to Dr. Ambedkar is to redouble our efforts to preserve the Constitution which endures as a lasting monument to the man who was one of the noblest sons of India."[17]

Therefore, in one voice most of the leading lights of the Constituent Assembly had great sense of gratitude and appreciation to Dr. Ambedkar for his contributions in the task of Constitution-making. They were quite high sounding in their appreciation that establishes Ambedkar as the Chief Architect of the Indian Constitution to the posterity. These were the words of the leaders who were the men of might and standing, therefore, it cannot be claimed that they appreciated Ambedkar just for the sake of appreciating. However, at different occasion the same people have also appreciated others alongside Ambedkar, which suggests that Ambedkar is not the sole architect, rather there are others also.

Ambedkar on Indian Constitution

There is always a flip side of every story. Dr. Ambedkar had his own views on Indian Constitution some of which were self-contradictory. To start with he was not in favour of the Constituent Assembly for framing free India's Constitution which he explained to the Cripps Mission, "It is quite obvious that the proposal for Constituent Assembly is intended to win over the Congress. How do the proposals deal with the Depressed Classes? To put it shortly, they are bound hand and foot and handed over to the caste Hindus. They offer them nothing, stone instead of bread. For the Constituent Assembly is nothing short of a betrayal of the Depressed Classes..."[18] He wrote to Winston Churchill, India's worst enemy, who had made a strong anti-India speech in the British Parliament, praising him. In it Ambedkar said that the Cabinet Mission proposals 'are a shameful betrayal of the cause of the 60 million Untouchables.' Subsequently he went to London to fight for the cause of Untouchables and to address a meeting of the Conservatives Indian Committee in the House of Commons. There he demanded the abrogation of the Poona Pact signed by himself and Mahatma Gandhi and demanded the restoration of Separate Electorates. Here was a man who considered himself as a sole spokesman for the Dalits and went to the extent of fielding 1,585 candidates for election to various Provincial Assemblies, of them only one got elected.[19]

Moreover, when he was elected to the Drafting Committee in 1946, he said, "I came into the Constituent Assembly with no greater aspiration than to safeguard the interest of the Scheduled Castes."[20] Though according to many sources, it is claimed that when he was elected the Chairman of the Drafting Committee, he left all his initial interest and contributed himself whole heartedly for giving a constitution to the newly born nation. He gave up all his personal wishes only for the general interest of the nation.

The true Constitutional philosophy of Ambedkar has been fully reflected in the course of Round Table Conference in England and in the Memorandum which he submitted to the Constitutional Assembly on behalf of All India Scheduled Caste Federation. In the plenary session of the Round Table Conference on 20th November 1930, he said: "We must have a government in which the men in power will give their undivided allegiance to the best interest of the country. We must have a government in which men in power, knowing where obedience will end and where resistance will begin, will not be afraid to amend social and economic code of life which the dictates of justice and expediency so urgently call for."[21]

In the memorandum submitted to the Constituent Assembly, Dr. Ambedkar stated that the intention of the Poona Pact to ensure the return of the representatives of the choice of the Scheduled Castes to the legislature has been completely nullified in the elections which took place in February 1946. He pointed out that an analysis of the data proved that the success of the Scheduled Castes candidates in the final election, depended on the choice of the castes Hindus and not on the wishes of the Scheduled Castes. It was also seen that in most cases the candidates who got the maximum votes in the primary elections were not elected in the final elections.[22]

Once, he delivered a speech in Lucknow and asked the Scheduled Castes, "That the Scheduled Castes cannot capture political power by joining the Congress. It is a big organisation and if we enter the Congress we will be a mere drop in the Ocean....Congress is a burning house and we cannot be prosperous by entering in it."[23]

On another occasion on September 2, 1953 he made a statement in Parliament in great angst, "I shall be the first person to burn the Constitution. I do not want it, it does not suit anybody. People always keep on saying to me: 'Oh, you are the maker of the Constitution'. My answer is yes: 'I was hack. What I was asked to do. I did, much against my wish'."[24] Whereas on completion of the task of writing the Constitution he said in Parliament on March 19, 1955 as to how elated he was, "I say it with a certain amount of pride that the Constitution which has been given to this country is a wonderful document. It has been said not by me but by many people.....it is the simplest and the easiest."[25] As for safeguarding the interest of the Dalits he said, "The provisions made in the Constitution for safeguarding the position of the Schedule Castes were not to my satisfaction. However, I accepted them for what there were worth." The man who hated Hindus, once even went to the extent of saying that "the Schedule Castes should give up their political aloofness and co-operate with other communities..."[26] On another occasion when he delivered a speech in Lucknow asked the Scheduled Castes, "That the Scheduled Castes cannot capture political power by joining the Congress. It is a big organisation and if we enter the Congress we will be a mere drop in the Ocean....Congress is a burning house and we cannot be prosperous by entering in it. [27]

Therefore, it makes it complex to understand how to comprehend and appreciate what Dr. Ambedkar really stood for. He seems to be highly appreciative of the Constitution on one occasion and a worst critique on another when he goes to the extent of burning it. He asked Dalit community on one occasion to refrain from Congress and on another occasion asked them to cooperate with all other political forces. He seems to project that Constitution as it evolved was not the handiwork of his own or was one according to his vision, rather it was according to the vision of Congress Working Committee, to which he referred as majority, and that he did whatever they asked him to do. Therefore, it is indeed a matter of concern as it fails to provide any consistent perspective of Ambedkar, about something that he delivered to his countrymen, and that for which he is being honoured.

Drafting the Constitution: The Controversies

There was a huge uproar in the year 2012 upon a cartoon made by the legendary cartoonist, Shankar on the tardy progress of Constitution making by the Constituent Assembly.[28] The MP stookumbrage in a politics of competitive grimace. For the followers of Dr. Ambedkar it was to insult a Prophet. Some of the followers also mocked the Indian civilisation and were aggrieved that a cartoon on Ambedkar published during his own time to which he did not take offence, was included in the NCERT book for Class XI.[29] Finally, laughter met frontally with slaughter as the Cartoon was withdrawn subsequently by a Parliamentary dictate. Though it was done to pacify the champions of Dalit's cause in India and their political masters; yet it speaks volume about the fact that how people in India react and go wild to negate history.

There is another controversy related to the very status of the 'Architect of Indian Constitution', so far as the history of Drafting of the Constitution is concerned. A group of scholars and critique have argued it as a tragedy that history is being falsified and the makers of Modern India are being forgotten. They have emphatically claimed that a kind of Talibanisation has been creeping in our society which wants to impose their own distorted version of history and culture by showing the power of "slaughter". Therefore, it makes it imperative to learn about the controversy regarding the process of drafting and the contributions of other people into it, to have better understanding about the real architect of Indian Constitution.

Naziruddin Ahmed, a Member of the Constituent Assembly, criticised the Dr. Ambedkar-led Drafting Committee as the "Drifting Committee" for its tardy pace. Dr. Ambedkar had to justify the delay by giving details about the time taken and the clauses in various constitutions across the world. This was the theme of Shankar's cartoon as well. Dr. Ambedkar did poke Naziruddin Ahmed for his famous criticism:

> "He calls it a Drifting Committee. Mr. Naziruddin must no doubt be pleased with his hit. But he evidently does not know that there is a difference between drift without mastery and drift with mastery. If the Drafting Committee was drifting, it was never without mastery over the situation. It was not merely angling with the off chance of catching a fish. It was searching in known waters to find the fish it was after."[30]

This amply demonstrates Dr. Ambedkar's aptitude to retort criticism with humour. It's the moment to rediscover political satire. However, one thing that makes it obvious that there was something wrong with the pace of constitution writing. Accordingly, the rage that was raised on inclusion of the Cartoon in NCERT text seems to be uncalled for.

The Architect of Indian Constitution: B.N. Rau[31] vs. B.R. Ambedkar

There is yet another controversy related to the real contributions in the task of Constitution writing. According to some sources it was B.N. Rau who did most of the work in his capacity of Constitutional Advisor to the Constituent Assembly. However, he has never been accorded any credit by later breed of political leaders. The reason could be that he did not command the status of an icon of any community, which could have been a vote bank. The contributions of B.N. Rau have been deliberated in academic writings and hence it makes it obvious that he was an unparalleled stalwart to this effect which becomes clear from the ensuing discussion.

Lord Wavell, the Viceroy, had declared his intention to call a Constituent Assembly on September 19, 1946. On October 22, 1945, he wrote to Lord Pethick Lawrence that he intended to appoint Sir Benegal Narsingh Rau in the Reforms Department. At Wavell's instance Rau had a long meeting with Nehru on November 21, 1945. It may be mentioned that Rau was a contemporary of Nehru at Cambridge and Nehru was an admirer of Rau's scholarship and achievements.[32] Subsequently, Rau was appointed as Constitutional Advisor on July 1, 1946. On July 11, 1946 Nehru as Congress President appointed a Committee of Seven Persons to collect material for the Consideration of the Constituent Assembly in 1946. Later, all the preparatory work was done by B.N. Rau. He collected precedents from Britain, Canada, USA, Australia, South Africa, Ireland, etc. Three Volumes of the Precedents were given to the members of the Assembly. He wrote a note for Dr. Rajendra Prasad and Nehru on March 9, 1947. Later, on March 17, 1947 he sent a questionnaire to members of provincial legislative assemblies. The same questionnaire was circulated to the members of the Constituent Assembly on May 5, 1947.[33]

Rau prepared a Draft Constitution in October 1947. This Draft was considered by the Drafting Committee. The revised Draft was circulated on February 21, 1948 and was the basis for discussion. Dr. Rau attended the meetings of all the Committees and prepared notes for the members. His comments occupy about 400 pages in B. Shiv Rao's[34] Book, which includes about 200 pages of the Minutes of the Drafting Committee. However, his name has been forgotten by both the Parliament and the nation. Followers of Dr. Ambedkar may cry from roof top that this again is blasphemy to the legacy of Dr. Ambedkar, but Ambedkar in his own concluding speech in the Constituent Assembly on penultimate date 25th November 1949 said:

> Sir, looking back on the work of the Constituent Assembly it will now be two years, eleven months and seventeen days since it first met on the 9th of December 1946. During this period the Constituent Assembly has altogether held eleven sessions. Out of these eleven sessions the first six were spent in passing the Objective Resolution and the consideration of the Reports of the Committees on Fundamental Rights, on Union Constitution, on Union Powers, on Provincial Constitution, on Minorities and on the Scheduled Areas and Scheduled Tribes. The seventh, eighth, ninth, tenth and the eleventh sessions were devoted to the consideration of the Draft Constitution. These eleven sessions of the Constituent Assembly have consumed 165 days. Out of these, the Assembly spent 114 days for the consideration of the Draft Constitution.

Coming to the Drafting Committee, it was elected by the Constituent Assembly on 29th August 1947. It held its first meeting on 30th August. Since August 30th it sat for 141 days during which it was engaged in the preparation of the Draft Constitution. The Draft Constitution as prepared by the Constitutional Advisor as a text for the Drafting Committee to work upon, consisted of 243 articles and 13 schedules. The first Draft Constitution as presented by the Drafting Committee to the Constituent Assembly contained 315 articles and 8 schedules. At the end of the consideration stage, the number of articles in the Draft Constitution increased to 386. In its final form, the Draft Constitution contains 395 articles and 8 schedules. The total number of amendments to the Draft Constitution tabled was approximately 7,635. Of them, the total numbers of amendments actually moved in the House were 2,473."[35]

Thus, Dr. Ambedkar himself admits that the Drafting Committee which he headed was not the architect of the Draft Constitution. B.N. Rau prepared the Draft Constitution consisting of 243 Articles and the Drafting Committee worked over it to expand it to 315 Articles. After the 2473 amendments, the final form of the Constitution emerged with 395 Articles. Dr. Ambedkar further appreciates the work of B.N. Rau in the same speech:

"The credit that is given to me does not really belong to me. It belongs partly to Sir B N Rau, the Constitutional Advisor to the Constituent Assembly who prepared a rough draft of the Constitution for the consideration of the Drafting Committee. A part of the credit must go to the members of the Drafting Committee who, as I have said, have sat for 141 days and without whose ingenuity of devise new formulae and capacity to tolerate and to accommodate different points of view, the task of framing the Constitution could not have come to so successful a conclusion. Much greater, share of the credit must go to Mr. S.N. Mukherji, the Chief Draftsman of the Constitution. His ability to put the most intricate proposals in the simplest and clearest legal form can rarely be equalled, nor his capacity for hard work."

Even, the President of the Constituent Assembly, Dr. Rajendra Prasad himself admired B.N. Rau on the day of signing Constitution:

"Dr. Ambedkar mentioned the names of these Committees.

> Several of these had as their Chairman either Pandit Jawaharlal Nehru or Sardar Patel to who thus goes the credit for the fundamentals of our Constitution. I have only to add that they all worked in a business-like manner and produced reports which were considered by the Assembly and their recommendations were adopted as the basis on which the Draft of the Constitution had to be prepared. This was done by Mr. B N Rau, who brought to bear on his task a detailed knowledge of Constitutions of other countries and an extensive knowledge of the conditions of this country as well as his own administrative experience. The Assembly then appointed the Drafting Committee which worked on the original draft prepared by Mr B N Rau and produced the Draft Constitution which was considered by the Assembly at great length at the second reading stage."[36]

Dr. Rajendra Prasad Concludes, "If B.R. Ambedkar was the skilful pilot of the Constitution through all its different stages, Shri B.N. Rau was the person who visualised the plan and laid its foundation. The opinions that he gave on any controversial point were full and judicious and based on a deep study of the subject. His services were highly appreciated even outside India and the Credit for preparing the framework of the Constitution of Burma goes to him in a large measure."[37]

Dr. Ambedkar even went on to explain that he did not deserve that much credit for the making of the Constitution, and even paid his gratitude to the members for extending him the Chairmanship of the Drafting Committee:

> "I came into the Constituent Assembly with no greater aspiration than to safeguard the interests of the scheduled castes. I had not the remotest idea that I would be called upon to undertake more responsible functions. I was therefore greatly surprised when the Assembly elected me to the Drafting Committee. I was more than surprised when the Drafting Committee elected me to be its Chairman. There were in the Drafting Committee men bigger, better and more competent than myself such as my friend Sir Alladi Krishnaswami Ayyar. I am grateful to the Constituent Assembly and the Drafting Committee for reposing in me so much trust and confidence and to have chosen me as their instrument and given me this opportunity of serving the country."[38]

Pandit Nehru on November 30, 1953, made an obituary reference to Rau in Lok Sabha stating, "He was intimately connected with the Constitution-making and he might well be called one of the principal architects of our Constitution."[39] Moreover, the Constituent Assembly's resolution setting up the Drafting Committee mentioned that it was being set up to "Scrutinise the Draft of the text of the Constitution prepared by the Constitutional Advisor giving effect to the decisions taken already in the Assembly and including all matters ancillary thereto or which have to be provided in such a Constitution, and to submit to the Assembly for consideration the text of the Draft Constitution as revised by the Committee."[40]

Therefore, there remain hardly any doubt that the Drafting Committee was conceived with specific task to scrutinise the Draft, then where is the question of 'writing the constitution' by Drafting Committee. Ambedkar himself, Rajendra Prasad, and J.L. Nehru have appreciated and recognised the task of 'Constitution Writing' executed by Rau in their speeches. It is a historical wrong that the name of Rau has been kept hidden in the pages of Constituent Assembly and Lok Sabha debates. Therefore, the need is to bring them out so that the future generations learn about their heroes the right way and their knowledge and information are not victimized by vested political interests.

Conclusion

Ambedkar is being debated today by different political parties. It would be debated with emotive inputs and also may be in violent manner. The debate and discussion however, must be welcomed as it provides an opportunity for the contemporary generation of youth and learners to know and learn more about their national heroes who made indelible contributions in the making of country and society. However, there lies the danger also because on most occasions the political parties endeavour to project their own beliefs on to Ambedkar, and many other national heroes and political icons. There is hardly any doubt that Ambedkar stood for complete annihilation of caste; therefore he must be crying in his grave the way political parties are competing for the Dalit vote bank by making the caste-based discrimination through the expansion of caste quotas. He was a modern thinker and a practitioner of pragmatic politics who refused to be bogged down by any particular ideology or religion. His spirit of Protestantism was deeply rooted into his social experiences that must be appreciated as he stood for fighting against it at all levels. He and most other leaders of the downtrodden castes and class stood for real empowerment of marginalized castes. However, the empowerment stands distorted today as it is happening but in the wrong direction. They stand politicised and have been reduced to a mere vote bank to be tempted and lured at the time of elections.

The important aspect that becomes obvious from the on-going debate is that he did not only think for Dalits but also for each and every common man of this country, which also establishes him as a true nationalist in real sense of the term. He was both a rebel and a rationalist. He established the goal of Constitution as social, economic and political democracy for the betterment of all Indians. Syamanandan Sahay rightly said in the Constituent Assembly, "The achievement of independence would go to the credit of Mahatmaji and its codification to one of Mahatmaji's worst critics, viz. the great architect of our Constitution Dr. Ambedkar."[41]

B.N. Rau, undoubtedly is creditworthy for preparing the foundations of Indian Constitution and setting the tone for debate in the Constituent Assembly about vision and philosophy of Indian Constitution. However, there must not also be any doubt that Ambedkar's role in drafting of the Indian Constitution has enabled the initiatives for abolition of Untouchability and the outlawing of all forms of social discriminations. It was his contributions that India could move forward towards the realization of its dream of creating an egalitarian social order, even though it still remains unfulfilled. It is unfortunate that even today for most political parties when elections come, they see Dalits as Hindus, but later they don't even like to sit with them.

The controversy about credit for the 'Father of Indian Constitution" or the 'Architect of Indian Constitution' is undoubtedly an unsettled one. It requires to be settled in right perspective. The credit which is due to B.N. Rau must be accorded to Rau by all means by the present breed of political leaders. Academicians, journalists, and intelligentsia must campaign for the same. However, such a campaign must not create another controversy by belittling the tremendous role of Ambedkar towards piloting the Constitution by entailing social, political and economic Justice into it, in accordance with his vision, philosophy and ideology. History at this stage stands distorted, and it must be rescued for larger benefit of the country and social institutions.

END NOTES

1. "War for Ambedkar", *The Times of India*, April 13, 2016.
2. Ibid.
3. Ibid.
4. As quoted in Kavitakait, "Dr. B.R. Ambedkar: The Father of Indian Constitution", www.legalserviceIndia.com published on December 12, 2013.
5. Gurnam Chand, "Dr. Ambedkar: Architect of the Indian Constitution", *Mainstream Weekly*, Vol. XLIX, No. 17, April 16, 2011.
6. "Dr. B.R. Ambedkar Biography—Life and Profile", www.culturalIndia.net Retrieved on February 5, 2011.
7. Ibid., no.5.
8. Mukesh Kumar Sablania, "Role of Dr. B.R. Ambedkar in the Constituent Assembly", available on www.countercurrents.org Retrieved on November 24, 2015.
9. "Ambedkar's Role in National Politics", www.latasinha.wordpress.com Retrieved on September 27, 2010. As quoted here K.V. Rao has made this remark, "No doubt, Ambedkar, a man of legal acumen, untiring industry, consummate skill and firmness, tempered with modernisation, made substantial contribution to the framing of the Constitution...My reading of the Constitution makes me feel that it is inappropriate to call Dr. Ambedkar, the father of the Constitution. If any people are entitled to be called so, they are Nehru and Patel, but I would like to call them the "Presiding Deities", the sources of all the ideas of the Constitution, the real makers of the Constitution. I would like to attribute fatherhood to them as well as to the members of the Drafting Committee in common, but I would not like to single out Dr. Ambedkar for this honour."
10. P.N. Krishna Mani, "Dr. B.R. Ambedkar: His Role in the Constituent Assembly", in *Dr. B.R. Ambedkar: The man and His Message*, (New Delhi: Prentice Hall of India, 1991), p.61
11. Constituent Assembly Debates, Vol. II, p.217. On 29th August 1947 passing one resolution the Constituent Assembly appointed a 'Drafting Committee' with seven members including Dr. Ambedkar, for preparing a draft of the Constitution of the independent India. The Seven members were Dr. B.R. Ambedkar (Chairman), N Gopalswami, Alladi Krishnaswami Ayyar, K.M. Munshi, Saijio Mola Saadulla, N. Madhava Rao and D. P. Khaitan.
12. Suresh Mane, *Some Reflections on the Constitutional Philosophy of Ambedkar*, Chapter Five, "Studies in Ambedkar" (Delhi: 1995), p. 67. As quoted in Mukesh Kumar Sablania, "Role of Dr. B.R. Ambedkar in the Constituent Assembly", available on www.countercurrents.org Retrieved on November 24, 2015.
13. P.T. Borale, *Dr. Ambedkar and the Constitution of India*, Chapter Eleven, "Political Idea and Leadership of Dr. B.R. Ambedkar, (Pune: Vishwanil Publications, 1989), p.110.
14. M.V. Paylee, *Constitutional Government in India*, (Bombay: Asia Publishing House, 1960), p.138.
15. Ibid., no.14, p.26.
16. Constituent Assembly Debates, November 26, 1949, Vol. XI, p.994.
17. As quoted in a M.V. Kamath's Book Review of a Book by Sheshrao Chavan, "The Constitution

of India: Role of Dr. B.R. Ambedkar" (Atlantic Publishers, 2014), available on www.freepressjournal.in Retrieved on November 5, 2015.

18. Ibid., no.17.
19. Ibid., no.17.
20. Constituent Assembly Debates, Vol. XI, p.973.
21. B.R. Ambedkar, "Writing and Speeches", Vol. I, 1979, p.353.
22. Thomas Mathew, *Constitution Making,* Chapter 13, "Ambedkar: Reform or Revolution (New Delhi: Segment Books, 1991), p.103.
23. Ibid., no.8.
24. Ibid., no.17.
25. Ibid., no.17.
26. Ibid., no.17.
27. Ibid., no.8.
28. "Ambedkar did not draft Constitution", www.ariseasia.blogspot.in Retrieved on November 24, 2015.
29. Ibid., no.28.
30. Ibid., no.28.
31. Sir Benegal Narsingh Rau (1887-1953) was an Indian Civil Servant, Jurist, Diplomat, and Statesman known for his key role in Drafting the Constitution of India. He was also India's representative to the United Nations Security Council from 1950 to 1952. His brothers were Governor of the Reserve Bank of India, Benegal Rama Rau, and Journalist and Politician Benegal Shiva Rao. He was entrusted with the job of revising entire Indian statutory code including Hindu Code Bill which he accomplished during the period 1935-37. He was knighted for this work by British Government in 1938. Later he was elevated as Judge of the Bengal High Court at Calcutta in 1939. The Indus Commission appointed in 1941 was headed by B N Rau. This Report is still the basis for water sharing between India and Pakistan. After retirement in 1944 he served as Prime Minister of Jammu and Kashmir state. He was appointed as the Constitutional Advisor to the Constituent Assembly with so much expertise in understanding world governments and political system with his administrative and legal experience.
32. Brij Kishore Sharma, "A Product of Joint Efforts", *Organiser,* www.organiser.org Retrieved on November 24, 2015.
33. Ibid., no.32.
34. Benegal Shiva Rao (1891-1975) was an Indian Journalist and Politician. He was also a member of the Constituent Assembly of India and an elected representative of the South Kanara Constituency in the First Lok Sabha. He was the correspondent of *The Hindu* and then of the *Manchester Guardian.* He was also a member of the Rajya Sabha from 1957 to 1960.
35. Constituent Assembly Debates, "Vol. XI, Lok Sabha Secretariat.
36. http://ParliamentofIndia.nic.in/ls/debates/vol11p12.htm Retrieved on November 24, 2015. See also "Ambedkar did not draft Constitution", www.ariseasia.blogspot.in Retrieved on November 24, 2015.
37. As quoted from Constituent Assembly Debates in "Ambedkar did not draft Constitution", www.ariseasia.blogspot.inretrieved on November 24, 2015.
38. Ibid., no.37.
39. Ibid., no.37.
40. Ibid., no.37.
41. Constituent Assembly Debate, Vol. V, p. 788.

2

Dr. B.R. Ambedkar's Critique of Elitist Nationalism

Anuradha Mukherjee

The elitist nationalism in pre-independence India was the center of attack by non-elitist nationalist thinkers who were apprehensive of the exploitative, hierarchical regime that prevailed in the name of *Varnashrama*. Caste system as an offshoot of *varnashrama* could not survive unless the inhuman practices of caste did not get the support of religion. B.R. Ambedkar led the strongest revolt against this system and in the process, bitterly criticised the casteist character of the independence movement led by leaders coming from upper castes and defined the whole scheme of nationalist policies as Brahmanical meaning elitist and non-inclusive. Ambedkar's approach from that of his predecessors like Jyotiba Phule (1827-1890) and Vithalrao Shinde (1873-1944) was different. Both these leaders had worked for the untouchable cause, but their works were not exclusively concentrated on the anti-Brahmin protest. Ambedkar differed from them in the sense that he attributed 'Brahmanism' to all kind of privileged upper classes and upper castes who denied social equality of the untouchables.

The nationalist discourses in colonial settings have a tendency to enlarge and emphasise the infallibility of traditional values in order to thwart the hegemon's claims of cultural supremacy. So it is not surprising to see the nationalist discourses of the Third World countries centering upon patriarchal, elitist and conservative views prescribed for the nation as the correct national imagery of liberation. At the same time, it is the colonial institutions that are the usherers of the new national narratives, woven around the past glories, like the educational institutions, the printing press, and the various public platforms shaped in the western political model. Glamourising the past through the modern institutions dominated the Indian political agenda during the struggle for independence with few questions about the shared past seen through the non-indigenous glasses of Western institutions. Dr. B.R. Ambedkar's critique of this imagery came from below and highlighted a different narrative with a different reproduction of the nation. Ambedkar's critique of the political, social and ideological appeals of nationalism as the perpetuation of disguised inequalities-a legacy of the caste-based social structure is highly relevant in the context of post-colonial nationhood.

The mainstream political discourse of this nationhood rested on cultural elitism which was essentially Brahmanical in character. Ambedkar dared to question the acceptability of this discourse itself. It was a challenge to the validity of a claim-a claim that pretended to encompass the multifarious within the core of one narrative. A common national identity had to be built so that a common national feeling could be created. This 'nation', in Ambedkar's vision', was not a true one so long it did not discard the socio-political dominance of the "varnashrama". Ambedkar was defiant against this Brahmanisation of India's political tradition. In October 1956, two months before his death, together with his some four hundred thousand followers, Ambedkar embraced Buddhism. It was his last act of defiance against an unjust socio-political order that constituted the core of the national body-politik of the mainstream political narrative of pre-independence India. If that narrative was directed at ousting foreign colonial hegemony, it certainly had nothing to do with the in-built socio-cultural and therefore political hegemony that continued to oppress the socio-political structure of India from time immemorial. The pre-independence chapter was only a watershed in that continued process, distinct by the British imperial rule of about two hundred years. The national consciousness emerged as a unitary whole thereby sweeping aside all other dependencies and dominations, marginalising the traditionally oppressed faces of humanity from its agenda. The nation must unite as one in order to shatter the colonial fetters. The age-old stories of deception were being lost somewhere in this totalistic construction of patriarchy and elitism asking for sacrifices needed to attain independence. If this legacy was contested at all, it was by religious minorities who could afford to be communal having communitarian interests. Outnumbering them were the faceless millions who did not have any other identity apart from the "Hindu" identity, but barely having a role to play in legislating in governance, in choosing the way to be ruled, in Rousseau's words, "to select the way to be governed".

It will be an understatement to say that the defiance to this status quo came from Dr. B.R. Ambedkar. In fact, it was for the first time in Indian history that defiance took a multi-pronged approach. He gave a clarion call to change the monolithical system of inhumanity by questioning the very root of its existence. This article proposes to suggest that it was by deconstructing the Brahminical canons of restriction, Dr. Ambedkar used his intellect to shatter the age-old cultural myth and the sanctions imposed by an elitist political order on the millions of Indian's poor down-trodden deprived masses and give them real human rights and power that they deserved like any other people of the world. Ambedkar visioned the political rise of Untouchables.

Dr. B.R. Ambedkar's perspective on Brahmanism as reflected in the scriptural texts and its legacy is a conjectural document of the multi-dimensional layers of Indian history and the undercurrents of long-lost voices of humanity. But this conjecture struck at the root of a very strong superstructure that pervaded almost all Indian political, social and economic thought since the post-Upanishadic era. This superstructure was "caste" which was seen by Ambedkar as a clever attempt to deify a cunning socio-economic device by giving it the sanctity of religion. Ambedkar gave an interpretation of ancient Indian history from the view point of one of its many subaltern life-experiences In doing so, he constructed a counter-narrative of the main nationalist historiography that celebrated India's ancient past, reconstructing the present based on that past.[1]

In India as in many formerly colonized states of Asia and Africa, the nationalist discourses were products of colonial nationalism. They had to be constructed in the effort to conceptualise the nationalist struggle for liberation from foreign rule. Most of these discourses were linear, homogeneous and patriarchic overlooking the heterogeneous, subaltern and women as secondary in relation to the first-order discourses of class and power.[2] The legacies of the past had to be woven in the colonial narrative by rewriting history with old ideologies presented in secular, Westernised forms which could fit in the multi-dimensional nature of Indian society.

Need for a Counter-narrative

Ambedkar's interpretation of the main narrative of Indian history as Brahmanic in his numerous writing on caste and the possible causes of this phenomenon, his relentless battle against the unjust social order prevalent in India, and his eventual conflict with the Indian National Congress and Mahatma Gandhi on this issue had created huge upheavals in the pre-independence socio-political scene of India at a time when political independence was its ultimate goal. It was a well-defined national trajectory where all other discourses were regarded unjust, untimely and even opportunist. In his many writings like "Who were the Shudras", "Annihilation of Caste", "Philosophy of Hinduism", "Untouchable and Untouchabilies" and many more, Ambedkar presented a critique of the mainstream Indian history which shows the incompleteness of modern state-centered nationalism against the vast assimilation of Vedic cultural history practiced throughout India from time immemorial. The contradictions and heterogeneity put into question the validity of a common nationalist program as the mouthpiece for all segments of people who did not share a common life-experience for centuries. The nationalist school regarded the national past as one of prosperity and general contentment.[3] Ambedkar's parable-like reconstructions of history questioning the validity and credibility of the Brahminic texts were attempts to modernize the nation-state in the European Enlightenment model whereby the link with the past is broken by doubts. His use of counter-narration was suitable for the construction of a new nation-state as a democracy, accommodating multi-religious, multi-national, and contending groups all the while attempting to resolve the contradictions peacefully as strategy of survival. Ambedkar's utterances on nationalism evolved out of this deep distrust of mainstream national discourse which in its every fiber talks of a self that continually excludes the other in texts, in rituals and in everyday life.

Ambedkar's critique of mainstream Indian political discourse was directed against the manipulation of power-relations that keep all modes of production and capital under its control. He saw it as consisting of two main aspects. Firstly, that Brahmanism as Brahminic texts defies morality by taking the place of morality. The ethics of Brahmanism was rule-following, while the author of the rules was the power strategy of the educated Elite, in this case the establishment with its pro-Brahminic power base. Secondly, Brahmanism aspired for political emancipation of the state. In these two spheres, individual's emancipation was pushed to the periphery. In the first notion. Brahmanism as priestly power and religious sanctions was the driving force of the society. It ruled the latter with canonical scriptures going against all norms of secular, humanitarian and moral considerations.[4] In the second notion, the Kshatriya king was merely a state-machine with its control in the hands of Brahmanism Ambedkar cited Shivaji's coronation as a case in point.[5]

Ambedkar's understanding of Brahmanism was that it was but another name for exploitation, but justified by a very clever construction of religious sanctions in the form of fundamental conceptions of Hindu life. This was an appropriation which did not have any challenger; although many reformers tried to soften the harshness with which the texts were interpreted Ambedkar challenged this appropriation and authority directly, on its own terms, questioning the grounds of its claims of supremacy. He accused straight away the interest groups to be benefitted by this scheme, i.e., those in power and whose interest it was to be perpetually in power. By a secular, historical conjectural analysis, he shows that all the elements of power were in their hands, i.e., knowledge, wealth and law. The heroic lores of the state would always uphold this system. 'Caste' as a pejorative term was coined by this powered class; *Varnavyavashtha* was a systemisation of this scheme of in equality, injustice and perpetual oppression. No elitist discourse, albeit national, ever addressed caste as a problematic, and therefore to Ambedkar, the national discourse of a glorified nation was unreal, deplorable and blatantly suppressive of other life-worlds within a common national agenda. That in the name of national integrity and cohesion, identities are crushed however legitimate they are is not a unique phenomenon in human civilisation as world-history shows us, but if that integrity is conceived without assuring the minimal criteria of people's welfare, then integrity itself is jeopardized and the nationalist discourse remains an incomplete project whose very in completeness demonstrates serious lacunae threatening stability of the nation-state. The inhuman ideologies of slavery and caste, the latter in the Indian context, blur the imagery of a glorious and righteous nation, oppressed by the foreign rule, and yet capable of being idealised by the merits of the country's collective virtues worthy of being named a civilized nation.

Project of Modernity Against Cast Legacy

Ambedkar wanted the nationalist agenda to take note of the lack of homogeneity and common life experience in its trajectory of equal citizenship and secularism. The Utopian homogeneity and real heterogeneity was for the first time displayed before the nation by Ambedkar's keen intellect. The powerful engines of legal and religious sanctions could not only keep caste going, as Ambedkar saw it, but they also glamourized and idolized the past in its unchangeability, its modernity project unable to come to terms with its legacy, its cultural hegemony being more powerful than its colonial hegemony. Ambedkar had to take the double role of a modernist and an interrupter, interpreting the traditional texts not in the light of modernity but as counter-narratives of mainstream cultural discourse. Thus, Ambedkar's criticism of Gandhism was actually the criticism of power-politics of Brahamanism that he reads into it. He did not see any emancipation for the Sudra-Ati Sudra-Untouchable Bahujan in the pre-independence national political discourse.

Conclusion

Ambedkar's attitude towards the British colonial power was a tactical one, as he said later that why they were his enemies so were the upper caste nationalists and "we cannot fight two enemies at once."[6] The Akhanda Bharat concept of the Indian Nationalist narrative was questioned by Ambedkar's critique of it, in which surfaced again and again, his assertion of plural identities voluntarily suppressed by Brahmanic Historiography. From the nationalist discourse of human beings as ideas Ambedkar creates a counter-narrative of human beings as political. It is from this viewpoint that Ambedkar's critique of our national political legacy must be seen. In this critique, the issues involved were the questions on how to provide a space to the identities in the post-colonial nation and how to subvert the pull of the pre-colonial Brahmanic hegemony in the post-colonial construction of the nation.

In this discourse, the most important issue that was born was that for the first time the negative stigma of being an untouchable was replaced by the very positive identity of being a Dalit, a person oppressed by socialized structure of oppression. The *antyaja* for the first time stood up for his human rights as guaranteed to all human beings in the modern, post-enlightenment meaning of rights. At the same time, the enemy or the oppressor was also categorically identified. It was not any more the law of Karma, or the cycle of birth and rebirth according to one's deeds that explained every misery, but the *Varna* division that perpetually exploited the lowest classes, the goldmine in Ambedkar's words[7]. Ambedkar's critique of elitist nationalism has in its core the questioning about a religion or culture and its inherent valves. The nation had to be constructed where nationalism as imposed by elitist domination strategy becomes unreal and superficial.

END NOTES

1. T.K. Oommen, *Nation, Civil Society and Social Movements*, Sage Publications, New Delhi, p. 85.
2. Debjani Ganguly, *Caste and Dalit Life Worlds: Postcolonial Perspectives,* Orient Longman Private Limited (South Asian Edition), New Delhi, 2008, p. 22.
3. Romila Thapar, *Ancient Indian Social History Some Interpretations*, Orient Longman Private Limited, 1979, New Delhi, 1978, p.13.
4. Babasaheb Ambedkar Writing and Speeches, Government of Maharashtra, Vol. 3, p.181.
5. Ibid., p.73.
6. Gail Omvedt, *Ambedkar: Towards an Enlightened India*, Penguin Books India, Delhi, 2004, p. 39.
7. B.R. Ambedkar: *What congress and Gandhi have done to the Untouchables*, Thacker & Company Ltd., Bombay, 1945, p. 196.

3

Relevance of B.R. Ambedkar's Economics in the Age of Globalisation

Binita Batsa

Introduction

Babasaheb Bhim Rao Ambedkar is usually recalled as the chief Architect of Indian Constitution, an eminent jurist and a renowned Dalit Leader. His contributions in the area of Indian Economy have attained less attention from the academic scholars in particular and people in general. Babasaheb had carried out an in depth study of Indian Economy and suggested several methods to overcome its problems. His works cover a vast area ranging from Indian Agriculture System, Indian Currency and Tax System, Industrialisation to the policy of the Free Market, which is considered as the prototype of globalisation. Therefore, it would be very improper to not admire him for his enormous contribution in the field of economics. This paper will attempt to elucidate the significance of the observations and suggestions made by Babasaheb in relation to the present Indian Economy which has embraced the ideals of Liberalisation, Privatisation and Globalisation in recent decades. In order to solve the problems of the agricultural sector, Babasaheb suggested a variety of measures. Among them, Collective farming, equal distribution of land, government support and subsidy for farming, minimum wage security were most prominent. He was a staunch opponent of Gold Exchange

Standards and advocated the policy of price stability instead of exchange rate stability. He was against a tax system which was based on discrimination and inequality. He believed that in order to utilise available resources, to reduce the dependence on imports and to ensure security to the labours, India should support industrialisation. He also championed the idea of women empowerment through economic policies. Babasaheb also backed the idea of the Free Economy with some precautionary measures. Most judicious economic norms espoused by the government of India overlap with these recommendations. This paper concludes that the ideas promoted by Babasaheb Ambedkar not only influenced the formation of economic policy of free India, they are far more relevant in the neoliberal paradigm of the present times.

Ambedkar's Postulation About the Small Land Holdings in India

The occasional paper released by the NITI Aayog on 16 December 2015 states that in Indian Economy, Agriculture is still the largest sector in terms of providing livelihood as 48.9 per cent workforce depends upon it. According to the same document, there are 5 key areas of agriculture which need immediate attention. Small size of farms is one among them. The document reads:

> "Over the generations, as families have grown, land holdings have come to be divided and fragmented into small economically unviable parcels and plots. Onerous leasing laws have prevented consolidation of these holdings. On the one hand, these small holdings force owners to seek alternative means of livelihood and on the other their plots remain uncultivated with no prospect of being joined to other plots to produce more viable holdings."

The data provided by the Agricultural Census also gives the same picture. According to this, there were about 121 million agricultural holdings during 2000-01. Around 99 million among them were small farmers. The document further interprets that the average size of land has declined from 2.3 hectare in 1970-71 to 1.37 hectare in 2000-01. Small and Marginal farmers comprise about 80 per cent of Indian Agriculture but there share in operated area is around 44 per cent. Therefore, the performance of small and marginal landholdings will determine the prospect of food security and the growth of sustainable agriculture.

Babasaheb Bhim Rao Ambedker had made the same analysis about a century ago. He did a comprehensive study of the agricultural system of India. It was Ambedkar who gestated the land reform plan in a real sense for the first time and also explained that why it is necessary for the development of Indian Agriculture system. He incorporated his ideas on Indian agriculture in his famous article, "Small Holdings in India and their Remedies" which was published in 1917. Another article "Status and Minorities" also demonstrate his in-depth knowledge about Indian Agriculture sector.

He said from a national point of view as well, the importance of primary sector is beyond question, but, the importance of agriculture is crucial for a country like India, which is almost dependent upon it. He condemned the definition of economic holdings based on consumption which was prevailing that time and enunciated that it should be defined from the point of view of production. According to Ambedkar, the inability to produce surplus was the fundamental problem of Indian Agriculture. Capital could not be generated due to the scarcity of surplus and it was unimaginable to utilise the resources without capital. The overall economic growth was adversely affected due to the awful condition of agriculture. He believed that the small land holdings are the main obstacle for the development of agriculture. In "Small holdings in India and their Remedies", he exposed the drawbacks of the small land holdings in following words:

> "The evils of small holdings no doubt, are many. But it would have been no slight mitigation of them if the small holdings were compact holdings. Unfortunately they are not....These small and scattered holdings have given a real cause for anxiety regarding our great national industry." [Small holdings in India and their Remedies, p. 3]

In order to solve the problems of the agricultural sector, Ambedkar suggested a variety of measures. Among them, Collective farming, equal distribution of land, government support and subsidy for farming, minimum wage security were most prominent. Stressing upon the need of cooperative farming he said:

"The better method is to introduce cooperative agriculture and to compel owners of small strips to join in cultivation." [Collection of Dr. Ambedkar's writings, published by the Government of Maharashtra in 1979]

Ambedkar as an Advocate of Industrialisation

Ambedkar reiterated that Industrialisation is essential for the faster development of India. Industries will help utilise the available raw materials, they will generate more and more jobs and the industrial production will lessen our import dependency. He suggested that government should come forward to take charge of the large scale industries as the private sector lack sufficient investments required for such industries. He also believed that nationalisation of large scale industries would mere down the exploitation of industrial labourers and would also render equal opportunities. But he agreed with the view that small industries can be put under the charge of private ownership. Ambedkar also emphasised that agricultural development and industrial development are complementary to each other and thus we should stop looking at them as two different objects. He proposed that Industrialisation could be the best way to motivate the additional labours to move from agriculture to other creative works. In one of his speeches he expressed his views on industrialisation in following words:

"India is caught between two sides of pincers, the one side of which is progressive pressure of population and the other is limited availability of land in relation to its needs. The result is that at the end of each decade, we are left with negative balance of population and production and a constant squeezing of standard of living and poverty. The population pressure is giving rise to an army of landless and dispersed families as well. Nothing can open possibilities of making agriculture profitable except a serious drive in favour of industrialisation..." [Dr. Babasaheb Ambedkar, Writings & Speeches, Vol. 1, Government of Maharashtra, p.477]

The First Five Year Plan (1951-56) which was based on Harrod-Domar Model strongly endorsed the idea of agricultural development and also instigated the process of Industrialisation. State was entitled to play a vital role in all the sectors of economy throughout this plan. The Second

Five Year Plan (1956-1961) was dedicated to the development of public sector to ensure the economic growth. This plan led the way for the establishment of heavy industries and hydroelectric power projects in India. India embraced the policy of privatisation following the economic crisis of late 1990s but the government still plays an influential role in the Industrialisation policy and the public sector companies are major engines of Indian economy.

Ambedkar: A Defender of Labourers' Rights

Ambedkar fought for the rights of labours from the beginning of his practice as a lawyer. He was aware of the fact that a large population of the labourers belongs to the downtrodden communities of Indian society and they have already suffered a lot due to their position in the society. He didn't want them to suffer in the hands of the capitalists. This was an important reason behind his support for nationalisation of large scale industries. Ambedkar favoured the formation of trade unions and their right to strike. He also supported the involvement of labours in the management of industries. He firmly believed that without social justice industrial peace can never be attained. Ambedkar was equally concerned for the agricultural labours. It was his efforts which led to the passage of several beneficial provisions for the labourers. Health Insurance Scheme, Provident Fund Act, Factory Amendment Act, Labour Disputes Act, Minimum Wage, The Legal Strike, Mines Maternity Benefit Act, Women Labour Welfare Fund, Women and Child, Labour Protection Act, Maternity Benefit for Women Labour, Restoration of Ban on Employment of Women on Underground Work in Coal Mines, Dearness Allowance (DA) to Workers, Leave Benefit to Piece Workers are central among them.

Ambedakar's View on the Problem of Currency

"The Problem of the Rupee" is the main source which throws light upon Ambedkar's view on currency. "The Problem of the Rupee" was his thesis in which he discussed the monetary issues in detail. He strongly opposed the idea of linking rupee with gold and suggested to do away with it; reason being linking with gold often leads to instability of currency. Further on, he said that such instability can have a detrimental effect on a country like India. In his view, Gold exchange standard can cause inflation and hike in prices. Thus, he advocated for gold standard with some modifications and enunciated that it will prove more favorable than the gold exchange standard. He suggested three important measures to maintain the equilibrium of an economy which are as follows:

- Stability of price should be the priority instead of exchange rate stability.
- Appropriate measures should be taken to control the deficits.
- Circular flow of money to be ensured.

The Governments of free India adhered on these principles for monetary regulation and steady economic growth.

Ambedkar's Thoughts on Tax

Ambedkar had established "Swatantra Majdur Party" in 1936. In its manifesto, he articulated his analysis on the tax system of India. He was against a tax system which was based on discrimination and inequality. He criticised the land revenue system and called it an unnecessary burden on the deprived section of our society. He suggested that the system of taxation should be such that it could help the government without affecting the people adversely. Tax should be imposed according to the capacity of the payers. He also supported the idea of tax exemption to a certain limit. This limit had to be equal for all.

Present day tax system of India more or less pursues the same tax model which was recommended by Ambedkar decades ago.

Champion of Women's Empowerment

Ambedkar was an ardent supporter of women empowerment. But he was aware of the fact that this goal could not be achieved without ensuring the economic rights of women. Therefore, he championed the idea of women empowerment through economic policies. He emphasised that the women should be provided equal opportunity. They should also get the freedom to choose their livelihood. Ambedkar's view on tyranny of the women is somewhat similar to the feminist thinking of modern India. To improve the economic condition of Hindu women, a bill called "Hindu Code Bill" was proposed in the Parliament. Ambedkar and the then Prime Minister

Pt. Jawaharlal Nehru were the principle initiator of this bill. The Hindu Code Bill was a major initiative in the direction of the uplifment of Hindu Women. The Bill granted women the right to divorce and maintenance. Monogamy was made compulsory. The bill also authorized the inter-caste marriages and adoption. Women got the share in property of her father and husband. Hindu Code Bill proved a mile stone in this regard. Apart from this, Ambedkar suggested a number of ways to help women labourers. These laws were essential to make sure the safety and security of women workers.

Supporter of Free Economy?

Ambedkar's support for Free Economy is an issue of contention among the scholars. Some scholars consider him as one of the first-generation free-market economist (Balakrishnan Chandrashekaran, Srinivasa Ambirajan, Narendra Jadhav). They use the writings of Ambedkar in favour of their argument. One of those arguments is given below:

> "...an obligation on the state to plan the economic life of the people on line which would lead to highest point of productivity without closing every avenue to private enterprise, and also provide for equitable distribution of wealth (Narendra Jadhav, 1991, p. 982).

These scholars also use Ambedkar's magnificent work, "The Problem of the Rupee" to portray him as a diehard supporter of free economy. In its first chapter, Ambedkar writes:

> "Trade is an important apparatus in a society, based on private property and pursuit of individual gain; without it, it would be difficult for its members to distribute the specialised products of their labour. Surely a lottery or an administrative device would be incompatible with its nature. Indeed, if it is to preserve its character, the only mode for the necessary distribution of the products of separate industry is that of private trading. But a trading society is unavoidably a pecuniary society, a society which of necessity carries on its transactions in terms of money. In fact, the distribution is not primarily an exchange of products against products, but products against money. In such a society, money therefore necessarily becomes the pivot on which everything revolves. With money as the focusing-point of all

> human efforts, interests, desires and ambitions, a trading society is bound to function in a regime of price, where successes and failures are results of nice calculations of price-outlay as against price-product." [The Problem of the Rupee, First Chapter, p. 1]

Another group of Scholars out rightly rejects the claims made by these scholars. They question that how come it is possible for a man like Ambedkar to support Free Market economy which is based on inequality? In a Free market it is assumed that the buyers and sellers are equal, but this assumption becomes complicated once it comes in practice. With given inequality of people in marketplace the free market becomes an instrument of exploitation. They further argue that Ambedkar was an upholder of State Socialism which is antithetical to the concept of Free Market. In-depth analysis of the works of Ambedkar suggests that his support for State Socialism is doubtless, but he also backed the idea of Free Economy with some precautionary measures.

Conclusion

B.R. Ambedkar was one of the first-generation Indian economists who adopted a holistic view on Indian Economy. His ideas on economy were full of regards for the social development. Ambedkar raised the issue of small land holdings which persisted even after the execution of land reforms and the consecutive governments have tried to find a viable solution for this problem. Ambedkar's vision on industrialisation is more relevant in the present-day situation. The credit of upholding the Indian economy goes to the industries. The growth of industries was unendurable without labour reforms and contribution of Ambedkar in this regard is unforgettable. Most judicious economic norms espoused by the government of India overlap with the recommendations made by Ambedkar. Thus, we can say that the ideas promoted by him not only influenced the formation of economic policy of free India, they are far more relevant in the neoliberal paradigm of the present times. In his recent interview in the *Economic Times*, RSS Joint Secretary Mr. Krishna Gopal rightly observes that, "Ambedkar's economics was a bridge between industrialisation and labour reforms. This is the relevance of Ambedkar today" [*source*: B.R. Ambedkar's Ideas on Economy need to be studied: Krishna Gopal, RSS Joint Secretary, *Economic Times*, 22 June 2015.]

END NOTES

1. Venkatesh Atherya, "A New Resonance," *Frontline*, Vol. 19, Issue 15, July 20 to August 02, 2002, at http://www.frontline.in/static/html/fl1915/19151150.htm.
2. R.G. Kadapatti and S.T. Bagalkoti, "Small farms and agricultural productivity A Macro Analysis," *International Journal of Social Science Studies*, Vol. 2, No. 3 July 2014, at http://dx.doi.org/10.11114/ijsss.v2i3.463.
3. Balakrishnan Chandrasekaran, B.R. Ambedkar, the Greatest Free Market Economist of India, in *Economics*, January 22, 2014.
4. Kavita Kait, Dr. B.R. Ambedkar's Role in Women Empowerment, Published on December 18, 2013, at http://www.legalservicesIndia.com/article/article/drbrambedkar%C3%A2% E2% 82%AC%E2%84%A2s-role-in-women-empowerment-1611-1.html.
5. B. Chandrasekaran, Ambedkar, the forgotten free-market economist, published on 14 April, 2011, at http://pragati.nationalinterest.in/2011/04/ambedkartheforgottenfree market economist/.
6. Anand Teltumbde, Babasaheb Ambedkar and the Neoliberal Economic Reforms, published on 11 September, 2011 on *Countercurrents.org*, at http://www.countercurrents.org/teltumbde110911.htm.
7. Krishna Gopal, BR Ambedkar's ideas on economy need to be studied *Economic Times*, June 22, 2015, at http://articles.economictimes.Indiatimes.com/2015-06-22/news/63708815_1_dr-ambedkar-caste-system-caste-discrimination
8. Bharti Chhibber, Globalisation and its Impact on Women: *A Critical Assessment, Mainstream,* Vol. XLVII, No. 21, May 9, 2009.
9. Shweta Wankhede, Impact of Dr. Ambedkar's Thoughts on Indian Economy, *Dr. Babasaheb Ambedkar International Association For Education, Japan*, at http://www.baiae.org/resources/articlesessays/113-impact-of-dr-ambedkar%E2%80%99s-thoughts-on-Indian-economy.html
10. Raising Agricultural Productivity and making Farming Remunerative for Farmers, An Occasional Paper of NITI Aayog, Government of India, 16 December 2015, pp. 5-11.
11. B.R. Ambedkar, Small Holdings in India and Their Remedies, Published in *Journal of the Indian Economic Society*, Vol. I. 1918, at http://www.ambedkar.org/ambcd/11.%20Small%20Holdings%20in%20India%20and%20their%20Remedies.htm
12. S.Mahendra Dev, Small Farmers in India: Challenges and Opportunities, *Indira Gandhi Institute of Development Research, Mumbai, June 2012*, at http://www.igidr.ac.in/pdf/publication/WP-2012-014.pdf
13. Narendra Jadhav, Dr. Ambedkar: Economic Thought & Philosophy, Published in 1992.
14. Bhimrao Ambedkar, The Problem of the Rupee.
15. Bhimrao Ambedkar, Small Holdings in India and Their Remedies, Published in Journal of the Indian Economic Society, Vol. I, 1918, at http://www.drbacmahad.org/speeches/small-holdings-in-India-and-their-remedies.pdf.

4

Dr. Ambedkar on Social Transformation: Some Riddles

Chandra Mohan Upadhyay

Political appropriation of an icon is hardly news. What is the new happening is the intellectuals rush to be in the right side of the discourse. A politician can be condoned but the intellectual cannot be. In zeal to appropriate Dr. Ambedkar "a thousand unkind cuts" are applied and the "assassins of the memory triumph merely realign a past figure to the needs of contemporary times".[1] The journey of Dr. Ambedkar from Bhimrao to Babasaheb has not been a linear process. It has got several halts, junctions, caves, cuts and curves. The current race to canonize him, has one predominant common character that is to bypass any or many such points to suit the analysis.

We start our discussion with the oft-quoted opinion of Jafferlot: "In terms of core objective of his politics, the interests of depressed classes were paramount."[2] Apart from him many other Scholars have underlined strategies adopted by Ambedkar, to summarize a few:

(i) He wanted to negotiate in order to create a space for himself.
(ii) He organised the depressed classes to strengthen them and his position, to negotiate with Britishers.
(iii) He tried to ensure a minimum fair space for depressed classes.

Denial of the ***past*** will only perpetuate the *myth-making* on the one side and **petulance** on the other. We cannot brush aside a whole three-decade of his struggles, which form the core of his ideas and ideals, as merely *'space creation effort'* as proposed by some scholars, particularly Suhas Pal Shikhar, is nothing but **naïve.** This is not the first time when for the sake of "declared principles and positions" the scholars and activists have tried to camouflage the debate. It reminds me the division of 'young and old' Marx and the subsequent effort by the avowed Marxist scholars to hide or rather bury the existence of 'young-Marx' altogether. The existence of at least two Ambedkars, one who 'organised the Dalits, created space' and crafted the constitution, the other who collaborated, cooperated and even conspired with Britishers to stem the rising tide of freedom movement, cannot be denied. My considered opinion is that instead of high-lighting or hiding the facts of our liking, let the truth prevail. Dr. Ambedkar is a complete entity and to divide him is to destroy him. Both the sides are inalienable part of his personality. Even Arundhati Roy has to admit the existence of many Ambedkars, though strongly denied by devout supporters "Ambedkar's circumstances forced him to be a revolutionary and to simultaneously put his foot in the door of the establishment whenever he got a chance to. His genius lay in his ability to use both these aspects of himself nimbly, and to great effect. Viewed through the prism of the present, however, it has meant that he left behind a dual and sometimes confusing legacy: Ambedkar the radical, and Ambedkar the father of the Indian Constitution."[3]

Dr. Ambedkar was truly a harbinger of change. He wanted the complete overhaul of the society. This overhaul was completely dependent on the transformation of individual. He like J.S. Mill before him believes that no lasting change can be made without changing the individual and only these changed individuals in turn change the society. No progress worth its name is acceptable to Dr. Ambedkar which is achieved by dwarfing the individual composing the society and state. In India the transformation of individual in particular and society in general was not possible until the two most pressing challenges or to be more precise the impediments are dealt with namely:

1. The curse of caste system and
2. The question of freedom.

The person fondly called 'Baba Saheb' himself decried hero-worship in politics as a "sure road to degradation and to eventual dictatorship'. Prof Upendra Baxi has correctly called Dr. Ambedkar as 'doer' 'not sloganeer'...Dr. Ambedkar shared the perspective of Jawaharlal Nehru somehow to combine the best (creative) elements that will compose an "organic whole", some form of "nationalism and political freedom" and "social freedom" and dream of a classless society". He also agreed for expeditious removal of "all invidious social and customary barriers" impending "the full development of the individual as well as of any group".[4] The major roadblock resisting the change was 'caste as a system', supported by **scriptures** as substructure. According to Dr. Ambedkar, "society is always composed of classes. Their basis may differ. They may be economic or intellectual or social, but an individual in a society is always a member of a class. This is universal fact and early Hindu society could not have been an exception to this rule, and as a matter of fact, we know it was not. So what was the class that first to make in to the caste, for class and caste, so to say, are next door neighbors and it is only the span that separates the two? A caste is "an enclosed class". The system is totally inhuman and unnatural, which is maintained through unnatural means.[5] In other words the caste system has incapacitated the masses and incarcerated their creative energies.

The subdivision of society is not unique to Hinduism. "The subdivision of a society is quite natural. But the unnatural thing about these subdivisions is that they have lost the open door character of the class system and have become the self-enclosed units called castes. The question is: were they compelled to close their doors and become endogamous, or did they close them of their own accord? I submit that there is a double line of the answer. Some closed the doors and others found it closed against them. The one is psychological interpretation and the other is mechanistic, but they are complementary and both are necessary to explain the phenomena of caste-formation in its entirety". There were mainly four classes and resultant castes but during course of time one new class emerged from shudra class that was atishudra or Dalit, which was lower in status than the fourth Varna. When the condition of the fourth class was wretched, it is easier to infer the condition of the fifth class. The Dalits are often called the out-caste or un-touchable. Dalits were deprived of basic human rights.[6]

Their degraded position was sanctified by the religious law books. Ambedkar asserts that caste is not based on division of labor. It is division of laborers. As an economic organisation also, caste is a harmful institution. He calls upon the Hindus to annihilate the caste which is a great hindrance to social solidarity and to set up a new social order based on the ideals of liberty, equality and fraternity in consonance with the principles of Democracy. He advocates inter-caste marriage as one of the solutions to the problem. But he stresses that the belief in the 'shastras' is the root cause of maintaining castes. He therefore suggests, "make every man and woman free from the thralldom of the 'shastras', cleanse their mind of the pernicious notions founded on the 'shastras' and he or she will inter-dine and intermarry".[7] According to Dr. Ambedkar, opines Sanjay Kumar Pandagale "the society must be based on reason and not on atrocious traditions of caste system. From the above deliberation it is clear that the Caste is a close system and Class is an open system. Education can lead an individual to move from Caste to Class, i.e. from close system to open system. In Caste system, an individual is confined only to his or her traditional occupation. So, there is a little scope to grow. But in Class, as it is open, an individual can grow as per his or her capability. And only education can bring this change"[8] If this argument is taken on face value, then the western societies which are free from the vices of caste system should be equal-societies. The likes of Babeuf and Blonc or Karl Marx have absolutely no business over there. Unfortunately the whole 'discourses on Inequality' was born there and our Babasaheb learnt his first lessons there itself. Let us discuss some of the important view-points of Dr. Ambedkar on 'caste system'.

Dr. Ambedkar compared the caste system to a multi-storied building, which has no gate, no entrance and even no staircases. You have to die in the story you are born. Dr. Ambedkar correctly underlines the most pernicious effects of the caste system that it promotes 'isolation as a virtue'. Caste is basically a kind of 'infection of Imitation', which produces graded inequalities. More importantly the caste system obliterates the distinction between victim and oppressor. It is against the above analysis or rather accusations, I have to evaluate and examine the views of Dr. Ambedkar in the light of some other greats of the field, who are not only renowned but respected for their works across the globe. Some of them need reproduction here. The renowned historian

Romila Thapar in her book 'Interpreting early India' has noted that "Senart (*Les Castes dans l'Inde*-1896) sought the answer to the origins of the caste in the constitution of family. Caste has the same rights over individuals as do early families in other ancient societies such as Greeks and Romans. Endogamous laws were also fundamental to these societies (e.g. the *jus connubii* of Rome). The laws of commensality in the caste tended to exclude the aliens from sacrifices and religious feasts, since a meal signifies sharing and equality. Even the fear of impurity and defilement has analogies from Greco-Roman parallels. The origin of the caste requires a multi-causal explanation."[9]

For Dr. Ambedkar the division of society was universal but division along caste-lines was not only unnatural but unique phenomenon of Hindu society. The renowned Indologist Bougle also examined the caste in the light of the definition of 'mechanical solidarity'. He began by investigating whether caste was indigenous to Hindu society or was common to all societies at some stage. He includes among the characteristics of caste the following four: hereditary specialization, hierarchy and the inequality of rights and a clear opposition between elementary groups. Bougle disagrees with the explanation that the *Brahmans* were the originators of the caste using it to divide and control society which he felt too great emphasis on religion".[10] For Bougle, writes Prof. Romila Thapar the prototypes of caste were not the *varnas* but the jatis which were lineage descendants and indicated the dominance of ancient familial exclusivism. Such exclusivism was not specifically Aryan; tribal societies are known to have had rigid rules of exogamy and commensality and fraternity taboos are also to be found among the Semites. According to Bougle the idea which generated the caste system, are not peculiar to the Hindus or the Aryans but were the common patrimony of primitive peoples.

The allegations of caste being stagnant and non-associative in character have acquired axiomatic character. And champions of this infallible theory have refused to renounce their principled stand. But the facts tell us a different story. There are ample proof of emergence of a community cutting across the caste and religious lines. In the normative text of Brahmanism, the ***Dharmashastras*** it is conceded that there were a variety of communities, determined by location, occupation and caste, and none of which were necessarily, writes

Romila Thapar "bound together by a common religious identity...in urban centers craftsmen of the same profession or of related profession formed organisations and guilds, such as '*gosthi*' and '*sreni*'."[11]

The Brahmanism or Hinduism has been more associative and open to adjustment than has been recognised. The presence of a uniform cultural-pattern across the length and breadth of India which may be termed as 'Hindu-Civilisation' is not without significance. Romila Thappar underlines the positive contributions of caste "it was again the assimilative character of caste which was fundamental to major social and economic changes from the late first millennium AD onwards, particularly in periods of state formation. It could be argued that the nature of caste underwent a historic change during this period—a change which has not been fully recognised by historians and sociologists.[12] This prowess cannot be brushed aside as merely "the capacity to eat dung and digest it."[13] The exchange between the high-culture of Brahmanism and the low-culture of local cults is generally known as the Sanskritisation of the latter. But there is another way round also. The high-culture has to bend in order to embrace the so called low-culture. The Viththala at Pandharpur and the Jagannath of Puri suddenly acquire centrality in Hinduism. This adaptability is seldom recognised in more positive ways. The multiplicity of cults and sects also reflects a multiplicity of beliefs. If two sruti-traditions are in conflict both are to be held as law.

This is fundamentally a different approach from that of religions, writes Romila Thappar, which would like to insist on a single interpretation arising out of a given theological framework.[14] The Vedas are the rock-bottom of Dharm i.e. the moral-order; even they may not satisfy someone. In such situation she should consult the scriptures, thereafter should seek the inspiration from noble deeds of the greats, not satisfied by even this option people should follow the commands of their conscience and the conscience is the ultimate court. No other religion allow this much liberty.

Even Acharya Kautilya maintains that while deciding a suit there might arise controversy between the rulings of Dharmshstra and jurisprudence, between jurisprudence and charit (the examples set by people of great character), between charit and edicts. In such situations the prior prevails over latter. Unlike the holy 'Bible' or the holy 'Koran' and despite their infallibility and transcendental character even the holy Vedas are not final word.

So far as the question of dismantling the scriptural base to realize the 'dreams' of Babsahebji is concerned, suffice is to say that many determinations of social development have had fallen flat on the ground like Hegel's march of 'Spirit', and Karl Marx's 'Withering-away of State' and this deterministic solution is bound to meet the same fate. Why the so called scriptures are essential for Hindu society and why they cannot be dismantled? India is the land of diversities and the one common ground that we have is our traditions and religion. The scriptures are the carriers of these traditions and religion. The scriptures ensure the continuity of culture and culture in turn "withstands the shocks, not a single mass of knowledge could do..."[15] Swamiji was not alone but the whole lot of freedom fighters from Lokmanya Tilak, Aurobindo, Lala Lajpat Rai to Mahatma Gandhi firmly maintained that some of the scriptures are national in character like Ramayana, Mahabharata and Gita and these are respected by all the Hindus despite several differences. The epics are basically civilisational symbols. They act like the vision documents and are constitutional in nature. They are the common points of references. "The germs of spirituality are stored up in our books".[16]

No nation and no society can commit suicide for some grand formulations how so ever lofty. Once you renounce the scriptures the chaos is the natural corollary. Once Your identity as a culture and civilisation is gone into the wind, several 'World-Class' religions with their hands out-stretched towards you are eager to embrace you in their larger 'brotherhood'. If this is the only recipe from the side of Babasaheb then this is also the surest way to disaster. Swami Vivekananda couldn't hide his dismay over such kinds of attitudes when he brilliantly highlighted the shortcomings of social and conscientious reformers like Buddha, Ramanujan and Kabir. "They raised the lower classes; they had all the wishes that these should come up, but they did not apply their energies to the spreading of Sanskrit language among the masses. Even the great Buddha made one false step when he stopped the Sanskrit language from being studied by masses. He wanted rapid and immediate results, and translated and preached in...Pali. That was great; it spread the ideas quickly...knowledge came but culture was not there. Knowledge is only skin-deep... and a little scratch brings out the old savage...something more is necessary; give them culture."[17] Swamiji also suggested the right ways to mitigate the caste conflicts. "Until you give the masses the culture, there can be no permanence in the raised condition of the masses. There will be another caste created...I tell you men who belong to lower castes, the only way to raise your condition, is to study Sanskrit. This fighting and writing and frothing against the higher castes is in vain, it does no good, and it creates fight and quarrel, and this race already divided, is going to divided more and more. "The only way to bring about the leveling of caste is to appropriate the culture, the education, which is the strength of the higher castes. That done you have what you want".[18] The annihilation of scriptures will not bring any of desired result. Instead it will create what has been aptly described by noted novelist Jhumpa Lahiri: "a generation of ABCDs in India, unaware of their culture, customs and traditions." Dr. Ambedkar was completely aware of the significant role of education in bringing the desired social transformation. He said, "Educate, Organise and Agitate". Here he had given a prime importance to education. He further added that, "The backward classes have come to realize that after all education is the greatest material benefit, for which they can fight. We may forego material benefits of civilisation but we cannot forego our rights and opportunities to reap the benefits of the highest education to the fullest extent. That the importance of this question from the point of view of the backward classes who have just realized that without education their existence is not safe."[19] He suffered a lot due to this caste system. Still in that system of discrimination, he succeeded to well educate himself. His own life is a shining example of the drastic changes ushered in by education.

A crusader against social and economic injustice and a great champion of human rights with a firm belief in democracy, he exhorted his audience at the All India Depressed Classes Conference: "It seems to me that there lies on us a very important duty to see that democracy does not vanish from the earth as the governing principle of human relationship. If we believe in it, we must both be true and loyal to it. We must not only be staunch in our faith in democracy, but we must resolve to see that whatever we do not help the enemies of democracy to uproot the principles of liberty, equality and fraternity."[20] For that he exhorted the Dalits to defend and support democracy and secularism to safeguard their rights, life and liberty.

A relentless champion of human rights and staunch believer in democracy, Dr. Ambedkar says: "Democracy is not a form of government, but a form of social organisation." Dr. Ambedkar believed that in democracy revolutionary changes in the economic and social life of the people are brought about without bloodshed. The conditions for that are as follows: "(1) there should not be glaring inequalities in society, that is, privilege for one class; (2) the existence of an opposition; (3) equality in law and administration; (4) observance of constitutional morality; (5) no tyranny of the majority; (6) moral order of society: and (7) public conscience." Addressing the Constituent Assembly, he suggested certain devices essential to maintain democracy: "(i) constitutional methods: (ii) not to lay liberties at the feet of a great man: (iii) make a political democracy a social democracy."[21] Dr. Ambedkar firmly believed that political democracy cannot succeed without social and economic democracy. For him political democracy is not an end in itself, but the most powerful means to achieve the social and economic ideals in society. State socialism within the framework of Parliamentary democracy can defeat dictatorship. Fundamental rights without economic security are of no use to the have-nots. "Social and economic democracy are tissue and the fiber of a political democracy." In his talk given on the Voice of America he argued that: "Democracy could not be equated with either republic or Parliamentary form of government. The roots of democracy lay not in the form of government, Parliamentary or otherwise. A democracy is a model of associated living. The roots of democracy are to be searched in social relationship, in terms of the associated life between people who form the society."[22] He was against coercive centralized institutional authority of state. It was against the privilege-based caste-system that Dr. Ambedkar rebelled and tried to replace the traditional and social morality with constitutional morality. Speaking on 4th November 1948 in Constituent Assembly, he said: "Constitutional morality is not a natural sentiment. It has to be cultivated. We must realize that our people have yet to learn. Democracy in India is only a top dressing on Indian soil, which is essentially undemocratic."[23] Indian society may be undemocratic, but some hard truths tell a different story altogether. The mother of modern democracy, a democracy without ills and evils of democracy, our famous Switzerland could accept women's equality only in 1973 by granting them right to vote. France the land of liberty, equality and fraternity reached this stage in 1945, USA in 1920 and the most progressive land the England in 1928. May I humbly ask how many countries qualify 'democratic test' of Dr. Ambedkar? Democracy has rightly been called a way of life apart from a form of government. This 'way of life' has to be learned. It is neither a gift of God nor a process of nature but is a habit to be acquired. India cannot squarely be blamed for rather shallow roots of democracy.

Dr. Ambedkar correctly underlined the need to strike a proper balance between liberty and equality in order to establish a just and egalitarian society. He emphasised on the need for liberty of movement, liberty of speech and liberty of action and political liberty to choose his government for securing "unalienable rights such as life, liberty and pursuit of happiness. Political liberty is really a deduction from the principle of human personality and equality." Liberty and equality exist together. One without the other is absurd. Commenting on failure of democracy in some countries, he said: "Parliamentary democracy developed a passion for liberty. It failed to realize the significance of equality and did not even endeavour to strike a balance between liberty and equality, with the result that liberty swallowed equality and has made democracy a name and a farce".[24] He was against all form of violence. A firm believer in the Buddhist doctrine of non-violence he asked his followers to 'agitate' for their rights in a peaceful manner. Violence undermines the spirit of democracy. He would never have supported Naxalites as being done by many of his supporters today.

The second major road-block to the process of social transformation is the rejection of villages as a basis of governance, so dear to the heart of Mahatma Gandhi, as they are 'a sink of localism, a den of ignorance, narrow-mindedness and communalism."[25] Instead he suggested the adoption of cities as the basic unit of governance. The cities are the epicenter of modernism, which ensures the freedom from traditions and heralds myriads of opportunities otherwise denied to the people of weaker section of society. It is high time to behold this remedy from the point of view of his one of the staunchest supporters and renowned scholar Arundhati Roy. While criticizing Gandhian utopia of village republic, she heaps praise on him " The impetus towards justice turned Ambedkar's gaze away from the village towards the city, towards urbanism, modernism and industrialisation—big cities, big dams, big irrigation projects. Ironically, this is the very model of "development" that hundreds of thousands of people today associate with injustice, a model that lays the environment to waste and involves the forcible displacement of millions of people from their villages and homes by mines, dams and other major infrastructural projects. Meanwhile, Gandhi—whose mythical village is so blind to appalling, inherent injustice—has, as ironically, become the talisman of these struggles for justice... Gandhi was prescient enough to recognise the seed of cataclysm that was implanted in the project of Western modernity. Gandhiji prophetically opined "God forbid that India should ever take to industrialism after the manner of the West. The economic imperialism of a single tiny island kingdom is today keeping the world in chains. If an entire nation of 300 million took to similar economic exploitation it would strip the world bare like locusts.[26] "As the earth warms up, as glaciers melt and forests disappear, Gandhi's words have turned out to be prophetic. But his horror of modern civilisation led him to eulogize a mythical Indian past that was, in his telling, just and beautiful. Ambedkar, on his part, was painfully aware of the iniquity of that past, but in his urgency to move away from it, he failed to recognise the catastrophic dangers of Western modernity."[27] Gandhi is probably first to remind the present generation about the necessity of recognizing our true needs and retrieve ourselves from the pangs of greed. "Civilisation in the real sense of the term consists not in multiplication, but deliberate and voluntary, reduction of wants which promotes real happiness and contentment and increases the capacity for servical."[28] This very insight of watching through the eyes of soul differentiated Gandhi from the rest.

Dr. Ambedkar was not very convinced with the ongoing freedom struggle in the country. For him the real freedom struggle had to concern itself with the emancipation of Dalits from the age-old bonds of caste. The first things should be first and in the lexical order of priority for Ambedkar the liberation of Dalits was prior to India's freedom. He said "It is foolish to take solace in the fact that because the Congress is fighting for the freedom of India, it is, therefore, fighting for the freedom of the people of India and of the lowest of the low," Ambedkar said. "The question whether the Congress is fighting for freedom has very little importance as compared to the question for whose freedom is the Congress fighting."[29] In 1931, when Ambedkar met Gandhi for the first time, Gandhi questioned him about his sharp criticism of the Congress.

"Gandhiji, I have no Homeland," was Ambedkar's famous reply. "No Untouchable worth the name will be proud of this land."[30]

Let us search the genuine answer to the question of 'whose freedom the congress is fighting'. Before the dawn of independence, India was truly termed the land of famines and floods. During infamous Bengal famine of 1943, more than nine million people perished. Most of them belonged to the very lower strata of society. According to noted economist Amartya Sen: "Contrary to the popular opinion of food availability deficiency (FAD), the actual availability of food increased during the (famine) period. Because the available food was very costly, only a few could manage to buy and rest perished".[32] who were rest? The rest were the poor people. Now the moot question is whether in free India anything really changed for the poor people? And the answer is a big YES. And the greatest beneficiaries of the change are the very people in whose name Dr. Ambedkar waged his life struggle. Not only in India but anywhere in democratic and free world no famine has ever taken place "No famine has ever taken place in the history of a functioning democracy."[32] Democracy is rightly called freedom and freedom is called power. It is clear that the Indian National Congress fought for the freedom of whole country, not for this and that section of society. Ambedkar's main concern was to privilege and legalize "constitutional morality" over the traditional, social morality of the caste system. His intentions cannot be doubted even by his staunchest of critics. Some of his solutions which form a kind of belief-system in his otherwise huge intellectual thought-monument are debatable and questionable. No living generation can pretend to survive, if it fails to equip itself with the critical-eye. No person, tradition or idea remains great by being 'unquestionable'. In the realm of immortality let there be struggle for survival among the best and fittest ideas.

END NOTES

1. Prof. Upendra Baxi: 'How not to recall an icon', *The Indian Express*, 18.04.2016.
2. Jafferlot Christopher: 'Which Ambedkar', *The Indian Express*, 26.12.2015.
3. Arundhati Roy: the doctor and the saint.
4. Prof. Upendra Baxi: 'How not to recall an icon', *The Indian Express*, 18.04.2016.
5. Dr. Babasaheb Ambedkar: writings and speeches, p.15.
6. Ibid.
7. Ibid
8. Sanjay Kumar Pandangale: Social philosophy of Dr. Ambedkar (Online available source).

9. Romila Thapar: 'Interpreting Early India', Oxford University Press, New Delhi, 1992, p.32.
10. Ibid., p.38
11. Ibid., pp.75-76.
12. Romila Thapar: 'the past and prejudice', p. 55.
13. Arun Shourie: 'worshiping False God' Rupa & Co, New Delhi, 1997, p.230.
14. Romila Thapar: 'Interpreting Early India', Oxford University Press, New Delhi, 1992, p.68.
15. Swami Vekananda: 'The complete works of Swami Vivekananda', Advait Ashram (Publication Dept.) Calcutta, 1986, p.281.
16. Ibid.
17. Ibid.
18. Ibid p.282.
19. Sanjay Kumar Pandangale, *Social Philosophy of Dr. Ambedkar* (Online available source).
20. Arundhati Roy, *The Doctor and the Saint*, p.11.
21. Shyam Chand: 'Dr. Ambedkar on Democracy', *Mainstream*, Vol. XLV-51, 08.12.2007.
22. Ibid.
23. Ambedkar said this during his speech delivered as Chairman of the Constitution Drafting Committee in the Constituent Assembly on 4 November 1948. CAD.
24. Shyam Chand: 'Dr. Ambedkar on Democracy', *Mainstream*, Vol. XLV-51, 08.12.2007.
25. Ambedkar said this during his speech delivered as Chairman of the Constitution Drafting Committee in the Constituent Assembly. CAD
26. Arundhati Roy: The doctor and the saint.
27. Ibid.
28. Mahatma Gandhi—'India of My Dreams', Rajpal & Sons, New Delhi 2008, p.30.
29. Arundhati Roy: The doctor and the saint.
30. Ibid.
31. Amartya Sen: wikepedia
32. Ibid.

5

Dr. B.R. Ambedkar's Philosophy on Education and its Relevance to the Present Education System in India

Daniel Debbarma

Dr. B.R. Ambedkar had a deep relation with education and his writings show expertise and in-depth analysis of the subject. He has been described as a philosopher, a patriot, scholar or a writer, the constitution maker, a social revolutionary, a humanistic thinker, or the socialist and he had also contributed a great deal to the cause of education. He mainly emphasized on education as a vital force for individual development and social change. Ambedkar realized education to be a priority for the society and for growth of individuals with character. His educational philosophy stresses on development of persons and their environment. Ambedkar also saw education as something that can create radical changes in an oppressed society and create avenues for change which are equal for all. His philosophy has great ideas for practical fulfillment and these ideas have the relevance to modern society. This paper highlights Ambedkar's mission, his thoughts, ideology, and strategy to strengthen our nation through education and its relevance in the present society. His contributions and vision towards education should be traced and nurtured. His thoughts resonate with the current academic discourse and hence make him relevant, to bring in a perspective which has been missing. The study is based on secondary data obtained from various texts, reference books, internet and various published journals and reports.

Dr. Bhimrao Ramji Ambedkar was born in a class considered low and outcast on 14th April 1891. He was a person with high intellect and was trained under the then distinguished scholars like John Dewey, Charles Beard and R.A. Seligman (Sirswal, 2011). He had given prime importance to education. He said that, "The backward classes have come to realize that after all education is the greatest material benefit for which they can fight. We may forego material benefits of civilization but we cannot forego our rights and opportunities to reap the benefits of the highest education fully". He suffered a lot due to caste system and still in that system of discrimination; he succeeded to well educate himself. He fought for the downtrodden and underprivileged selflessly. The man who suffered bitter humiliation became the first Minister for Law in free India and shaped the country's Constitution. He belonged to 20th century and his educational philosophy struck roots in the western pragmatic philosopher called John Dewey's theory of education. Therefore, Ambedkar approached the problem of educational upliftment of the masses as a pragmatist. He believed that education is one of the basic needs along with food, clothing, shelter and medicine. Ambedkar was very particular in developing the primary education and he says "The objective of primary education is to see that every child that enters the portals of a primary school does leave it only at a stage when it becomes literate and continues to be literate throughout the rest of his life." He put all his efforts to guarantee the education without any discrimination to all the citizens of independent India. He said "Education is something which ought to be brought within the reach of every one". This paper is an attempt to draw an outline of Dr. B.R. Ambedkar's Philosophy of education and social change. It is astonishing to realize that Ambedkar's opinions and perceptions on education are not being recognized. Present education system in India has different aims and objectives with regard to our needs and these are incompetent for individual and social growth. Dr. B.R. Ambedkar's philosophy on education enlightens us with clear understanding of the nature of our society and its relevance to the present education system in India.

Ambedkar's Philosophy on Education

His Educational philosophy stresses on development of persons and their environment. Ambedkar also saw education as something that can create radical changes in an oppressed society and create avenues for change which are equal for all. Ambedkar realized education to be a priority for the society and for growth of individuals with character. When Ambedkar talked about knowledge, he listed two purposes of knowledge: first, to acquire it for the betterment of others and secondly to use it for one's own betterment. The basic theme of his philosophy of education is inculcating the values of liberty, equality, fraternity, justice and moral character among the boys and girls of all classes. He emphasized on three components as objectives for policy makers: (1) Recasting the aims and purposes of education, (2) Education as an instrument of substantive equality, (3) Women's education (Velaskar, 2012). His contribution ranges from educational reforms made by the British Indian government in the education system from before independence to the post-Independence era. Ambedkar enthusiastically supported schooling that inculcates human rights education, education that teaches human dignity and justice in India. Ambedkar had explained the importance of education in his written testimony before the University Reform Committee set up by the Municipal Government regarding Mumbai University reforms. He discussed various issues related to education and also the reasons for the failure of the education system.

Dr. Ambedkar's Concept of Educate, Agitate and Organize

"Educate, Agitate and Organize" are three final words of Dr. B.R. Ambedkar. It has given meaningful massage to the people towards a meaningful development. Being a Buddhist, Babasaheb gave these slogans based on Buddhist philosophy. One may question as to why we must follow a particular order of these final words of Dr. Ambedkar.

Education has an enormous impact on the human society. Through education an individual is able to acquire knowledge, self confidence, dignified living and self attainment. It plays an important role in eradication of poverty of the society. Ignorance and poverty go hand in hand and for this, Education is the only weapon to break this vicious circle. It trains the human mind to think and take the right decision. In other words, man becomes a rational animal when he is educated.

According to Babasaheb the word 'Agitate' does not mean to agitate physically; it is a mental revolution in its place. Agitated mind, as Dr. Ambedkar presumed, would force educated people to form organizations and they would act to fix the problems. It does not mean to go out and start protesting violently on the streets without getting educated. On should be educated first in order to agitate for a better cause. Agitate means the agitation of thoughts in our mind in order to move to the next level i.e. to organize. So one needs to be educated first and then learn to agitate so that he or she can collectively organize. Agitated minds for a common mission will help them to unite and struggle for their common goal as one force.

Dr. B.R. Ambedkar insisted on his Dalit people "to educate, to organize and to struggle" for their own betterment by using whatever educational facilities they have. He recognized that lack of education was the main cause for the backwardness of poor people. Education is an effective instrument of mass movement to safeguard life and liberty.

Role of Recent Policies, Commissions and Acts in Education

Since Independence, the educational development initiatives have brought lot of changes in the country. The dream of Dr. B.R. Ambedkar to educate every child has been nearly fulfilled. His philosophy of education has been brought into practical reality by various education Policies, Commissions and Acts of the country.

After Independence, India had two national education policies: the National Policy on Education 1968 and the National Policy on Education 1986. The focal concerns of the NPE 1968, which were based on the Kothari Commission Report (1964-66), revolved around ensuring compulsory elementary education and equalizing educational opportunities. The NPE 1986 continued many of the key focuses of 1968 policy and also brought-in quality concerns through its recommendations of making elementary school education child-centered, creating provision for recruitment of teachers and for enhancement of infrastructure. Recently, the Government of India has announced the formulation of 3rd New National Education Policy 2015-16 (NPE) through a 'consultative' process. It has sought responses from various stakeholders in education on a set of themes and questions for school and higher education levels. While these are the national policies of education in India, there are several significant developments that have impacted last two policies and have shaped or are shaping the school education sector. Among these, three recent significant ones are: the Children's Right to Free and Compulsory Education Act, 2009 (RTE), the National Curriculum Framework 2005 (NCF), and the Justice Verma Commission on Teacher Education 2012 (JVC). These documents underline the conception of education as children's right and outline a framework to reform 'quality' of school education. While the RTE Act is meant to operationalise the Article 21A of the Indian constitution which makes elementary education a justifiable right of the children of ages 6 to 14, the NCF 2005 may be seen as defining what educational/ curricular experience should be like and the JVC charts the revamping of teacher education in the country to reform teaching–learning in schools.

It's Relevance in Present India

Keeping in mind the educational philosophy of Dr. B.R. Ambedkar the present scenario of education in India will indicate the level of educational development we reached in present India today.

Literacy Rates

The literacy rate of both male and female is given in the Table 1 from 1951 to 2011 census of India. From 1951 to 1971 the literacy age is from 5 years and above. From 1981 to 2011 the age of literacy starts from 7 years and above.

Table 1: Literacy Rates (%age)

Census Year	Persons	Males	Females
1951	18.3	27.2	8.9
1961	28.3	40.4	15.4
1971	34.5	46.0	22.0
1981	43.6	56.4	29.8
1991	52.2	64.1	39.3
2001	64.8	75.3	53.7
2011	73.0	80.9	64.6

1951-1971: Aged 5+; 1981-2011: Aged 7+.

Source: Census of India, 2011.

The Table 1 depicts that the percentage of literacy rate has drastically increased from 1951 to 2011. After the Independence from 1951 to 2011 there is an increase from 18.3 percent to 73.0 percent. However the percentage of female still remains low compared to male with the difference of 16.3 percent as per last 2011 census report. The dream of Dr. B.R. Ambedkar on female literacy has been achieved to some extent since Independence but the female literacy needs more focus. Without equal progress of both men and women the society cannot achieve all round development. Ignorance and poverty go hand in hand and for this, Literacy is the only weapon to break this vicious circle.

Table 2: Adult Literacy Rate among BRICSAM Countries

BRICSAM Countries	Adult Literacy Rate (%)
Mexico	93.4
Indonesia	92.0
India	62.8
Brazil	90.4
China	92.0
South Africa	93.0
Russia	99.7

Source: UNESCO Institute for Statistics (2012).

The Table 2 depicts the Adult Literacy Rate among BRICSAM countries. It is seen that the Adult Literacy rate of Mexico is 93.4, Indonesia 92.0, India 62.8, Brazil 90.4, China 92.0, South Africa 93.0 and Russia 99.7. India has the lowest Adult Literacy Rate by only 62.8 percent. The Adult literacy gap between India and rest of the BRICSAM countries is seen with a difference by 30.61 percent. Russia has the highest literacy rate of 99.7 percent and India with lowest rate of only 62.8 percent.

Table 3: Disparities in Literacy Across Gender, Social Groups and Location

Rural						Urban					
ST			SC			ST			SC		
M	F	T	M	F	T	M	F	T	M	F	T
66.8	46.9	56.9	72.6	52.6	62.8	83.2	70.3	76.8	83.3	68.6	76.2

Source: Census of India, 2011.

From the given Table 3, we can see there are huge disparities in literacy across gender, social group and location. In the rural area the literacy rate of ST is lowest including both male and female. In the urban area the literacy rate of ST is comparatively similar to SC category. But both ST and SC categories are lower in rural areas. The female literacy rate is low in both social groups and location. The female literacy rate in rural in lower with 67.8 percent compared to female literacy in urban area of 84.1. The comparative table also depicts the overall differences between urban and rural locations.

Table 4: Enrolment of Students in 2013-14 (Provisional)

(In lakhs)

Level	All			SC			ST		
	Boys	**Girls**	**Total**	**Boys**	**Girls**	**Total**	**Boys**	**Girls**	**Total**
I-V	672	628	1300	135	126	261	75	70	145
VI-VIII	337	320	657	66	63	128	33	31	64
IX-X	195	175	370	35	32	68	16	15	32
Senior Secondary (XI-XII)	117	104	222	20	18	39	7	6	14
Higher Education	163	133	296	20	16	36	7	6	13

Source: Educational statistics at a glance (2014), Government of India, MHRD, New Delhi.

From the given Table 4, the enrolment of students in 2013- 14 both at different levels and categories have been shown. From the table it is clear that the weaker section of the society like Scheduled Caste (SC) and Scheduled Tribe (ST) both are comparatively very low in enrolments against overall enrolment of students in the country. The table also shows the decreasing level of enrolments in all the categories from lower to higher education level. The ST category students' enrolment is lower in all the levels compared to SC category comparatively. The female enrolments in all the categories are lower compared to male literacy rate. The table depicts the fall of literacy rate from primary to higher education and this indicates the level of quality education as it goes higher. The gross enrolment at primary level has no meaning if it fails to educate them at higher level. So, maintain the rate of literacy percentage at higher education level is also important.

Table 5: Drop-Out Rates in School Education in 2013-14 (Provisional)

Level	All			SC			ST		
	Boys	**Girls**	**Total**	**Boys**	**Girls**	**Total**	**Boys**	**Girls**	**Total**
I-V	21.2	18.3	19.8	17.7	15.4	16.6	31.9	30.7	31.3
I-VIII	39.2	32.9	36.3	42.4	34.4	38.8	49.8	46.4	48.2
I-X	48.1	46.7	47.4	51.8	48.0	50.1	63.2	61.4	62.4

Source: Educational statistics at a glance (2014), Government of India, MHRD, New Delhi.

The Table 5 shows the Drop-Out rates in school education in 2013-14 both 'level-wise' and 'category-wise'. In both SC and ST category, the education level decreases as it goes higher from lower level to the upper levels (class I to X). The Drop-Out rates from class I-V level is 19.8, from class I-VIII is 36.3 and from Class I-X is 47.4. Similarly, in the cases of SC and ST categories the dropout rates keep on increasing as it goes on to the higher levels. So, the Drop-Out rates are found to be more increasing at higher levels in India.

Table 6: Lowest Average Schooling Years

Countries →	India	Indonesia	Brazil	China	Mexico	South Africa	Russia
Mean Years of Schooling received by people from ages 25 and above	4.4	5.8	7.2	7.5	8.5	8.5	11.7

Source: UNESCO Institute for Statistics (2012).

The Mean years of schooling received by people ages of 25 years and above are connected with dropout rates in higher education. If the schooling years is less the competency level of the student will also be less. Among the lowest Mean years of schooling received by people ages 25 and above is India. The above Table 6 shows the comparison of average schooling years. The lowest average schooling years are found to be in India with 4.4 percent followed by Indonesia and Brazil with 5.8 and 7.2 likewise. Subsequently China, Mexico, South Africa and Russia also has low Mean years of schooling received by people ages 25 and above with 7.5, 8.5, 8.5 and 11.7 respectively.

The Table 7 depicts the percentages of out of school children by religion including Hindu, Muslim, Christian and Others. In Rural areas the percentage of out of school children belonging to Hindu religion is

2.73 percent whereas in Urban area the percentage is 1.95. In case of Muslim, the percentage of children out of school in Rural area is 4.34 and in Urban area is 4.58. Among the Christians the percentage of children out of school in Rural area is 1.77 and in Urban area is 1.06 percent. It is found that the school children belonging to Hindu and Muslim have the highest percentage of out of school children by religion in India.

Table 7: Out of School Children by Religion in India (%)

	Hindu	Muslim	Christian	Others	Total
Rural	2.97	4.34	1.77	1.33	3.13
Urban	1.95	4.58	1.06	1.06	2.54

Source: Census of India, 2011.

From the given Table 8, we can see the percentages of children with special needs out of school. All Physically or Mentally Challenged has a percentage of 28.07, Mental Disability children is 35.97, Visual Disability 17.64, Hearing Disability 19.31, Speech Disability 34.82, Orthopedic Disability 23.72 and Multiple Disability 44.13 percent of school children with special disability that is out of school. Among them the children with Disabilities mental, speech and multiple has the highest percentage in out of school.

Table 8: Out of School Children with Special Needs (%)

Types of Disability	All Physically or Mentally Challenged	Mental Disability	Visual Disability	Hearing Disability	Speech Disability	Orthopedic Disability	Multiple Disability
% of out of school Children with special needs	28.07	35.97	17.64	19.31	34.82	23.72	44.13

From Table 9, we can see that the public spending on education is highest in South Africa. Brazil has the percentage of 5.8 percent, followed by Mexico 5.2 percent, then China 4 percent, India 3.8 and Indonesia 2.7 percent. Indonesia and India are among the less public spending on education among BRICSAM countries.

Table 9: Public Spending on Education

Countries	*Indonesia*	*India*	*China*	*Mexico*	*Brazil*	*South Africa*
Public expenditure on education as % of GDP (2011)	2.8	3.8	4.0	5.2	5.8	6

Source: UNESCO Institute for Statistics (2012).

Conclusion

From the given reports and data it is found that the educational status of Scheduled Castes (SCs) and Scheduled Tribes (STs) is much lower in comparison to other communities in our country even today. The NCERT says, "Across the country, enormous strides towards establishing schools within the reach of every habitation have been made. Attempts to put larger number of children through schooling have proved to be successful. But pockets of children still remain to be reached-children from the socially weaker sections, those belonging to the scheduled castes and tribes, those belonging to the minority groups, and particularly girls, in each of these groups. The need of the hour is to identify the extraordinary socio-cultural circumstances which restrict these children from accessing schools". The education system till this date projects itself as a tool for empowerment of marginalized and weaker sections of the society, but in practice it conveniently sabotages the same process of empowerment when it magnifies the importance of 'quality' in the present education system. Ambedkar's philosophy of education is not only on equal opportunity for all children but also to provide quality in education. Even toady much of the focus is on 'quantity education' (free and compulsory) and not emphasized on 'quality education'. As a result the dropout and stagnation still remains very high compared to other developed countries. The present education system should focus on creating not only academically qualified citizens rather nurture educated and empowered citizens thereby making them capable of seeking their self justice and rights. Teachers and trainers also need to promote an education that works towards the objectives of self-actualization and a just society. With such collective efforts, education can play a great role in the sensitization and creation of citizens who are aware of the injustice in the society and also motivate them to face challenge.

REFERENCES

Educational statistics at a glance (2014), Government of India, Ministry of Human Resource Development, Bureau of planning, monitoring and statistics, New Delhi.

Elementary education in India Trends 2005 to 2014, Sarva Shiksha Abhiyan (SSA), Published by National University of Educational Planning And Aministration, New Delhi, India.

Encyclopedia of Philosophy of Education: www.educao.pro.br/;links.html

http://mospi.nic.in/Mospi_New/site/inner.aspx?status=3&menu_id=31

https://www.cigionline.org/project/bricsam

Kotzee, B (2013), "Introduction: Education, Social Epistomology and Virtue Epistomology", *Journal of Philosophy of Education*, Vol. 47, No. 2

Mukherji, N. (2002), "Academic Philosophy in India", *Economic and Political Weekly*, Vol. XXXVII, No. 10

Rafaqi, M (2013), "Dalit Education and Government Policies," *Research Journal of Humanities and Social Sciences*. Vol.3. issue. 3.

Registrar General of India. Census of India, 2011, http://censusindia.gov.in/2011-common/Census DataSummary.html

School Education of India (2013), U-DISE 2013-14, National University of Educational Planning and Administration 17-B, Sri Aurobindo Marg, New Delhi 110016 (India)

Secondary Education India, State report cards (2013), Rashtrya Madhyamik Shikha Abhiyan, (RMSA) U-Dise, Published by National University of Educational Planning And Aministration, New Delhi, India.

Sirswal, R.D. (2011), Dr. Ambedkar's Ideas on Education and Social Change, *Weslyan Journal of Research*, Vol. 4, No.1.

State Report Cards 2013-14 (2013), U-DISE 2013-14, National University of Educational Planning and Administration 17-B, Sri Aurobindo Marg, New Delhi 110016 (India).

UNESCO Institute for Statistics (2012), www.uis.unesco.org

Valeskar, P. (2012), "Education for Liberation: Ambedkar's Thoughts and Dalit Women's Perspective", *Sage*, 9 (2) 245-271

6

Ambedkar's Idea of Social Justice

Deepak Yadav

Ambedkar's legacy as a socio-political reformer has a deep impact on modern India. In post-Independent India, his socio-political thought is respected across the political spectrum. His initiatives have influenced various spheres of life and transformed the way India today looks at socio-economic policies, education and affirmative action through socio-economic and legal incentives. His reputation as a scholar led to his appointment as free India's first law minister, and chairman of the committee for drafting the constitution. He passionately believed in individual freedom and criticised caste society.

The social justice is an application of the concept of distributive justice to the wealth, assets, privileges and advantages that accumulate within a society or state because the essence of justice is the attainment of the common goods as distinguished from the goods of individuals even of the majority. There have been two major conceptions of social justice one embodying the notion of merit and deserve, the other those of needs and equality. The first conception involves ending of hereditary privileges and an open society in which people have the chance to display their capability. It is expressed in equality of opportunity and careers open to talents. The second conception implies that goods should be allocated according to each person's varied needs. As it aims to make people materially equal, it entails an idea of equality.

In the Indian context, justice as seen was an important social value in terms of the strict observance of Dharma or the enforcement of a social order based on the *Varna-Ashram Vyavastha* reflected in an elaborate caste system. This established order, according to Ambedkar, was based on graded inequality and was legitimized by Hindu Law, which completely neglected liberty, equality, fraternity, democracy and human rights. He was also of the view that the system of graded inequality was not notional but legal and penal as it entailed strict enforcement of Hindu Law which meant different things to different castes and people and contained no notion of equal treatment to all. This fact has been highlighted by Ambedkar thus: "Hindu Law is the law of the established order and was made by the "touchables". The Untouchables had nothing to do except to obey it and respect it. The untouchables have no right against the touchables. For them there is no equal right, no justice, which is due to them, and nothing is allowed to them. Nothing is due to them except what the touchables are prepared to grant. The Untouchables must not insist on rights. They should pray for mercy and favour and rest content with what is offered.[1]

Dr. Ambedkar himself was a victim of caste discrimination. His parents hailed from the Hindu Mahar caste, which was viewed as "untouchable" by the upper class. Due to this, Ambedkar had to face severe discriminations from every corner of the society. The discrimination and humiliation haunted Ambedkar even at the Army school, run by British government. Fearing social outcry, the teachers would segregate the students of lower class from that of Brahmins and other upper classes. The untouchable students were often asked by the teacher to sit outside the class. After shifting to Satara, he was admitted to a local school but the change of school did not change the fate of young Bhimrao. Discrimination followed wherever he went. In 1908, Ambedkar got the opportunity to study at the Elphinstone College. Besides clearing all the exams successfully Ambedkar also obtained a scholarship of twenty five rupees a month from the Gayakwad ruler of Baroda, Sahyaji Rao III. Political Science and Economics were the subjects in which he graduated from the Bombay University in 1912. Ambedkar decided to use the money for higher studies in the USA.

Dr. Bhimrao Ambedkar was not only a visionary political leader and social reformer but also a scholar and a thinker. He has written extensively on various social and political matters. Some of his important writings include, *Annihilation of Caste, Who Were the Shudras, The Untouchables, Buddha and His Dharma,* etc. His thinking was based on a deep faith in the goals of equity and liberty. Liberalism and the philosophy of John Dewey also influenced his thinking. Jotirao Phule and Buddha have exercised great influence on Ambedkar's ideas on the society, religion and morality. His political ideas were also influenced his legal approach. Ambedkar's personal sufferings, his scholarship and his constant attention to the problem of bringing about equality for the downtrodden untouchable community forms the basis of his thinking and writings. He was the man of his own destiny who dared to take on the unjust Hindu social order head on.

Dr. Ambedkar was merciless in his denunciations of pettiness, perversities and the hypocrisies of Brahminism which to him was a wicked and mischievous agent of social exploitation of the backward and untouchable section of Hindu society. He ultimately got solace in the teachings of Lord Buddha whom he treated as messiah of downtrodden who preached the philosophy of complete egalitarian society based on non-violence.

To mobilize his followers he established organisations like Bahishkrit Hitkarini Sabha, Independent Labour Party and later All India Scheduled Caste Federation. He led a number of temple entry movements/*satyagrahas*, mobilised the untouchables, established many educational institutions and propagated his views from the newspapers like *Mooknayak, Bahishkrit Bharat,* and *Janta.* Despite facing backlash from Congress, he participated in the Round Table Conference in order to protect and defend the interests of the untouchables. He was in the favour of continuation of British rule till Dalits and backwards become self-dependent because he believed that once Britishers leave the country, upper castes will capture the power and they will reinforce the caste system. Although, he was particularly critical of the British administration on account of it's over expensive character and the general neglect of public welfare. He knew that abrupt departure of British would result in to political domination of the upper castes.

Ambedkar on Caste System in India

Ambedkar's main battle was against the caste system. According to him caste system had made Hindu society stagnant. Due to the caste system Hindu society has lost the upward mobility and is unable to accommodate people from outside to its fold. This drawback poses permanent problems for the integration. The *Jat Pat Todak Mandal*, a social reformist organisation of Lahore, in 1936, invited Dr B.R. Ambedkar to deliver the presidential address of its annual conference on the topic of the caste system in India. Ambedkar sent the manuscript of his speech titled The Annihilation of Caste. However, the organising committee found some of his views, particularly his critique of the Vedas and his inclination to leave the Hindu fold, unacceptable. It, therefore, suggested to Ambedkar that he delete these views, to which he replied that "he would not change even a comma". The speech thus remained undelivered. Ambedkar subsequently published it in May 1936.

Among the numerous writings and speeches of Ambedkar that run into thousands of pages, The *Annihilation of Caste* is indeed his magnum opus. Judged by any criterion such as content, logic, argument, language, diction, exposition, urge and, above all, the force, it is a manifesto of social emancipation, and occupies a place similar to what The Communist Manifesto once did in the world communist movement. Since the book is polemical in nature, Ambedkar did not elaborate much on the agonies, indignities, humiliation and overall sufferings of the Shudras, and particularly the untouchables. He only gave illustrations of how they were deprived of education and freedom of occupation and were subjected to stigmatized manual labour, all resulting in their virtual economic slavery, how they were segregated and deprived of basic rights such as drinking water even from public wells, and above all how they were made victims of social persecutions. But, according to Ambedkar, worse and unparalleled, the Hindu Dharmashastras gave legitimacy to the doctrine of Chaturvarna and the caste system. The infamous Manusmriti dehumanized the Sudras and untouchables, ruled the Hindu psyche for centuries and created the greatest obstacle to any serious attempt at eradicating the caste system. This made Ambedkar publically burn the Manusmriti on the occasion of his historical Mahad Satyagraha in 1927 for establishing the right of untouchables to drink the water of the Chawdar tank in Mahad town in Maharashtra.[2]

Hindu society has failed to satisfy the test of being a homogeneous society. It is only a collection of different castes which is the biggest obstacle in the path of national integration and the national spirit. Caste system permanently perpetuates injustice to the lower strata of the society. They are denied education, equal opportunity, livelihood and human dignity. Lower caste people born in poverty, live in poverty and die in poverty without any hope of change in their fate. Therefore, the battle for removal of poverty and untouchability becomes the battle for human rights and justice.

In his work *Who Were the Shudras?*, Ambedkar attempted to explain the formation of Untouchables. He saw the Shudras, who form the lowest caste in the ritual hierarchy of the Hindu caste system, as being separate from Untouchables. Ambedkar oversaw the transformation of his political party into the Scheduled Castes Federation, although it performed poorly in the elections held in 1946 for the Constituent Assembly of India. In his 1948 sequel to *Who Were the Shudras?* Which he titled *The Untouchables: A Thesis on the Origins of Untouchability*, Ambedkar said that: "The Hindu Civilisation is a diabolical contrivance to suppress and enslave humanity. Its proper name would be infamy. What else can be said of a civilisation which has produced a mass of people who are treated as an entity beyond human intercourse and whose mere touch is enough to cause pollution?." In this book Ambedkar argues that the Shudras were originally Aryans belonging to the Kshatriya class.

Ambedkar further argues that the Brahmins brought about the degradation of the Shudras. Relations have also been drawn between the wide acceptance of Mahars in Hinduism as outcasts and untouchables due to their affirmation to Buddhist practices. In a separate chapter, Dr. Ambedkar has shown that ill effects of caste system have spread even in Islam in South Asian countries. While justifying the partition of India, he condemned the practice of child marriage, as well as the mistreatment of women, in Muslim society.[3]

Due to Ambedkar's prominence and popular support amongst the untouchable community, he was invited to attend the Second Round Table Conference in London in 1932. Gandhi fiercely opposed a separate electorate for untouchables, fearing that such an arrangement would split the Hindu community into two groups. In 1932, when the British had agreed with Ambedkar and announced a Communal Award of a separate electorate, Gandhi protested by fasting while imprisoned in the Yerwada Central Jail of Poona. The fast provoked huge civil unrest across India and orthodox Hindu leaders, Congress politicians and activists such as Madan Mohan Malaviya and Palwankar Baloo organised joint meetings with Ambedkar and his supporters at Yerwada. Fearing a communal reprisal and genocidal acts against untouchables, Ambedkar was coerced into agreeing with Gandhi.[4] This agreement saw Gandhi end his fast and Ambedkar drop his demand for a separate electorate, was called as Poona Pact. Instead, a certain number of seats were reserved specifically for untouchables (who in the agreement were called the "Depressed Class").[5]

The confrontation between Ambedkar and Gandhi was a historic one. It had its beginnings in the Round Table Conferences of 1930-32. Ambedkar had gone for the first, as the prime representative of Dalits, or Untouchables. But when Gandhi finally decided to attend the second conference, he argued fervently that he represented the Untouchables, because they were an integral part of the Hindu fold—which he represented. To Ambedkar, the Untouchables were not a part of the Hindus but "a part apart" (a phrase he had once applied to himself), a uniquely oppressed people. They could accept, even welcome, the coming of independence and its inevitable domination by the Congress (i.e. by caste Hindus), but they needed "safeguards".

Ambedkar had originally felt that with universal suffrage, reserved seats would be sufficient. But universal suffrage was not given, and the issues at the conference revolved around separate electorates. Gandhi was reconciled to giving this to Muslims; he had already accepted their identity as a separate community. Not so for Dalits. When the Ramsay MacDonald Award gave separate electorates to Dalits, he protested with a fast unto death and this brought him into direct confrontation with Ambedkar.[6]

According to Ambedkar, untouchability was partly a result of Brahminic superiority. Untouchability resulted from the conflict between Brahmanism and Buddhism. He believed that in Indian society we found mixture of various races living together for centuries.

Therefore the idea that untouchables belongs to some inferior or defeated race was unacceptable. For this question Ambedkar provides a socio-anthropological answer. Originally India has a large number of unsettled tribes and frequently they came in to conflict with other wandering tribes. These wandering tribes were defeated and their members got scattered and became the part of the larger settled tribes. But, their social status remained inferior to the settled tribes. The next round of conflict between the outsiders and settled tribes took place on the issue of religion and beef eating. Ambedkar argues that to meet the challenge of Buddhism, Brahmanism adopted complete non-killing, renunciation of meet eating and worshiping of cows. The outsiders who were followers of Buddhism tradionally ate the meat of dead animals. Since they did not suspend the practice of meat eating, they were ex-communicated. The ex-communication was later justified by incorporating it in the religious scriptures. Thus, untouchability became a permanent and sacred part of religion.

Ambedkar ultimately suggested that inter-caste marriage is the only remedy to destroy caste. In The Annihilation of Caste, Ambedkar's critique of the Hindu social order was so strong that Mahatma Gandhi, in Harijan, described Ambedkar as a "challenge to Hinduism". Ambedkar replied to Gandhi in his usual uncompromising manner. Ambedkar did not spare the socialists or the communists either. He vehemently attacked the communists for their doctrinaire approach to caste in treating it as the superstructure and argued that unless they dealt with caste as a basic structural problem, no worthwhile social change, let alone a socialist revolution, was possible.

Ambedkar on Social Reforms

Social reforms were always on the top priority of Dr. Ambedkar. He believed that economic and political issues should be resolved only after achieving the goal of social justice. If priority is given to the issue of political emancipation, it would mean transfer of power from British rule to the upper caste Hindus, who are equally distant from the lower castes. Thus injustice against untouchables and backward sections of the society will remain and egalitarian society will become a distant dream for them. Similarly, the idea that economic progress will resolve all social problems was based on immature prediction according to

Ambedkar. Casteism is the expression of mental slavery of the Hindus. It has perpetuated age old injustices to the people of lower castes who have been living in misery for no faults of their own.

According to Ambedkar social reform consisted of the reforms in the family system and religious life. Family reform means abolition of child marriages, sati, *purda* system, widow remarriage, inter caste marriages, etc. Upliftment of women was always on the top of agenda of Ambedkar and he strongly criticised the degradation of women in the Indian society. He vehemently opposed Hindu religion for not providing right to property to the women. Later on after independence, he prepared Hindu Code Bill which took care of the cause of women and giving them right to property. The operation of caste, both at the systemic level and at the functioning of patriarchy, the growing caste/class divide in feminist political discourses made Ambedkar's views on women's oppression, social democracy, caste and Hindu social order significant to modern Indian feminist thinking. The contemporary social realities warrant close examination of the wide range of his topics, the width of his vision, the depth of his analysis, and the rationality of his outlook and the essential humanity of his suggestions for practical action. For the Indian Women's Movement, Ambedkar provides a powerful source of inspiration to formulate a feminist political agenda which simultaneously addresses the issues of class, caste and gender.

Ambedkar's legacy as a socio-political reformer had a deep impact on modern India. He believed that "political democracy without social and economic justice is meaningless." In post-Independent India his socio-political thought has acquired respect across the political spectrum. His initiatives have influenced various spheres of life and transformed the way India looks today. His reputation as a scholar led to his appointment as free India's first law minister, and chairman of the committee responsible to draft the constitution. He passionately believed in the freedom of the individual and criticised orthodox Hindu society. His condemnation of Hinduism and its foundation of caste system, made him controversial and unpopular among the upper caste Hindus. His conversion to Buddhism sparked a revival of interest in Buddhist philosophy in India and abroad.[8]

Ambedkar on Affirmative Action

The British government had allowed separate electorates for "depressed classes" in the 1932. This provision was made at the insistence of the untouchables' representatives, B.R. Ambedkar from the province of Bombay and Rao Bahadur Rettamalle Srinivasan of Madras—the two most active areas of reform—who felt, in the face of demands for separate constituencies from all other minorities, that proper elected representatives could only be elected by untouchables themselves. Mohandas K. Gandhi, then in prison for activities against the government in the interests of independence, thought separate electorates were too divisive and began a "fast unto death." Under pressure due to deteriorating health of Mahatma Gandhi, Ambedkar gave up his demand but bargained for reserved seats for untouchables in all elected bodies to be elected by the general electorate.

Ambedkar was a firm believer that education and knowledge will greatly improve the conditions of untouchables. Education makes man enlightened, makes him aware of his self-respect and also helps him to lead a better economic life. One of the major causes of the degradation of the untouchables was due to the denial of education. By 1935 it had become clear that untouchable castes must be listed to determine who exactly would be eligible for the reserved seats and for educational and economic benefits.

The criteria for listing stipulated specific castes in specific areas that were denied religious rights of entry into temples and civil rights of entry to public places and the use of wells. The word *specific* was necessary because the ways of identifying who is an untouchable can vary. Occupation is not always a reliable guide. Laundrymen (Dhobis) and barbers may be untouchables in certain areas of the north but not in the state of Maharashtra. The new term *scheduled castes,* those on a list or schedule, was applied to 429 castes.[9]

Ambedkar criticised the British policy of education for not adequately encouraging the education among the lower castes. He felt painful that even during the British rule; the upper castes have the monopoly on the education system. Ambedkar wanted Dalits and backwards to go for the liberal as well as technical education. He was lover of the secular character of education and opposed religious control of it. He warned that only a secular character of education will inculcate the values of liberty and equality among the students.

Upon India's independence on 15 August 1947, the new Congress-led government invited Ambedkar to serve as the nation's first law minister, which he accepted. On 29 August, Ambedkar was appointed Chairman of the Constitution Drafting Committee, charged by the Assembly to write India's new Constitution. Granville Austin has described the Indian Constitution drafted by Ambedkar as 'first and foremost a social document'. 'The majority of India's constitutional provisions are either directly arrived at furthering the aim of social revolution or attempt to foster this revolution by establishing conditions necessary for its achievement. [10]

The text prepared by Ambedkar provided constitutional guarantees and protections for a wide range of civil liberties for individual citizens, including freedom of religion, the abolition of untouchability and the outlawing of all forms of discrimination. Ambedkar argued for extensive economic and social rights for women, and also won the Assembly's support for introducing a system of reservations of jobs in the civil services, schools and colleges for members of scheduled castes and scheduled tribes, a system akin to affirmative action. India's lawmakers hoped to eradicate the socio-economic inequalities and lack of opportunities for India's depressed classes through these measures. The Constitution was adopted on 26 November 1949 by the Constituent Assembly.

Ambedkar was the firm believer in the principles of liberty, equality and fraternity and these were guiding principles of his all the writings. But he knew that economic disparity and social injustices are detrimental of liberties. Therefore, political democracy without social democracy and economic justice is meaningless. Equality and liberty can only be realized when there are economic resources at the disposal of millions of downtrodden in the society. Social justice means equal social opportunities shall be available to everyone to develop their personalities which is associated with equality and social rights. According to Ambedkar, his Justice is based on moral values and self-respect. Three types of justices' i.e. social, political and economic are the corner stone of the Indian constitution.

The principles of liberty, equality and fraternity are not to be treated as separated items in a trinity. They form a union of trinity in the sense that to divorce one from the other is to defeat the very purpose of democracy. These principles are fundamental rocks of a just social order and had their origin from French Revolution. He admits that 'justice and liberty' are the two basic ideas of all political thoughts. Every society needs some sort of concept concerning that structure. Justice is the basic concept of social values and holds any society together.

According to Ambedkar, liberty has been divided into two categories namely Civil Liberty and Political Liberty. Ambedkar's notions of civil liberty deals with three basic opinions are; Liberty of movement, Liberty of speech and Liberty of action. Civil liberties are often formally guaranteed in Indian constitution but ignored in practice which came from Bill of Rights. Civil right is often used to refer to one or more of these liberties or indirectly to the obligation of government to protect Dalits from violations of one or more of their civil liberties.

Conversion to Buddhism

According to Dr. B.R. Ambedkar "foundation of religion is essential to life and practices of the society" and religion is the part of one's social inheritance. Religion to him was the driving force to human activity. He acclaimed that "man cannot live by bread alone, he has a mind which needs food for thought".[12] In the search for a faith to mobilize and liberate the Untouchables, Ambedkar's lifelong reading of scholarly works on the history and teachings of Buddhism included more than twenty thousand volumes of rich collections throughout his school years and subsequent visits to New York, London, and Bonn. Ambedkar's frequent exposure to living Buddhist traditions in Burma, Sri Lanka, and other countries, and his appreciation of Buddhist art in various places such as the Ellora and Ajanta caves might have influenced on his religious endeavour too.

Ambedkar had considered converting to Sikhism, which saw oppression as something to be fought against and which for that reason appealed also to other leaders of scheduled castes. He rejected the idea after meeting with leaders of the Sikh community and concluding that his conversion might result in him having what scholar Stephen P. Cohen describes as a "second-rate status" among Sikhs.[13]

He studied Buddhism all his life, and around 1950, he turned his attention fully to Buddhism and travelled to Ceylon (now Sri Lanka) to attend a meeting of the World Fellowship of Buddhists. While dedicating a new Buddhist Vihara near Pune, Ambedkar announced that he was writing a book on Buddhism and that as soon as it was finished, he planned to make a formal conversion to Buddhism. [14] Ambedkar twice visited Burma in 1954; the second time in order to attend the third conference of the World Fellowship of Buddhists in Rangoon. [15] In 1955, he founded the Bharatiya Bauddha Mahasabha, or the Buddhist Society of India. He completed his final work, *The Buddha and His Dhamma*, in 1956. It was published posthumously.[16]

After meetings with the Sri Lankan Buddhist monk Hammalawa Saddhatissa, Ambedkar organised a formal public ceremony for himself and his supporters in Nagpur on 14 October 1956. Accepting the Three Refuges and Five Precepts from a Buddhist monk in the traditional manner, Ambedkar completed his own conversion, along with his wife. He then proceeded to convert some 500,000 of his supporters who were gathered around him. He prescribed the 22 Vows for these converts, after the Three Jewels and Five Precepts. He then traveled to Kathmandu in Nepal to attend the Fourth World Buddhist Conference.[17] D.C. Ahir claim that due to Ambedkar's influence as the architect of Indian constitution the Ashoka Chakra was put on the Indian flag and lions from the Ashokan pillar at Sarnath were adopted as the National Emblem.[18]

Ambedkar pleaded for constitutional safeguards to SCs and STs not as altruistic concessions or humanitarian doles. He wanted historical oppression and miseries caused to the depressed classes to be corrected through the reservation policy and its application. He wanted the SCs and STs to lift themselves with their bootstrap and stand up to the competition of the world at large. That is why he accepted the stipulation of 10 years' time for the minorities to cope up. He believed that it is wrong for the majority to deny the existence of minorities and it is equally wrong for the minorities to perpetuate themselves. The movement the majority loses the habit of discriminating the minority; the minorities will have no ground to exist. It is obvious from this that Ambedkar did not want the minorities nor the SCs and STs to develop a "permanent interest" in the "backwardness".[19]

Conclusion

Dr. Ambedkar was a social prophet for the untouchables. His rise to the national politics was not less important than Gandhi. Search for the complete equality brought him closer to Buddhism. There is no doubt that he was a patriot and would not be opposed of national integration. Whatever might have been the origin of the caste system, it has been the most unjust social order in actual practice. Hence Ambedkar deserves the credit having made Hindus aware of the great tension generating social problems, which must be tackled; otherwise they may eventually bring about the doom not only of the Hindu society but to the whole political system as well. It was beyond doubt that he awakened the self-respect of millions of downtrodden from the slavery of servitude, who had been exploited for centuries in the name of caste system. He became the voice of voiceless and taught and gave untouchables an alternate vision to become free forever from the bondage of casteism. Conversion to Buddhism gave him and his people long lasting solace to live in casteless and egalitarian society.

END NOTES

1. Ambedkar, B.R. (1946), "*Who Were Shudras?*" Bombay, Thacker and Company, pp.16-17.
2. Bhalchandra Mungerkar, "Annihilating caste", *Frontline*, Vol. 28, Issue 15, Jul.16-29, 2011.
3. Ambedkar, Bhimrao Ramji (1946), "Chapter X: Social Stagnation". *Pakistan and the Partition of India*, Bombay: Thackers Publishers, pp. 215-219.
4. Omvedt, Gail (2012), "A Part That Parted", *Outlook,* August 20, New Delhi, pp.14-17.
5. Vasant G. Gandhi, "Gandhi's Epic Fast", http://www.mkgandhi.org/articles/epic_fast.ht.
6. Omvedt, Gail op.cit., pp.14-*17*.
7. Ambedkar, B.R. (1946), "*Who Were Shudras*?", Bombay, Thacker & Co., pp.57-65.
8. Naik, C.D. (2003), "Buddhist Developments in East and West Since 1950: An Outline of World Buddhism and Ambedkarism Today in Nutshell". *Thoughts and philosophy of Doctor B.R. Ambedkar* (First edn.). New Delhi: Sarup & Sons. p. 12.
9. Untouchability—The Beginnings of "affirmative Action", see at http://science.jrank.org/pages/11541/Untouchability-Beginnings-Affirmative-Action.html
10. Granville Austin (1999), *The Indian Constitution: Cornerstone of a Nation*, Oxford University Press, p.23.
11. Gopal Guru (2002), Ambedkar's Idea of Social Justice in Ghanshyam Shah (ed), *Dalits and the State,* Concept Publishing Company, New Delhi.
12. Keer, "Mhatma Jyotiran, Phooley—Father of Social Revolution", Bombay, p.39.
13. Cohen, Stephen P. (May 1969), "The Untouchable Soldier: Caste, Politics, and the Indian Army", *The Journal of Asian Studies*, 28 (3): 460.
14. Sangharakshita (2006), "Milestone on the Road to conversion", *Ambedkar and Buddhism* (1st South Asian edn.). New Delhi: Motilal Banarsidass Publishers. p.72.
15. Ganguly, Debjani and Docker, John (eds.) (2007), *Rethinking Gandhi and Nonviolent*

Relationality: Global Perspectives, Routledge studies in the modern history of Asia, London: Routledge. p. 257.

16. Quack, Johannes (2011), *Disenchanting India: Organised Rationalism and Criticism of Religion in India*, Oxford University Press. p. 88.
17. Buddha or Karl Marx – Editorial Note in the source publication: Babasaheb Ambedkar: Writings and Speeches, Vol.3.
18. Ahir D.C., "*Buddhism and Ambedkar*", p.185.
19. Yadav, Susma, "Dr. B.R. Ambedkar: The vision of social justice", *Just in Print*, December 15, 2014.

7

Babasahib Ambedkar: Contemporary Relevance for the Indian Youth

J.S. Rajput

When one refers to the Constitution of India, it is just impossible not to recall and salute with adulation the outstanding contributions of Dr. B.R. Ambedkar. His concluding speech in the Constituent Assembly is a historic document. Delivered on November 25, 1949, just a day prior to the formal acceptance of the Constitution of India, he made a superb incisive analysis of the past and its impact on the present. His scholarly understanding of Indian culture and civilisation sharpened his capacities to envision the future. Armed with that insight, he referred to the hopes, aspirations of the people of the newly emerging independent India. Simultaneously, he also very clearly placed on record the apprehensions that could mar the fulfillment of the goals of national welfare. His apprehensions have come astonishingly true in the context of those who had condemned the Constitution during its making! He knew how they would try their best to sabotage what "We the people" were giving to ourselves on January 26, 1950. He was particularly apprehensive of the Communists and the Socialists of his days. We find how numerous factions of the Communist and leftists perpetually strive to damage the democratic process without an iota of concern for the progress and development of the 'proletariat'. The devotees of socialism, within the Congress and also outside it, have now come in their true colours. State governments headed by Socialists in UP and by the Left Front in Kerala did little to ameliorate the deprivations in the lives of the deprived, exploited and depressed. Not only this, those who introduced the term 'Socialist' in the Preamble of the Constitution in 1976 formally renounced it in 1991. The other addition—"secular"—is used only for one purpose: how to ensure the votes of the Muslim Community in the next election? Those who unscrupulously misuse socialist and secular still claim to be the protagonists of communal harmony and national integration! The communists, socialists and 'those who think alike' consistently shout hoarse as being the sole protectors of the rights of the weaker sections. They never hesitate to sabotage democratic functioning of the Parliament, the first critical requirement for the smooth implementation of democratic values and hence, of the Constitution. Dr. Ambedkar had very rightly visualised who would be exploiting religious and caste diversity for petty electoral games. Obviously this they do at the cost of the national interests. Having envisioned the future scenario in full perfection, Dr. Ambedkar put it in the following words:

> "The condemnation of the Constitution largely comes from two quarters, the Communist Party and the Socialist Party. Why do they condemn the Constitution? Is it because it is really a bad Constitution? I venture to say no'. The Communist Party wants a Constitution based upon the principle of the Dictatorship of the Proletariat. They condemn the Constitution because it is based upon Parliamentary democracy. The Socialists want two things. The first thing they want is that if they come in power, the Constitution must give them the freedom to nationalize or socialize all private property without payment of compensation. The second thing that the Socialists want is that the Fundamental Rights mentioned in the Constitution must be absolute and without any limitations so that if their Party fails to come into power, they would have the unfettered freedom not merely to criticise, but also to overthrow the State." (Ambedkar, 1949)

While the Communist parties have transitioned to innumerable factions, the Socialists too, did not lag behind. Together, they have just confirmed what Dr. Ambedkar had anticipated based on his in-depth understanding and vision. He knew that these two would not hesitate to come together whenever they smell a chance to damage the cause espoused in the Constitution of India. Who can forgive the Communists for what they did in 1942 Quit India movement, during Chinese invasion of 1962, just to recall only two of the umpteen instances? Communists and other leftists fully exploited the weakness of the Indian National Congress when the minority government of Indira Gandhi had to seek their support for survival. They had their plans ready: prepare people and towards that bargain for control over institutions and use education to propagate ideology. Further, institutions like ICHR, ICCR, and ICSSR were most suited strategically to sabotage the ancient culture and history of India and Indians. To achieve these objectives, these institutions were crowded with academicians who were identified dexterously on the single point criterion: they must tow the ideological line! Even reputed scholars who were unwilling to function under ideological compulsions were just discarded, and even maligned consistently. The Jawaharlal Nehru University was handed over to them on the platter and is at present, the hub centre of leftist ideology in a cocoon that none else is allowed to even attempt to penetrate. Anyone who is not like them is communal. JNU is only one amongst many that exemplify the success of the leftist strategy. Their institutional hegemony has been challenged only in 1999 and 2014. The manner eminent scholars, authors and poets come together in; say, '*Award Wapsi*' clearly exposes the agenda to sabotage democracy in the country.

The Current Scenario

With their hegemony at stake, academics bound by ideological considerations, including some being actively associated with political parties of leftist hue, became restless and is targeting the young to play their game. This is the genesis of what happened at FTII, Pune, Central University Hyderabad, JNU and Jadhavpur! The manner leftist political leaders rushed to JNU without verifying the facts; to express their solidarity with elements that shouted anti-national slogans and wanted to break India in to pieces to get the *Azadi* of their interpretations. JNU is, without any doubt, a pampered institution in a country that still runs substantial numbers of its schools without teachers and blackboards, schools where drinking water and functional toilets are still a luxury. Even if the weak defense of outside elements is accepted, how could they have such a free access to JNU and its hostels and participate in programmes? How could some young person's be allowed to stay in hostels for decades together and indulge in active party politics while other coming from far-off places are forced to rent rooms outside the campus? Most astonishing part of these developments was their projection as a struggle to stop atrocities against the Dalits! Is this the level of understanding of the principles espoused by Babasahib Ambedkar amongst young persons and their mentors? Did they ever care to understand the spirit of Dr. Ambedkar when he was handling the issue of reservations? Will they have the courage to accept that Babasahib was not in favour of reservations for indefinite period? Why don't they have the courage to sit across the table and discuss with those who may be protagonists of having a fresh look on the nature of reservations? They could learn to put their view point against any group or ideology that may not 'think alike'! There is so much to learnt from the handling of opposite view point by Babasahib in the Constituent Assembly alone, if one remains ignorant on how he handled adversities in past. He never ran away from debate and dialogue. That needed scholarship and persistent pursuit of knowledge. That is one trait of immense value to young persons who may have political inclinations and a desire to serve the downtrodden.

Understanding the Visionary

It is rather painful and disappointing to find ambitious young people mentioning his name, talking of working for the welfare of the weak and downtrodden but ignoring the width of Babasahib's vision and the urge to understand India and its people. Without such and understanding, no effective contribution is possible. This is what M.K. Gandhi was advised by Gopal Krishna Gokhale when he returned to India after successfully leading struggles in South Africa. He followed his advice in the right spirit. Jawaharlal Nehru never had that advantage and its consequences manifested in umpteen situations and decisions. JNU which could very rightly boost of its national character and the presence of young persons from weaker sections of society in reasonably good numbers could have developed as a great centre of making them understand India, understand Gandhi, Ambedkar, Patel, and Nehru, and not ignore Swami Vivekananda, Sri Aurobindo and Swami Dayananda Saraswati. It should have allowed discussions and debates on varied strategies to ameliorate the life and living of those who were dearest Dr. Ambedkar. At the same time, JNU could have become a leading light on how the Indian tradition of Knowledge creation, dissemination and utilization, sustains its relevance, that it discards none and neglects none. No Think Tank establishment can confine itself in a single cocoon and bar entry to those who do not think alike, or are not liked by the dominant group for one reason or the other!

As against such expectations, is it not an amazing situation, if not amusing in a manner, that those who shout slogans against their own country, celebrate Afzal Guru as a martyr, rejoice on the massacre of 73 CRPF Jawans in Chhattisgarh shout hoarse on what they call 'growing intolerance' in India. Move outside JNU: a farmer Judge of the Supreme Court of India speaks in a public gathering in Kolkata and finds fault with the judgment of his brother judges in the case of Afzal Guru. A farmer Home minister, too, had expressed his grave reservations how justice was not delivered in case of Afzal Guru. He, too, was addressing an informed invited audience on increasing intolerance in India! Which other country would permit organisation of 'cultural evenings' that celebrate the martyrdom of attackers on its Parliament, on Bombay and killers of hundreds of innocent people?

They complain how the Constitutional guarantee of freedom of expression is being throttled by the central government! Here is an institution of higher learning that is supposed to create a sense of pride amongst all on being Indians instead pampers to anti-national sentiments and, offering a weak defense, expecting people to trust them and believe that it was just a handiwork of few outside elements. Is it freedom of expression to shout from rooftops that Jammu and Kashmir is under illegal occupation of India? Did Babasahib Ambedkar ever think that way? Such fringe groups respect none, not even their own country and their Icons whom they 'pledge' to follow but never even try to understand the depth of their thoughts and their vision for India and Indians. May be, these young persons are ignorant of what happened during Emergency imposed during 1975-77. The leftists were with Mrs. Gandhi and she in turn permitted them to play their ideological objectives in institutions of higher learning to prepare a generation that would be willing to denounce India, Indians and all of its ancient culture and heritage The contrast is very clear: Dr Ambedkar had his genuine issues with the Hindu Society, its traditions and abhorrent practices like untouchabilty, he never lost faith in the democratic traditions of India. He converted to Buddhism, which meant immeasurable respect and regard for Gautama, the Buddha. However, he traces the origin of Sanghas created by the Buddha, to ancient Indian practices:

> "It is not that India did not know what Democracy is. There was a time when India was studded with republics, and even where there were monarchies, they were either elected or limited. They were never absolute. It is not that India did not know Parliaments or Parliamentary Procedure. A study of the Buddhist Bhikshu Sanghas discloses that not only there were Parliaments—for the Sanghas were nothing but Parliaments—but Sanghas knew and observed all the rules of Parliamentary procedure known to modern times. They had rules regarding seating arrangements, rules regarding the motions, Resolutions, Whip, Counting of Votes, Voting by Ballot, Censure motion, Regularization, Res Judicata, etc., Although these rules of Parliamentary procedures were applied by the Buddha to the meetings of the Sanghas, he must have borrowed them from the rules of the Political Assemblies functioning in the country in his times." (Ambedkar, 1949).

Fathom the Future

The youth of India would be greatly benefitted if they study the deep-rooted concerns of Dr. Ambedkar on the day he was reflecting upon the work he and others had accomplished in the Constituent Assembly. He posed a query that has eternal relevance: "If we wish to maintain democracy not merely in form, but also in fact, what must we do? First; 'We must abandon the bloody methods of revolution. It means we must abandon the method of civil disobedience, non-cooperation and Satyagraha'. Will our Hon'ble Parliamentarians pay heed to this advice, or ever have time to think that if they really respect Dr. Ambedkar, they should better be in their seats in the Parliament instead of shouting slogans in the well of the House every day! Those who see Naxalism and Maoism as the only path to redeem their dreams would better devote time in libraries and also in fields and forests to visualise how this sentence unveils the strategy of growth and development for India and particularly its weak, deprived, downtrodden and Dalits.

Attacking an individual, a political party, an organisation or even a Prime Minister brings nothing worthwhile to anyone. Protest is a fundamental democratic right but only so long as the intent itself is an outcome of truly democratic considerations. That implies honesty and integrity towards people, community and the nation.

Such qualities of intellectual honesty that emerge from sustained scholarly pursuit require in-depth researches in personality of Babasahib by the young of today. Many would scarcely believe that Dr. Ambedkar wanted "the executive Committee of All India Scheduled Caste Federation to pass a resolution on September 10, 1949 in support of making Samskrit the official language of India". He however, withdrew the resolution as it was opposed by some young members of the Executive Committee. One of them, Sri B.P. Maurya, had a change of heart and in a letter dated February 14, 2002, addressed to the author of this piece, he wrote:

> "It is an admitted fact that Sanskrit is the most scientific language. It is also admitted that Sanskrit is an ancient language, which has very accurate grammar. It will be appreciated by well-meaning persons if Sanskrit is included in Modern Indian Languages.
>
> I had the privilege to work with Babasahib Dr. B.R. Ambedkar for a long period of ten years. I had been the member of the National executive Committee of Scheduled Caste Federation. Once, I think during the year 1949, he wanted the National executive Committee of the Scheduled Caste Federation should pass the resolution that Sanskrit should be made the national language of free India.. Because of my inexperience, I opposed the resolution. Ultimately the idea of the resolution was dropped. But Babasahib Ambedkar made a Press Statement wherein he stated that Sanskrit should be made national language of free India" (Maurya, 2001).

It is clear from the above how much convinced Dr. Ambedkar was of not only the greatness of Sanskrit as a language but its being part of the great Indian heritage. It also establishes he had no ill will or rancor against any community. After all, Sanskrit was considered to be the language of privilege of the Brahmins and Dr. Ambedkar was fighting against the Brahminical order! To him, national unity and integrity were paramount, other social aberrations could be handled separately and he did that with aplomb and great success.

An accomplished scholar of ancient Indian tradition of knowledge pursuit and its impact, Dr. Murli Manohar Joshi (2016) infers that 'Dr. Ambedkar's engagement with Sanskrit was inspired by keen desire to find out the truth about Aryan invasion'. Dr. Ambedkar asserts that: 'The Vedas did not know any such race as the Aryan race' and also that 'There is no evidence of any invasion of India by the Aryan race' or of any conquest of those supposed to be the natives of India. He was very clear, based upon the anthropometry evidence that 'Brahmins and untouchables belong to the same race'. Now it has been established on the basis of latest scientific knowledge and evidence that his conclusions were, indeed, correct. As a great scholar, he could visualise the vested interests behind the Aryan Invasion Theory, made in-depth studies and found incontrovertible evidence to demolish it. This in itself becomes a great contribution towards reforms in Hindu Society and, simultaneously, in achieving national unity and integration that had suffered considerably because of this transplanted and divisive 'theory'

People do understand that freedom any nation depends on its inner strength, national unity, social cohesion and religious amity. There could be external elements active in India who would like communal clashes and distrust amongst religions to be fanned on one pretext or the other. It is not a cliché but a reality that eternal vigilance is the price of liberty. In the same speech Dr. Ambedkar continues:

> "Here I could have ended. But my mind is so full of the future of our country that I feel I ought to take this occasion to give expression to some of my reflections thereon. On 26th January 1950, India will be an independent country (Cheers). What would happen to her independence? Will she maintain her independence or will she lose it again? This is the first thought that comes to my mind. It is not that India was never an independent country. The point is that she once lost the independence she had. Will she lost it a second time? It is this thought which makes me most anxious for the future. What perturbs me greatly is the fact that not only India has once before lost her independence, but she lost it by the infidelity and treachery of some of her own people. In the invasion of Sind by Mahommed-Bin-Kasim, the military commanders of King Dahar

accepted bribes from the agents of Mahommed-Bin-Kasim and refused to fight on the side of their King. It was Jaichand who invited Mahommed Gohri to invade India and fight against Prithvi Raj and promised him the help of himself and the Solanki Kings. When Shivaji was fighting for the liberation of Hindus, the other Maratha noblemen and the Rajput Kings were fighting the battle on the side of Moghul Emperors. When the British were trying to destroy the Sikh Rulers, Gulab Singh, their principal commander sat silent and did not help to save the Sikh Kingdom. In 1857, when a large part of India had declared a war of independence against the British, the Sikhs stood and watched the event as silent spectators" (Ambedkar, 1949).

Will History Repeat Itself?

In 1949, Dr. Ambedkar's foremost concern was India retaining its freedom and not to suffer the 'treachery and infidelity' of its own people, once again! Those who swear by the name of Dr. Ambedkar and shout slogans against India and how they would like it to be dismembered probably forget what would happen to their 'ideology' if India becomes unstable and loses its *ikhlaq* in comity of nations? His anxiety deserves to become the anxiety of everyone at this juncture of India's history:

> "Will history repeat itself? It is this thought which fills me with anxiety. This anxiety is deepened by the realization of the fact that in addition to our old enemies in the form of castes and creeds we are going to have many political parties with diverse and opposing political creeds. Will Indian place the country above their creed or will they place creed above country? I do not know. But this much is certain that if the parties place creed above country, our independence will be put in jeopardy a second time and probably be lost forever. This eventuality we must all resolutely guard against. We must be determined to defend our independence with the last drop of our blood. (Cheers.)
>
> On the 26th of January 1950, India would be a democratic country in the sense that India from that day would have a government of the people, by the people and for the people. The same thought comes to my mind. What would happen to her democratic Constitution? Will she be able to maintain it or will she lost it again this is the second thought that comes to my mind and makes me as anxious as the first" (Ambedkar, 1949).

A person of great conviction he was a real optimist with full faith in India and its Constitution. He suggests ways and means how to proceed ahead and implement the Constitution 'not merely in form, but also in fact'. The first suggestion was to stick to the Constitutional means to achieve identified goals and objectives. This in simple words means 'politics with principles'. In free and independent India there is no place for striking work, disturbing the working in institutions and wasting man-hours, burning and damaging public properties. Even disturbing Parliament for days together just cannot be justified by any manner or means. Indian youth must learn to appreciate the difference: what was fully justified during freedom struggle just cannot be applied in the process of national reconstruction. If this process is disturbed even in one place or in one institution, it retards the process of ameliorating the miseries of those who are still waiting to see better days and lead a dignified life. His second suggestion was to remain conscious of the devastating repercussions of hero worship as the same could become a 'sure road to degradation and to eventual dictatorship'. India witnessed it during 1975-77 in its worst form. Youth must involve themselves in free and frank analysis of the rise of caste-based and family-based regional parties and how these have led to the revival of a decimating caste system and parochialism. How do they view the dynastic transition of power in the 21st century? The third suggestion of Dr. Ambedkar is indeed of immense relevance in the total personality development of the young of India who are privileged to be in colleges and universities. He exhorts them not to be content only with the political democracy alone but 'must make our political democracy social democracy as well'. We were, and still are, a 'society based on graded inequality'. When he utters the following words in the Constituent Assembly, his scholarly vision is augmented by emotionality and pragmatism:

> "On 26th of January 1950, we are going to enter into a life of contradictions. In politics we will have equality and in social and economic life we will have inequality. In politics we will be recognizing the principle of one man one vote and one vote one value. In our social and economic life, we shall, by reason of our social and economic structure, continue to deny the principle of one man one value. How long shall we continue to live with this life of Contradictions? How long shall we continue to deny

equality in our social and economic life? If we continue to deny it for long, we shall do so only by putting our political democracy in peril" (Ambedkar, 1049).

It is for the young of India to realize that not only political democracy but also our social democracy seems to have been hijacked by vested interests. The tyranny of the rich and resourceful manifests in huge scandals and windfall gains to some and these go on practically unchecked. When millions of food grains are lost because of management inefficiency and corruption, heart-rending stories of men, women and children are reported dead because of hunger! Huge amounts sanctioned for irrigation projects vanish in thin air and people die because of no availability of water! Government of the people and by the people is all fine but what people look forward is the 'government for the people'. Looking into the realm of immense alternatives interpretations of systems of governance, the agenda before the youth is to scrutinize the present systems dispassionately—free from ideological boundaries—and present possible solutions before the country and those in power. None would be able to ignore them. This is what one expects from institutions that must function as' national think tanks', should prioritize their programmes, courses, surveys and researches. Many of our universities and institutions are found rather weak on this front. The concerns are known, many like river and air pollution come up before everyone rather on daily basis but solutions are yet to found and plans formulated accordingly implemented. Every government and every system of governance requires scholarly intellectual inputs from those who are fully devoted to their areas of academic pursuit sand have grown up to interpret things with highest levels of humanly achievable objectivity. These expectations from the young of India would find reflection in the Educational background and the way Dr. Ambedkar philosophized education based on his own scholarship and vision.

On Education

It may generally be difficult for the young of today to fathom the measure of humiliation and demoralization that was inflicted on the so-classified 'untouchables'. When once called to come to the Black Board to solve a problem in geometry by the teacher, other children rushed to remove their Tiffin boxes from the vicinity lest these get polluted by the presence of this' untouchable boy'! Enduring innumerable such inflictions, he marched ahead with determination, became Babasahib Ambedkar millions and millions. He led them through a movement of social transformation that has given them inner strength, made them conscious of their rights, and also of duties. He alerted them to their right to equality, and elaborated how it was their right not only to access but also to success. While social reforms did form a major component of the agenda of freedom struggle, the conditions on social and religious front were not conducive to concede the 'eternal equality of all human beings'. Dr. Ambedkar evolved as a scholar in true sense; he realized 'ignorance' as the root cause of evils like untouchabilty in the social firmament, and envisioned the solution in: "knowledge is the foundations of man's life". He translated it into pragmatic terms: Give up the idea that parents give '*Janma*' to the child and not destiny (*Karma*). They can mould the destiny of their children by giving them education". On the broader canvas, Dr. Ambedkar was convinced that no democracy would function effectively unless masses were taken out of the veil of ignorance through education. He was convinced that larger social transformation can be brought about 'neither by mere counting heads nor by breaking of heads, but by appealing to head as well as heart'. He was worried about the fate of democracy in independent India if the demolition of the 'rock of ignorance and glaring social inequalities' was not accomplished well within the right time.

When one reflects on the state of education; and particularly elementary education; in India it is indeed amazing to recall the initial direction to the state to provide free and compulsory education to 'all children till they attain fourteen years of age'. The target remains unfulfilled till date, and in spite of the RTE Act of 2009 according to which it was to achieve for all children in the 6-14 years of age by March 2013. The issue is not only of numbers and percentages but of the very spirit contained in the Constitution of India to create an egalitarian democratic society. Are the weaker sections getting their share of good quality education as available to others? Certainly Not! Who is not familiar with the continued erosion of the credibility of public funded schools? The upper echelons of the society are still reluctant to give the weaker sections their due. Under the 25 per cent seats available to weaker sections in the eligible private schools, out of estimated 22 lakh seats, only 3 lakh have been filled. And that is less than 15 per cent. What is the way out? On October 5, 1927, Dr. Ambedkar offered a solution: "Backward classes have come to realize that after all education is the greatest material benefit for which they can fight. We may forgo material benefits of civilisation, but we cannot forget our right and opportunity to reap benefit of the highest education to the fullest extent". His dream for the emancipation of the weaker sections was that of 'higher education, higher employment, and better ways of earning a living'. In the days of increasing commercialization of education, it is relevant to recall his views: "Education ought to be cheapened in all possible ways and to the greatest possible extent. I urge this plea because I feel that we are arriving at a stage when lower orders of society are just getting in to high schools, middle schools and colleges, and policy of this department therefore ought to be to make higher education as cheap to lower classes as it can be possible be made". Unfortunately, good quality education still remains an elusive dream for most of the weaker sections, and that deserves greater state intervention. (Rajput, 2016)

It is customary to recall three famous words of Dr. Ambedkar that have an everlasting relevance. He repeatedly "urged upon women to overcome inferiority complex and behave with their husbands on par, educate themselves and become economically independent. He asked them not to become slaves of their husbands" (Pawar, 2015). He encouraged women to come forward, be part of agitations and assert their identity everywhere. He, thus, offered a ray of hope and an avenue for women emancipation and empowerment. It was for the young of today, particularly those interested in the empowerment of women to study and analyze what continues to impede women getting their due. Dr. Ambedkar gave a very important message to his followers in a conclave in 1942: "Educate, Agitate and Organise"! Interestingly, it is not 'educate, organise and agitate'! An educated mind must become an enlightened mind, equipped to analyze and think of creative solutions to significant issues and concerns facing not only him but' his people', and that would include all the people. A rightfully 'agitated mind' shall invariably focus on solutions and not on destruction and revenge. To him, 'organise' would imply a collective action for the betterment of the lot of his people around him. Subsequently, his canvas of activity and action could expand manifold and become wider, as it happened with Dr, Ambedkar himself.

A sustained study of Babasahib's journey of life, his thoughts, philosophy, principles and contributions could guide the youth of today to understand India, its culture, society, societal aberrations the need to fully eradicate practices that were an outcome of tyrannical groups. Here the importance of dialogue and free discussion and exchange of ideas deserves total acceptance. From this solutions must emerge, equality of access and success to one and all must become the hallmark of every initiative, whether public or private. The remnants of casteism, untouchability, isolation, discrimination though in there last stage, are to be totally and completely wiped out. Educational discrimination must end. Poverty, misery and hunger must be removed in real sense. That should be the aim and goal of life of the enlightened and educated youth. There could be no better tribute to him than the acceptance of such a mission.

END NOTES

1. This article is an outcome of authors understanding of the Speech DR. Babasahib Ambedkar delivered in the Constituent Assembly on November 25, 1949, a day prior to the acceptance of the Constitution of India. This speech is available on the internet, and several other publications, including the official version of the Constituent assembly Debates. It is quoted above under reference (Ambedkar, 1949).
2. The author is convinced that this one speech if studied, analyzed and internalized by the youth of India could bring about an attitudinal transformation amongst the young of India in schools and colleges.
3. Maurya, B.P. (2001), Personal communication dated February 14, 2001 to Professor J.S Rajput, the Then Director of the NCERT, who was under attack for having proposed that Sanskrit be given due importance.
4. Murli Manohar Joshi (2016), 'Ambedkar wanted Sanskrit as Nat/l Language", The Times of India, April 25, 2016
5. Rajput, J.S. (2016), 'Realize Babasahib's Dream of Education for the Weak', The New Indian express Magazine, Chennai, March 18, 2016
6. Pawar, J.V. (2015), "Dr. B.R. Ambedkar's Social revolution", Bhashya Prakashan, Mumbai

8

Dr. Ambedkar, Gandhi and the Dalit Movement

Krishan Gopal

Dr. B.R. Ambedkar, the leader of the depressed classes of his time (1891-1956) should be viewed as a social scientist, reformist, thinker, writer, statesman and constitutional authority. He is known as the messiah of the social revolution against all kinds of oppressive and discriminative practices prevailing in our social structure. He was vehemently opposed to the caste system and the practice of untouchability as propounded on religious grounds. To do away with these social evils Dr. Ambedkar evolved a theory of safeguards and protections for the backward classes and weaker sections of society for the cause of social justice and equality, which he evolved on the basis of his experience of discrimination and inequalities during his childhood. He, therefore, developed a concept of social justice and security of its own kind along with political equality and sought its due place in the constitutional law of India. For his relentless struggle Dr. Ambedkar was dubbed as the 'Modern Manu' or social reformer who, throughout his life, wrote extensively on the political and social problems facing Indian society. He was concerned with problems, namely, caste system, untouchability, backwardness and exploitation. On his part he suggested numerous solutions to transform the Indian society on the basis of democratic values, secular credentials and social equality. In that sense, Babasaheb was a man of thought and action, as his political and social philosophy revolves around humanism, equality, liberal democracy, secularism and social cohesion. During his life-period, he struggled for the cause of social justice and organised the scheduled castes to seek their due place in the new democratic order.

From his childhood, Ambedkar was opposed to the Hindu code based on caste-system, which has segregated individuals into compartments and units on the basis of birth and parental vocation or occupation. According to him the caste system is unique in the world; it contributed to economic imperialism, political tyranny and social fascism of the Brahmins in India society. For him, the caste system of the Hindu society, based on ascription and social dominance, is like a steel frame of Hinduism. He felt that the caste concept in India was more ancient than the Vedas and no such comparable institution can be found elsewhere, encompassing features like complexity, exploitation, discrimination and rigidity of caste-system as prevailing in India. Dr. Ambedkar viewed the institution of caste as inhuman, undemocratic and authoritarian and so he regarded it contrary to the very concept of social justice and economic equality. His firm belief was that the caste system would retard the social unity and generate caste conflicts and wars in society, cutting at the roots of democracy. He, therefore, preferred to follow the political approach in dealing with the problems of untouchables and identified their interests, by propounding a theory of safeguards and reservations as a solution.

To achieve this purpose, he considered the awakening of the inner consciousness of the depressed classes as of foremost importance. He wanted that the Dalits should gain self-pride, self-improvement and self-confidence so as to have an equal share in the society. For this mission, the first Mahar Conference of Untouchables and Non-Brahmins was convened in 1927 in a town of South of Bombay and the issues relating to psychological dimensions of untouchability, creating self-pride, ways and means of redressing their grievances via legal means in a Parliamentary democracy, etc., were discussed therein. While seeking solution to the problems on hand Dr. Ambedkar gathered the impression that only untouchables could lead untouchables; and he never sought the support of any caste Hindu-led groups for his mission, namely, social justice and equality. It is pertinent to mention that when he launched his Satyagraha to establish equality among the

Hindus by asking the people to allow the Harijans to enter the temples, he was not support by either Gandhiji or Hindu leaders or the Indian National Congress. Nevertheless, he was committed to reforming Hinduism itself with the help of legal and constitutional means. After Independence, while quitting the Nehru Cabinet in 1951 he realized that the conversion of the Harijans into Buddhism was the only alternative to escape from the dominance of Hinduism (i.e. Brahamanism) and from the curse of untouchability, so as to enjoy and equal status and to live with pride and self-respect on par with others in the Hindu community. Dr. Ambedkar founded the Buddhist Society of India, in 1954, for this purpose and since then, it has revived its proselytism in earnestness.

It is true that Gandhiji himself denounced the practice of untouchability operating in the Hindu society and launched the anti-untouchability campaign for awakening the consciousness of the Hindus to the wrongs inflicted on the Harijan community. He also aroused the Harijans to their rights and status. But Dr. Ambedkar was not satisfied with the political approach of Gandhiji and his bona-fides. Consequently, Dr. Ambedkar emerged as a prominent leader of the Harijan community at the time of the Poona Pact in Sept., 1932. He vehemently criticised the way of handling the problems of the Harijans by Gandhiji, thus expressing a lack of faith in the path of Truth and Ahimsa as a means in bringing a change of heart of the Hindus. In fact, Gandhiji viewed untouchability as a political problem and not as a social problem. But Dr. Ambedkar was afraid that the Gandhian approach in dealing the problem of untouchability was likely to make caste Hindus more powerful and untouchables weaker. Dr. Ambedkar's vociferous criticism in this regard resulted into some sort of a personality clash between the two leaders of great stature.

Against this backdrop, it is worthwhile to mention the acrimony between Gandhiji and Dr. Ambedkar over the upliftment of untouchables, dating back to the Second Round Table Conference in London in 1931, in which Gandhi vehemently opposed Ambedkar's demand for separate electorates for the Dalits. The intense feelings of the Dalits against Gandhi was manifested by black flag demonstrations against him on his return to Bombay. Dr. Ambedkar himself did not mince words when it came to criticizing Gandhi. He said: "I insist that if I dislike Gandhi, it is because I love India more.... The worship of

Gandhi and service to India are two very different things and may even be contradictory of each other". In another scathing comment he said: " I hate all the Mahatmas and firmly believe that they should be done away with. I am of the opinion that their existence is a curse to the nation in which they are born. They try to perpetuate blind faith in place of intelligence and reason."

In 1932, the Communal Award of the British government granted separate electorates for the depressed classes. M.K. Gandhi took up a fast unto death in his prison cell in Poona, protesting that separate electorates were a device which would separate the untouchables from Hindu society for ever. As Gandhi weakened, Dr. Ambedkar capitulated, but only when some Hindu leaders pledged their help in the removal of untouchability, and agreed that the untouchables would have seats in all elected bodies. Dr. Ambedkar, however, never reconciled himself to this outcome. According to him, it forced the Dalits to agree to live at the mercy of the Hindus. Subsequent events showed that Gandhi was wrong when he claimed in August, 1934 that 'untouchability was on its last legs'. On the contrary, the impact of the evil still persists, even 69 years after Independence. According to the Commissioner of Scheduled Castes and Scheduled Tribes, there are many areas where these weaker sections are denied even common access to drinking water. There has been a sharp increase in the atrocities on them, and their socio-economic conditions are fast deteriorating, despite the Dalit movement.

The Dalit movement has never benefited from mere electoral participation. It would be useful to consider the record of Dr. Ambedkar's first political party, the Independence Labour Party, which was born in great optimism to fight the elections of 1937, The first in which the Scheduled Castes had designated seats. It won 11 of the 15 seats reserved for the SCs in the Bombay Province. The Congress won the rest. But Ambedkar's electoral success was of absolutely no use in passing legislation as long as his party was a small and lonely minority in a legislature dominated by the majority party. The party was second only to the Muslim League as an opposition party to the Congress in Bombay, and it functioned with vigour, but had little effect. Not even the protest against the use of Gandhi's term 'Harijan' for untouchables was heard. Even Dr. Ambedkar too realized after his defeat in the 1952 general elections that the problems of Dalit could not be solved by a caste-based party. Hence, he wanted to convert the Scheduled Caste Federation (CSCF), the organisation in existence at that time, into a broad-based party. This did not happen during his life time. After his death, his followers simply renamed SCF the Republican Party, but failed to achieve the unity of all the oppressed classes as desired by him.

An objective study of the role played by Dr. B.R. Ambedkar in a proper historical perspective reveals that it suffers from two factors, namely: (i) the mindless deification of the man by his followers and (ii) the reluctance of the country's intellectual elite to shed its deep prejudice against Dr. Ambedkar. His deification only exposes the bankruptcy of the Dalit leaders today, for Ambedkar was a man of action and resented being idolized. He believed that a society which idolized and raised a man to the level of God, had set on the path of destruction. For this, the mainstream political leaders are equally to be blamed. They have silently conspired, with their eyes on the vote bank, to allow, abet and encourage the idolization of the great man to a disgusting level. Likewise, the second obstacle is more formidable. The prejudice of the Indian intellectuals against Dr. Ambedkar is based on three factors: his role in the national movement, his confrontation with Mahatma Gandhi and the lingering influence of Manu, the codifier of the Hindu Law, on the psyche of the Indian thinkers. Our intellectuals and thinkers, although not casteist in outlook, have been prejudice by the caste system operating within the country. B.R. Ambedkar was perhaps afraid that Manu's influence would continue for a long time. Manu, who had ordained that the status of an untouchable, no matter how old or venerated, will always be lower than the lowliest of caste Hindu. And this fear coloured Dr. Ambedkar's perspectives throughout his life. Not without reason though, since the caste system has taken such deep roots in the Hindu subconscious, that even today, 69 years after Independence, a Dalit celebrity is tolerated, encouraged or patronized, but rarely accepted with warmth or given equal status. Dr. Ambedkar's first priority was social reform. To him annihilation of the caste system and ensuring the basic human and political rights to the untouchables was a task of paramount importance. He said that the level of society cannot raised unless those at the bottom are given their due. All his early struggles, to secure for the lower castes a right to enter temples, to draw water from common wells, and later his fight to the Hindu Code Bill, were directed towards this objective. Dr. Ambedkar's strategies and tactics ought to be viewed against this background. If he openly regarded the British as the "deliverers" of the untouchables, it was essentially a tactic. He cared little if the Hindu orthodoxy was alienated because he was certain that the caste system left no scope for the high castes to help the untouchables.

Dr. Ambedkar's cooperation with the Simon Commission and the first Round Table Conference, both boycotted by the Congress Party, earned him the wrath of the Congressmen. From then on, he was abused as a stooge of the British. His championing of the idea of separate electorates for the untouchables evoked violent resentment among nationalists, Congressmen and orthodox Hindu groups. The echoes of the vilification campaign against Dr. Ambedkar have still not died. Likewise, Mahatma Gandhi's famous fast unto death to oppose separate electorates for the untouchables caused extreme bitterness on both sides. The Mahatma himself, Congressmen and the Hindus at large, thought that Dr. Ambedkar was seeking to divide the country. They cried that Ambedkar was holding the whole of Hindu society and the Mahatma to ransom. In the eyes of the depressed, however, Gandhi's fast was a diabolical poly to crush the aspirations of the untouchables and the same time to win the confidence of the Hindu orthodoxy. "Why does not the Mahatma go on a fast unto death to wipe out untouchability?" Dr. Ambedkar asked, only to capitulate in the face of pressure from the entire nation. But up to the end of his life, he did not forgive Mahatma Gandhi for coercing him into signing the Poona Pact. The bitterness of that confrontation lingers even today. Dr. Ambedkar's followers and critics alike thrust on him a kind of greatness he never wanted, the former out of naive adulation and the latter with a deliberate design. Ambedkar's predicament was peculiar in the world's social history because of the unique viciousness of the caste system. For him fighting for the dignity of the lower castes was the most human endeavour, a supreme contribution in enhancing the consciousness of the universal mind. And he did it with zeal, caring little for the wrath of the "tyrannical majority".

Since Indian Government marked the year 2015 to celebrate the 125th Birth Anniversary of Dalit icon and architect of Indian Constitution B.R. Ambedkar, three question questions have arisen. First, if Indians, by and large, accepted the new Constitutional regime of the independent nation-state and continue to both abide by the idea of equal citizenship and respect the rule of law, then why do caste prejudice, caste violence and social inequality based on caste hierarchy persist in such a rampant way? Second, if Babasaheb unequivocally won the argument against Gandhi, then why did not more people, Dalits as well as caste Hindus, follow him into Buddhism? Why are there numerically so few Ambedkarite Buddhists even today? Third, if the 2014 general election produces a national government led by the Hindu Right, then what kind of attitudes toward caste can we expect will re-enter the public imagination, through the backdoor, if not explicitly and programmatically? Given that Hindutva is founded on a hatred of Gandhi, a dislike of all Gandhian values, and literally, the assassination of the person of Gandhi together with all that he stood for, will we see a glorification of Caturvarnya, greater caste pride, a renewed confidence in the religious legitimacy of caste differentiation, and newer forms of humiliation and exclusion inflicted upon Dalits?

It is high time we turned and returned to Dr. Ambedkar—not just within the confines of the Dalit community, whatever its undeniably special relationship with its greatest leader—but as Indians on the verge of entering into a reactionary phase in our political history. Whether through his conflict with Gandhi, or his rejection of Hinduism and adoption of Buddhism; whether through his work on the making of the Constitution and his creation of the basic outlines of a reservation policy, or a as a believer in associational forms of collective life, fraternity, equal citizenship and fundamental rights—in all respects, Ambedkar suggested the way forward to a more egalitarian, democratic, and enlightened society than India has ever been. Only by retaining a commitment to his radically progressive vision not just for Dalits, but also for caste Hindus, and for India as a whole, will we be able to survive what promises to be a dark chapter in the political life of the nation.

The acceptance of Ambedkar does not necessarily equate itself with the spread of an anti-caste ethos. Today, Ambedkar certainly outshines every other leader in terms of public acceptance. No other leader can rival him in the number of statues, pictures, congregations, books, research, organisations, songs, or any other marker of popularity of/

on him. Curiously, his pictures has become a fixture even in movies and television episodes. However, the incidences of casteism as indicated by cases of caste discrimination, caste atrocities, caste associations and caste discourses, etc. also show parallel growth. This paradoxical phenomenon can be explained only by separating the real Ambedkar from the unreal one, cast into the icons constructed by vested interests to thwart the consciousness of radical change ever germinating in Dalit masses. These icons package the enigmatic real Ambedkar into a simplistic symbol: an architect of the Constitution, a great nationalist, the father of reservations, a staunch anti-communist, a liberal democrat, a great Parliamentarian, a saviour of Dalits, a bodhisattva, etc. These icons of the harmless, status quo-ist Ambedkar have been proliferated all over and over-shadow a possible, radical view of the real Ambedkar.

Notwithstanding the intrigues behind the promotion of such icons by vested interests with active support from the state, the evolution of Ambedkar, the pragmatist sans any ideological fixation, all through his life, makes him intrinsically difficult to understand. A young Ambedkar who theorized castes as the enclosed classes, the enclosure being provided by the system of endogamy and exogamy, expecting the larger Hindu society to wake up and undertake social reforms like intermarriage in order to open up castes into classes is in contrast to the post-Mahad Ambedkar, disillusioned by the rabid reactions from caste Hindus, turning his sights to politics to accomplish his objective. Were his threats of conversions to Islam for a separate political identity for Dalits, or to force caste Hindus to consider social reforms? Then there is a the Ambedkar of the 1930s, anxious to expand his constituency to the working classes sans castes, who founded the Independent Labour Party (ILP), arguably the first Left party in India, and walked with the communists but at the same time one who declared his resolve to convert to some other religion to escape castes. What about the Ambedkar of the 1940s, who returns to the caste, dissolves the ILP and forms the Scheduled Castes Federation, shuns agitational politics and joins the colonial government as labour minister or the one who wrote States and Minorities propounding state socialism be hardcoded into the proposed Constitution of free India? Or Ambedkar, the staunchest opponent of the Congress or the one who cooperated with the Congress in joining the all-party government and accepted its support to get into the Constituent Assembly? Or even the Ambedkar who developed the representation logic culmination in reservations, expecting that a few advanced elements from among Dalits would help the community progress or the one who publicly lamented that educated Dalits had let him down? Or the Ambedkar who was the architect of the Constitution and advised Dalits to adopt only constitutional methods for a resolution of their problems or the one who disowned it in the harshest possible terms and spoke of being the first person to burn it down? And finally, the Ambedkar who kept referring to Marx as a quasi-benchmark to assess his decisions? Or the one who embraced Buddhism and created the ultimate bulwark against communism in India to use the words of one of his scholars, Eleanor Zelliot, or even the one who would favourably compare Buddha and Marx just a few days before bidding adieu to the world, saying their goal was the same but that they differed in the ways of achieving them—Buddha's being better than Marx's? There are just a few broad vignettes of him, problematic in typifying him in a simplistic manner. If one goes deeper, one is bound to face far more serious problems.

Ambedkar is surely needed as long as the virus of caste lingers in this land. Ambedkar is equally important in contemporary world to cope up with the emerging challenges.

END NOTES

1. https://en.wikipedia.org/wiki/Bildungsroman accessed on 26th March, 2016
2. http://www.folomojo.com/16-great-quotes-of-dr-babasaheb-ambedkar-that-explain-why-he-is-on-google-doodle-in-8-different-countries/ accessed on 26th March, 2016
3. Raut, Nitin, Ambedkar on Population Policy contemporary Relevance, Shipra Publications: New Delhi: 2014 pp 2-3.)
4. Baisantry, D.K., Ambedkar The Total Revolutionary: Segment Book distributors: New Delhi: 1991 pp 9-10
5. http://www.mapsofIndia.com/on-this-day/14th-october-1956-b.r.-ambedkar-converts-to-buddhism-along-with-365000-followers accessed on 26th March, 2016.
6. Jadhav, Narendra, Ambedkar Speaks Vol. 1: Konark Publishers: New Delhi: 2013 pp. 282-3)
7. Dr. Baba Saheb Ambedkar Writings and Speeches, edited by Vasant Moon ambedkar\vol-14-II\vol14-II-02.indd
8. Dr. Baba Saheb Ambedkar Writings and Speeches, ambedkar\vol-017\vol17-01-05.indd
9. Dr. Baba Saheb Ambedkar Writings and Speeches, ambedkar\vol-017\vol17-01-05.indd

9

Dr. B.R. Ambedkar on Indian Women

Koushiki Dasgupta

So far has been the modern democratic movements are concerned, women empowerment movements are an important part of this trend. Women empowerment movements are related with wider social political developments of a country; however, each and every example of this sort of movements should be treated on the grounds of time and space. In post independent India, the question of women empowerment has been treated by post colonialists as a trope to justify the west being a 'saviour' and the others as 'victims'. The so-called binaries of a 'saviour' and a 'victim' must be read within the same framework of homogeneity which has been assigned to third world women and their problems irrespective of their primordial identities. Western feminists have a tendency to view third world women as homogeneous coherent identity and simultaneously as a universal powerless group subject to similar exploitations in every historical and political junctures. It should be pointed out the range of gender experiences and the dynamism of women's movements inpost-colonial countries was quite different from the others. The growth and development of feminist thoughts were diverse in those countries where 'colonial' and 'patriarchal'—this duel paradigms of exploitation had created an unusual mode of social structure and its legacies were unique as well. In India too, women's movements had never ever been organised on unlined fashion, rather multiple voices and multiples histories were documented within and outside the arena of women movements. The preoccupation of Dalit understandings of gender history could been viewed as the most suitable example of this trend from 1990s, and women as 'subaltern' were heard against the mainstream feminist thoughts in India. One of the very interesting feature of this new trend was to identity an exclusive voice of the women as 'Dalit' and the others as 'non-Dalit' or to the extent Brahmanical. However, the word 'Brahmanical' itself is problematic. This new paradigm has traced the binaries of 'upper' and 'low' in women's movements and somehow questioned the entire structure of the existing narratives. Even though the patriarchal structure is quite strong among the Dalit movement itself, the Dalit feminists have traced out the channels of patriarchy within the wider women movements where the upper class/caste women had failed to become the voice of the marginal or the lower. It is to be mention here that the position of Dalit women in Indian history is quite vague and formless because the dualities of, 'Dalithood' and 'womanhood' had always created problems for a total history of Dalit women. Right from 1920s these women were seen in political realm as well clamouring for political issues, they were lacking the very spirit and voice required for pure consciousness from within. Dr B.R. Ambedkar could have been cited as the first to be realising the real nature of Dalithood for women. He was the man first put forward the question of equality and justice for Dalit women. He raised his voice against the Hindu social order through his renowned journal *Mook Nayakin*, 1920 and *Bahiskrit Bharatin*, 1927. Through these journals he spoke on the gender equality, women and problems of women and other depressed class. He also proposed family planning measures for women in Bombay Legislative Assembly.

Unfortunately the role of Ambedkar is not widely discussed in the realm of Dalit women movement movements since he was not a social reformer like Raja Ram Mohan Roy or an activist like Gandhi. Ambedkar is more familiar either as an anti-caste leader or simply as the father of Indian constitution. His political and social ideas, in fact, received serious attention only after his death in 1956. What is important is that Ambedkar not only searched for the roots of social stigmas or castism in the Hindu society, he equally looked for the ways of women's empowerment in the true sense of the term. Ambedkar should not be read only as anti-caste leader rather a philosopher who dealt with the issues like women consciousness and transforming that consciousness for an overall change in the social matrix. In Dhanajay Keer's *Dr Ambedkar: Life and Mission'*, Gail Omvedt's, *Dalit and the Democratic Revolution: Dr Ambedkar and the Dalit movement in Colonial India*, M.S. Gore's, *The Social Context of an Ideology: Ambedkar's Political and Social Thought'* and in others writings the references on Dalit women have been raised but the role of Ambedkar in lifting up women awareness or empowering all women, didn't appear separately. Throughout his career Ambedkar devoted his attention equally to the questions of SC/ ST development, anti-caste issues and on Indian women in various occasions. The truly believed that unless the Indian women come forward for their rescue, nobody would do anything from outside. He was very much aware of the fact textual discourses like the *Manusmriti*, contributed a lot for the degeneration of women in society, that in 1927 he burnt up a copy of the said text along with his Dalit women followers like Shantabai Dani, Gita Bai Gayakwad or Meena Bai Shivraj. On the other hand Ambedkar knew it well if there was *Manusmriti* for women in ancient India, there was the liberating message of Buddhism too. While law givers like Manu had tried to chain women into social customs, there was Buddha too who offered women the noble path of liberation and knowledge. Thus while taking amount liberation and empowerment for women, Ambedkar looked back at Buddha, not at Europe.

Amdebkar's entire understanding on the women question was based primary on caste, since caste an as institution was related to the condition of women in Hindu society. Therefore, he took caste as a consolidated structure of oppression against the basic human values and women being the most vulnerable section of the society were easily kept under castiest surveillance. For him, Hindu social order didn't speak for individuality, only talk about class or Varna, thus made the Shudras and women suffer as being part of their social-hierarchical and sexiest positions. Since the entire structure of oppression was legitimised as per law and in order to remove the handicaps of Indian women, Dr. Ambedkar proposed the Hindu Code Bill to codify the various versions of law prevailing in Hindu society in India as well as to codify the rules of Hindu law scattered in the decisions of the High courts or at the Privy council. Being India's first Law Minister and the chairman of the drafting committee of the constituent assembly. Dr. Ambedkar brought forward the Hindu Code Bill with an objective redefine the Hindu society. "...if you want to maintain the Hindu system, the Hindu culture, the Hindu society does not hesitate to repair where repair is necessary. The Bill asks for nothing more than repairing those parts of the Hindu system which have almost become dilapidated."[1] The Bill was introduced to the constituent assembly on 11 April, 1957, to free up personal laws so as to liberate the individual and ensure equality before law. The Bill mainly focussed on right to property, order of succession to the property and maintenance, marriage, divorce, adoption, minority and guardianship. No doubt the revolutionary character of the Bill had invited serious opposition form the conservation elements of the Parliament and passing of the Bill was delayed for more than four years. Ultimately in despair Dr. Ambedkar resigned from the legislature on 10 October, 1951. A brief overview of the Bill would highlight that, (i) the female member of the Hindu family was given full rights in matters of property, marriage, divorce, adoption, maintenance, inheritance, minority and guardianship; (ii) the family members were encouraged to come tighter for in matters affecting their mutual interests; (iii) all members of the Hindu family were entrusted with individual freedom and equality; (iv) women were given safeguard from dowry, disease and hunger; (v) to give them the right to knowledge and be economically strong at the time of crises; (vi) In accordance with the novelty of the Indian constitution the bill proposed to restructure the Hindu society ensuring liberty, equality, justice, individual dignity and national fraternity. The successful function these provisions were possible if only caste restrictions were abolished forever. Answering on this core issue, Ambedkar declared, "...The Bill says that if members of a Hindu community wants to follow the orthodox system which requires that marriage shall not be valid unless the bride and bridegroom belong to the same Varna, the same caste or the same sub caste, there is nothing in this code which can prevent him from giving effect to his wishes or living effect to what he regards as his dharma. In a same way if one Hindu who is a reformist and who does not believe in Varna, caste or sub caste, chooses to marry a girl outside his Varna, outside his caste, outside his sub caste, the law regards his marriage also as valid.. So far as the marriage law is concerned there is, therefore, no kind of imposition at all. The *vaidhikas*, the orthodox are left free to do what they think is right according to their dharma. The reformers who do not allow dharma but who follow reason, who follow conscience, have also been left to follow their reason and their conscience." The House had inhibitions regarding the Bill, however, Dr Ambedkar raised those issues which were never on the floor earlier. Each and every aspect of this Bill was related to the question of women empowerment. On the marriage question Ambedkar believed that the existing law of the Hindu society only recognise traditional religious marriages but the proposed Bill does not differentiate between traditional religious marriages and social contractual marriages. There are five provisions for a legal region marriage. Firstly, the age of the bridegroom should be eighteen and the bride should be of fourteen. Secondly, none of the parties should have living wife or husband at the time of marriage. Thirdly, the bridegroom and the bride should not have any illicit affair. Fourthly, both of them should not be in close blood relations and lastly, none of the parties should have mental illness. The basic difference between traditional marriage system and the proposed new system was on the issue of caste. The Bill didn't want to prioritise the issue of caste in any form while in traditional marriages caste remained at the centre of consideration. Very naturally the proposed Bill was strongly critiqued by the conservatives as they thought that the proposed omission of the caste question from Hindu marriages would misbalance the society and people would be undisciplined. With this question of marriage, the idea of monogamy and polygamy was closely associated. Dr Ambedkar unequivocally supported monogamy and proposed to ban polygamy. "...I must point out the I do not think any member in this house will be able to point out having regard to customary law or having regard to our Shastra that a Hindu husband had all times an unfettered, unqualified right to polygamy. That was never the case. Even today in certain parts of South India there are people who follow this, a section of the Nattukottai Chattiyars—the case has been reported in the Reports of the Privy council itself, I am not depending on mere heresy of evidence—but among the Nattukottai Chettiyars there is a custom that a husband cannot marry a second wife unless he obtains the consent of his wife. Secondly, when consent is obtained, he must allot to her certain property, which I think in the Tamil language is called 'moppu'. That property becomes her absolute property so that if after her consent the husband marries and ill-treats her, she has a certain amount of economic competence in her own hands to lead son independent life. I cite this as an illustration to show that there has not been an unqualified right for polygamy."[3] Dr. Ambedkar had shown several other examples like one from *Arhashastra* that polygamy was not permitted unconditionally in Hindu society and proposed monogamy as the ultimate rule of life. Other that marriages, Dr. Ambedkar also spoke on divorce, adoption, guardianship, inheritance and most importantly on uniform civil code.

Hindu code Bill couldn't get the legal recognition; however, the bill was divided into four later in the forms of Hindu Marriage Act, 1955, the Hindu Succession Act, 1956, the Hindu Minority and Guardianship Act, 1956, the Hindu Adoption and Maintenance Act, 1956. The Hindu Marriage Act, 1955 included mainly, (i) legitimisation of illegitimate children; (ii) custody of children; (iii) age of marriage for females; (iv) provisions for alimony, etc. The Hindu Succession Act, 1956 included (i) widow's right to adopt son and daughter; (ii) control on property; (iii) scheme of succession, etc. The Hindu Minority and Guardianship Act, 1956 included (i) empowerment of mothers in terms of appointing the guardian for children; (ii) father's right to appoint a guardian for the minor. The Adoption and Maintenance Act, 1956 included (i) adoption of male and female child without any difference; (ii) permission to wives for adopting a child even during the lifetime of her husband; (iii) wives became indispensible partner while taking the decision on adoption or giving a child for adoption. The entire structure of the laws in the bill was meant for limbering the women in every sense. He not only searched for the nature of inequalities in Hindu society but also sought out the remedies from within, through the help of law. The Hindu Code Bill and the subsequent laws had become the milestone of women empowerment in India.

Dr. Ambedkar always focussed on the need to educate women especially the Dalit women and involved them in all the social movements. He had a belief on the organised form of women movements, that at the All India Depressed Classes Women's Conference in 1940, he expressed, "I am a great believer in women's organisations. I know what they can do to improve the condition of the society if they are convinced."[4] He maintained that education, organisation and agitation was meant for women since women were not so different from the downtrodden, their mental and physical inhibitions were similar and so that their dialogue and treatment could not be different. Reform of the Hindu family and reform of the Hindu social structure, therefore was necessary to provide women the actual agency in larger social movements, Thus, Dr. Ambedkar looked into each minute issues related to the life and status of women. He was confident that the women would have to liberate themselves from the clutches of caste hierarchy and oppression. The promotion of inter-caste marriages in fact appeared to be a tool for unmaking the caste structure because Ambedkar for the first time promoted companionate marriages and declared husband as sexual partners, not the master or the mentor. Such an idea had negated the question of women subjectivity and gave woman the right to choose her husband and right to determine her marriage. On Dalit perspective of women's liberation. Ambedkar stated, "The question of annihilation of untouchability is more an issue for women than for men. You gave birth to us me and other people treat us even worse than they would treat animals... at places even our shadows are not allowed. Others acquire positions of prestige in offices and government but we, bon to you, are not even given the least prestigious jobs. For, we are considered to be of lowly status... How are we in any way different from the children of kayastha or other savarna women sitting in this Sabha? You must remember that you have as much of character as the Brahmin women and yet why is it that their progeny is acceptable to all but those born to you are so insulted that they are denied even the basic right to be human? Have you ever given this a though? Why is birth from your womb considered a sin?' (*Bahishkrut Bharat*, 1928, speech of Dr. Ambedkar at the Mahad Satyagraha Parishad). His in-depth study on the relation between caste and subordination of women made him aware that the caste system being a hierarchical one, the lower the position of the women in the hierarchy the more intense her exploitation. Legal provisions and united movements by the women themselves would change the situation, be liberated, in one day or other. He fervently supported the Maternity Benefit Bill, the Abortion Act, the birth control proposals and others to make women confident and eligible for ruling out her own destiny. His critics had always felt that the Hindu Code Bill would shatter the fundamental design of Hindu society, however, his indomitable will and rational speeches moved the House for a second thought on the Bill. The Hindu Code Bill should be taken as a water shade in the history of women's movement in India. Whatever the position the women had achieved in contemporary time is mostly due to the efforts of Dr. Ambedkar. He challenged the hegemony of an old structure and tried to deconstruct it with legal provisions and social movements. In his capacity as the Chairman of the Drafting Committee of the Constituent Assembly, he provided a legal frame to free India and figured out a workable constitution for all.

Although Dr. Ambedkar failed to succeed in getting passed the Hindu Code Bill, he put the ball rolling & laid the foundation of equality for the women of India. Women can now have custody of child, no marriage before age of 18 years, Provision of alimony (maintenance allowance from husband on getting legally separation). Widow can now adopt a child, rights over parental property, a uniform scheme for succession to the property of a Hindu female who dies intestate (not having made a will). All these are possible mostly due to efforts of Dr. Ambedkar. He was not a Dalit hero alone, but as saviours of the Indian women. Ambedkar made real efforts in understanding the reality about the women in India, and campaigned practical reformist measures for the upliftment of women. These measures established the foundation of the legislation for providing opportunities to women so that they could have a position of equality. Unlike Gandhi, Phule or Raja Rammohan Roy, he questioned the hierarchical social order and sought remedies form constitutional rights. He also spoke on the Muslim women about wearing veil, their religious traditions and marriages; however his basic interest was on Hindu society. Pandit Nehru called him the symbol of revolt against all oppressive features of Hindu society and he himself declared, 'unity is meaningless without the accompaniment of women. Education is fruitless without educated women, and agitation is incomplete without the strength of women.'

END NOTES

1. Dr Babasaheb Ambedkar: Writing and Speeches, Vol 14, pt.1, Government of Maharashtra, Mumbai, 1955, p.283.
2. Ibid.
3. Ibid, 268-69.
4. Ibid.

REFERENCES

Barnwal, Bijay K., "Dr. B.R. Ambedkar's Quest for Gender Equality: Its Relevance in Contemporary Feminist Discourse", *Online International Interdisciplinary Research Journal* (Bi-Monthly), Volume IV, Issue II, Mar.-Apr. 2014.

More, Dr. Vijay G., "Dr. B.R. Ambedkar's Contribution for Women's Rights", *Variorum, Multi Disciplinary e Research Journal,* Vol. 2, Issue I, August 2011.

Dhanvijay, Ms. Vaishali, „DR. Babasaheb Ambedkar's efforts for women empowerment and present status of women in society , *Electronic International Interdisciplinary Research Journal* (*EIIRJ*), (Bi-Monthly).

Volume I, Issue II, April 2012.

Shashi, S.S. (ed), "Ambedkar and Social Justice", Volume II, Director Publications Division, Ministry of Information and Broadcasting, Government of India, Patiala House, New Delhi, 1992.

Bharati, T., "Ambedkar and Uplift of Women," published in an edited book Ambedkar and Social Justice, Volume II, 1992, p. 264.

10

The Messiah of the Vulnerable Segment of Society: A Study on the Relevance of Dr. Ambedkar in Today's India

Mridusmita Baruah

> *"Man was born free, and he is everywhere in chains. Those who think themselves the masters of others are indeed greater slaves than they."*
> — **Jean-Jacques Rousseau**

In literary criticism, the word *Bildungsroman* (a German word meaning: *"novel of formation, education, culture"*), is a literary genre that focuses on the psychological and moral growth of the protagonist from youth to adulthood in which character change is extremely important.[1] Here in this research paper an overview of the Messiah of the downtrodden, Dr. Ambedkar's entire development of personality can be studied. His life is one of sheer challenges and success of the highest order.

The leader of India's untouchables in the decades leading up to Indian Independence, the architect of the Indian Constitution and the celebrated convert to Buddhism, Ambedkar began life as a pre modern man. As a member of the Mahar Community, required by Hindu Law to perform menial work and avoid polluting contact with the upper classes. But over his long career Ambedkar evolved into Berger's modern man, who rejected the sacred canopy Hinduism, systematically studied the religious options available in India and finally adopted the Buddhism as the faith that met the complex requirements of reason and morality he stipulated along the way. This is how he turned out to be the most highly educated man in India, the father of his people, lawyer and legislator, author, orator, labour leader, cabinet minister and educator.

Dr. B.R. Ambedkar the messiah for the downtrodden and the architect of Indian Constitution graced this planet on 14th April, 1891. As he was born in a socially backward family, Ambedkar was the victim of caste discrimination, inequality and prejudice prevalent in the Indian Society during that time. However, he courageously fought against all odds, and attained higher education thus becoming the first ever untouchable to attain the same. No sooner after completing his studies, he launched himself politically fighting for the rights of the depressed class and inequality practiced in the society. He was a crusader of social equality and justice. Academically trained as a jurist, he went on to become the first Law Minister of Free India and the framer or chief architect of the Constitution of India. In his later years, he converted himself to Buddhism religion to free him from the perils of caste differences that was practiced by Hindus.

On 14 October 1956, less than two months before he died, B.R. Ambedkar, the chief architect of India's Constitution and one of the towering intellects of modern India, converted to Buddhism along with some 365,000 of his followers in Nagpur after a traditional ceremony. (Deekshabhoomi Stupa in Nagpur.)

He graduated from Elphinstone College in Mumbai and thereafter was awarded a scholarship to attend Columbia University in New York from where he obtained a Doctorate. After this he moved to United Kingdom in 1916 where he studied at the London School of Economics and was awarded the degree of Barrister-at-Law by Gray's Inn. After returning to India he worked for the depressed classes and became their messiah. When he served as Labour Minister in the Viceroy's Council, Dr. Ambedkar successfully led the struggle for reduction of work day from 12 hours a day to 8 hours in 1942. He was truly a visionary in the sense that he single handedly established the Central Technical Power Board, the National Power Grid System and the Central Technical Power Board. He even had a major role in establishing the Damodar Valley Project and Hirakud Project.

Dr. Ambedkar always believed in liberating the society from the social evils like untouchability, superstition, illiteracy and backwardness through education. Education for him is the main weapon against all the social evils prevalent in the society. He was even a crusader for gender equality and fought for equal rights for women in inheritance and marriage.

Thanks to his fierce battle against the Indian caste system, his lifelong campaign for women's rights and his priceless contribution towards the labour movement, Ambedkar is widely regarded as one of the greatest leaders of the 20th century.[2]

Dr. Ambedkar was a strong supporter of birth control measures. In fact, he was the only political leader in India, who strongly advocated the cause of birth control. Dr. Ambedkar founded the Independent Labour Party as a Political Party in 1936. He had defined the problem of over population in the Election Manifesto of his Independent Labour Party and said that, over population was the major cause of poverty in India. It was mentioned in the aims of the party that "The Party, however, believes that the fragmentation of the holdings and the consequent poverty of the agriculturists are mainly due to the pressure of population on land and unless the pressure is relieved by draining off the excess population subsisting on land, fragmentation will continue, and the condition of the agriculturists will remain as poverty stricken as it is today." [3]

Since time immemorial the Depressed Classes have been subjected to untold sufferings and persecutions. In ancient India their condition was no better than chattels. The rationalistic ideas and the doctrine of "Liberty, Equality and Fraternity" which the Western invaders brought with them remained confined for a long time to the upper strata of the population. In their imperialistic interest they used and misused the Depressed Classes.

From the very beginning of his public career, Dr. Ambedkar passed for an independent and separate position for the Schedule Castes in the Country's body politics. He met the then Secretary of State for India Mr. Montague when he came to India in 1917. In his evidence before the Southborough Committee in 1918, he said that the Depressed Classes were not a chunk of the Hindu block and demanded for them separate representation.[4]

Ambedkar used his education to spearhead the cause of equality, fraternity and liberty. He wrote several books and columns highlighting the fundamental and human rights of all people. To close the gap of inequality inflicted on Dalits for centuries, he canvassed for reservation in education and employment for Dalits, and won. Human rights are more talked about than practiced in India. Dr. Ambedkar, himself a victim of the denial of rights, made sure that fundamental rights were enshrined in our Constitution, benefiting generations to come.

Ambedkar was deeply conscious of the dangers of social and economic inequality, and his words ring true even today: "How long shall we continue to deny equality in our social and economic life? If we continue to deny it for long, we will do so only by putting our political democracy in peril," he said when India was becoming a republic. "We must remove this contradiction at the earliest possible moment or else those who suffer from inequality will blow up the structure of political democracy which this Assembly has so laboriously built up."[5]

On women he said, "I am a great believer in women's organisation. I know what they can do to improve the condition of society if they are convinced. In the eradication of social evils, they have rendered great services. I will testify to that from my own experience. Ever since I began to work among the Depressed Class, I made it a point to carry women along with men".[6]

{Address in Marathi at the All India Depressed Classes Women's Conference second session Nagpur, July 20, 1942}

Ambedkar further went on saying that "The sovereignty of scriptures of all religions must come to an end if we want to have a united integrated modern India."

Dr. Ambedkar had a very liberal approach for women folk and he wished to have equal footing for women along with their male counterparts. He believed that society will progress only when women are empowered and thus upheld women's right to higher education and employment. He was very much vocal about the Hindu Code Bill and in this context he said that, "I maintain that today we cannot have a Hindu law like the one which was propounded by our ancestors. In those days Hindus lived in an exclusive way. The impact of civilisation and other religions had not begun so far as Hindus were concerned.

Now in every Code, in the Muslim Law, in the Christian Law, and in the Hindu law we have got principles which are not germane to those laws alone but which as a matter of Act have been made universal by the impact of other forces. For instance, in this Hindu Code we have got monogamy which is a special feature of the Christian Law. The authors of the Hindu Code want daughters to be given a share of the property. Now this was not known to Hindu law, so far as married daughters were concerned for a very long time. Of course, there is no practice or principle which has not been experimented upon at one time or other by the Hindus."[7]

Dr. B.R. Ambedkar was conscious enough regarding the census of India and he expressed his opinion on Indian Census on 26th October 1947, as follows:

> "The Census of India has over a number of decades ceased to be an operation in demography. It has become a Political affair. Every community seems to be attempting to artificially argument its numbers at the cost of some other community for the sake of capturing greater and greater degree of political power in its own hands. The Scheduled Castes seem to have been made a common victim for the satisfaction of the combined greed of the other communities who through their propagandists or enumerators are able to control the operations and the results of the Census."[8] This shows his enterprising nature regarding the upliftment of the vulnerable section of the society. He was a firm practitioner of Democratic form of Government where the common people are a direct beneficiary. According to him, Democracy is not a form of Government, but a form of social organisation. Democracy is not merely a form of Government. It is primarily a mode of associated living, of conjoint communicated experience. It is essentially an attitude of respect and reverence towards our fellow men.

In his election manifesto of Scheduled Caste Federation way back in 1952 he described the problems of raising the backward classes and problems of poverty along with many other features. The Problem of poverty is thus a double edged problem. From one point of view it is a problem of more production both in Agriculture and in Industry. From another point of view, it is a problem of controlling the excessive growth of population. Both sides are equally important. While the rapid industrialisation of the country is very essential in the opinion of the Federation agriculture is bound to remain the foundation of India's economy. The Federation holds that for increased production in agriculture the following plan must be adopted:

(i) Agriculture must be mechanized. Agriculture in India can never become prosperous so long as the method of cultivation remains primitive.
(ii) To make mechanized farming possible, cultivation on small holdings must be replaced by large farms.
(iii) To increase the yield, there must be provision for adequate manuring and for the supply of healthy seeds.

He even mentioned about the problems of Foreign Policy in terms of China and Pakistan and how our own state Kashmir is affected till date. This we can see in the recent developments between the two conflicting countries.

In terms of the question of resources he raised the following points to bring a balance in the economy. The Scheduled Castes Federation suggests the following ways of raising finances for the development of the country:

(i) Reduction of Expenditure over the Army.
(ii) Re-levy of the Salt tax.
(iii) Abolition of prohibition and the saving of Excise Revenue.
(iv) Nationalisation of Insurance.[9]

Dr. Ambedkar was such a foresighted leader that he could speak on problem of black market, inflation, big business power and the related terms which is relevant in today's time as well. No other leader can have such a tall claim as Dr. B.R. Ambedkar when it comes to discussing and implementation of plans on a futuristic way. He is such a colossal figure in India that in every aspect of our life we remember his able leadership and guidance. This is evident in all his speeches and actions. He was one heroic figure who practiced what he really preached.

To conclude this discourse, it will be very apt to mention that Dr. Ambedkar is so relevant even today as he had a very futuristic mindset and he was a visionary in the true sense of the term this is evident in all his services to the society. He was such an enterprising and renaissance hero that he could foresee much beyond his age and time.

He lived ahead of his time which is why under his able leadership the Country could achieve so much. He had the faculty to reform a society full of flaws and this we attribute to his various educational acumen and experience globally.

END NOTES

1. https://en.wikipedia.org/wiki/Bildungsroman accessed on 26th March, 2016.
2. http://www.folomojo.com/16-great-quotes-of-dr-babasaheb-ambedkar-that-explain-why-he-is-on-google-doodle-in-8-different-countries/ accessed on 26th March, 2016.
3. Raut, Nitin, and Ambedkar on Population Policy contemporary Relevance, Shipra Publications: New Delhi: 2014 pp 2-3).
4. Baisantry, D.K., Ambedkar The Total Revolutionary: Segment Book distributors: New Delhi: 1991 pp 9-10.
5. http://www.mapsofIndia.com/on-this-day/14th-october-1956-b.r.-ambedkar-converts-to-buddhism-along-with-365000-followers accessed on 26th March, 2016.
6. Jadhav, Narendra, Ambedkar Speaks Vol. 1: Konark Publishers: New Delhi: 2013 pp. 282-3)
7. Dr. Baba Saheb Ambedkar Writings and Speeches, edited by Vasant Moon ambedkar\vol-14-II\vol14-II-02.indd
8. Dr. Baba Saheb Ambedkar Writings and Speeches, ambedkar\vol-017\vol17-01-05.indd
9. Ibid.

11

Ambedkar's Contribution on Water Resource Sector Development in India

Nitumoni Kakati

India's water resource sector developments can be traced back from the pre independence period and Dr. B.R. Ambedkar made a substantial contribution in this prospect. Ambedkar was very keen to build India an economically strong nation and this led to formulated polices for planned economic development. For development of the nation water resource sector is one of most important area and Ambedkar was directly involved to formulating policies for the nation's water sector development. In this regard Ambedkar initiated to establish two powerful organisations namely Central Waterways, Irrigation and Navigation Commission and Central Technical Power Board in mid-1940s. Ambedkar's role and initiations in this sector led to formulation of concrete policy and strategy in the post-independence era. As a consequence a number of multipurpose river valley projects were set up in Independent India. Nevertheless his strategy remains very important in present day's dam's development model. In this context, this paper seeks to examine Ambedkar's contributions and roles on water resource sector development in India.

Dr. Bhimrao Ramji Ambedkar (1891-1956) popularly known as Babasaheb Ambedkar, was an eminent scholar, statesmen, social revolutionarily and his contributions tremendously helped to evolution and development of modern India. He was well known as the main architect of the Indian Constitution and leader of oppressed. Ambedkar played a very crucial in the socio-economic and political transformation of India during the pre-independence and post-independence India. He was served as a member of Viceroy's Executive Council of the British India from 1942 to 1946, Ambedkar was handled a very important portfolio including Labour and Employment, Energy, Minerals and Water management. During his tenure as a Viceroy's Executive Council Ambedkar have guided in the formation of a new definite all India water resource development policy. Under erudite leadership of Babasahib, the central government policy regarding water resources and hydroelectric power development was evolved and given a concrete shape during the pre-independence period as well as the post independent India (Jadhav 2015).

Ambedkar's Contributions on Water Resource Development

Ambedkar had played a major role in shaping the new water policy during the British India and the Independent India. Ambedkar argued that industrialisation and agricultural growth could enhance the Indian economy and for development of these two sectors he laid the foundation for the development of infrastructure in India such as irrigation, electric power, communication, roads and transport services as well as the technical manpower.

Development of electric power is crucial for industrial and agricultural development. Ambedkar emphasises on improvement of irrigation facilities which can help to increase of agricultural productivity. Babasaheb was the president of Policy Committee on Irrigation and Electric power and by virtue his position Ambedkar was significantly helped in formulation the policy and action plan for the optional development of water and power resources in India [Central Water Commission (CWC) 2016]. In a conference on Development of Orissa Rivers Ambedkar expressed his views about proper conservation and utilisation of water resources. Most significantly Babasaheb was the men in 1950's, who recommended interlinking of rivers for proper management of flood and drought.

In 1942, July, the formulation and planning and development of Irrigation and Hydroelectric power became major concerns of the

Labour Department (CWC 2016). And as an in charge of Labour Department Ambedkar's roles is very crucial for evolution and adoptions of new policies for water resources development including the Hydroelectricity development of the country. Because Ambedkar knows that electricity became important for the country's economic development and emphasised on productions cheap and abundant electricity for the nation (Kamble 2014). Thus, in the early 1940's the Labour department began to national planning for the development irrigation and waterways, navigation, as well as electricity generation and Ambedkar's contribution's was very remarkable in this context.

Creation of Two Central Technical Expert Bodies

Ambedkar was the main exponent in foundation of two main technical bodies at the center to undertake planned development of water resources sector. He was emphasised to formulation central technical bodies for proper planning, utilization and management of water resources. His major achievements were the establishment of these two technical organisations i.e. Central Waterways Irrigation and Navigation Commission and Central Technical Power Board and these organisations presently known as Central Water Commission and Central Electricity Commission.

The proposal for creation of Central Irrigation and Water Advisory body was approved by Dr. Ambedkar and strongly condemned to control the water sector. In a year later on 5th April 1945 Ambedkar and his labour department team constituted Central Waterways, Irrigation and Navigation Commission (CWINC) with its headquarters in Delhi, with A.N. Khosla as its first chairmen (1945-53). Ambedkar stated for CWINC "I visualise that the growth of this body in course of time, into a very big organisation with its activities spread over the entire length and breadth of India, and its assistance and advice eagerly sought by all provinces and states, to the end that the natural resources of any region may be exploited for maximum benefit and unified development."

Another important powerful organisation established by the efforts Babasaheb was Central Technical Power Board (CTPB). CTPB was established for power system development, hydropower station sites, hydroelectric surveys analysing problem of electricity generation and thermal power stations investigation.

Nevertheless, Ambedkar believed that expansion of electric industry and development of hydroelectric power were inextricably connected with the development of industries and food production. On the other hand expansion of irrigation, conservation of soil and control of floods had a direct bearing on food supply and people's general content and prosperity (Kamble 2014). Moreover, CWINC and CTPB two organisations widely contributed for development of irrigation and power in the country.

Thus, through establishment of these technical organisations Ambedkar and his labour department laid down the foundation for a new water policy on the eve of independence, preparing the ground for the prosperity of the emergent nation (Thorat 1998).

Establishment of River Valley Authority

Another important contribution of Ambedkar was establishment of the River Valley Authority for water resource development on the basis of multipurpose river valley basin. Babasaheb concerned on the concepts of comprehensive planning with multipurpose projects through a Multipurpose River Valley Development Authority and he thought that it has the most important mechanism to controlling of inter-state river waters. Dr. Ambedkar wanted to evolve a policy which would utilise the water resources of the country to the best advantage of everybody and the Tennessee Valley Scheme of USA would be an ideal model to emulate. TVA was the first ever River Valley authority in the world established in USA in the early 1930's. In influence of TVA, in mid 1940's, India was adopted the river valley authority model and Ambedkar was instrumental in ushering in the coordinated development of the Damodar basin by the Central Government (Thorat 1998).

Significantly, the concept of river valley authority/cooperation was adopted to overcome constitutional problem regarding the jurisdictions of central-state governments to develop irrigation and hydroelectricity on the inter-state rivers. A river is flows more than one state or provinces and setup of an inter-state river valley project it is very difficult and to overcome this problem through an appropriate mechanism and set up of an independent authority or cooperation. Thus, the River Valley Authority model was adopted for proper management and control of water through the multipurpose projects on inter-state rivers and Ambedkar was the first person in India has made efforts for establishment of river valley authority in India. For example, in 1948 India's first ever river valley cooperation Damodar Valley Development Cooperation (DVDC) was set up in Bengal.

Adoption of the Concepts of Multipurpose River Valley Projects

Since the pre independence times flood has the one of the major problems in the India and Ambedkar rightly visualised that the multipurpose river valley project can be the best prospect to controlling of a river. On the other hand to increased the irrigation facilities in the agricultural fields and developed of power generation and navigations, the best way is to set up of a multipurpose river valley projects on the rivers. Ambedkar argued that the multipurpose river valley project not only deals with the flood project but also it is benefited for irrigation, electricity, navigation, etc. As a cabinet minister Ambedkar took the lead in developing of multipurpose river valley projects in the eve of Independence and he was set up the various projects in the British India for example Damudar Valley project. Because of flood problem the Damodar Valley is known as "Sorrow of Bengal" (Thorat 1998). In 1943 the valley was severely affected from the flood and the Ambedkar took the matter seriously. To overcome the flood problem in the valley under the guidance Babasaheb plan was executed and the DVDC was constituted and the entire work of Damodar Valley was given over to DVDC. Ambedkar argued that the project of damming the Damodar should have as its purpose not merely stopping the flood but also include the generation of electricity and supply of water for irrigation, navigation and industrial use. There have not been enough realisations that our policy for water-ways must be multipurpose policy so as to include all possible uses of water. The Sone River Valley Project was another multipurpose scheme, which the Labour Department initiated during 1944-45. River Sone rises in Madhya Pradesh and flows onward to Uttar Pradesh before merging with the Ganga. On November, 1944 the Government of the United Provinces drew the attention of the Labour Department to the potentialities of development of Sone river and decided to build a river valley project. It was during the time of Dr. Ambedkar, the Labour Department treated the Sone Valley Project as a multipurpose river management scheme covering not only the potentialities for irrigation by canals and perennial hydro power for the area but also for increased irrigation utilisation of such power for pumping from the tube wells or from the river and increased fertility by the dewatering in water logged area. Provision of cheap power for industrial development, improved supply of water for navigation on the Ganga and improved flood control were other important considerations (CWC 2016).

Apart from the Damodar Valley project and Sone River Valley projects, the Hirakud dam project on the river Mahanadi and the Kosi and others on river Chambal and rivers of the Deccan are the major initiatives of the 1940's. All these projects were conceived essentially for multipurpose development with flood control, irrigation, navigation, domestic water supply, hydropower and other purposes.

Hirakud dam is the longest dam built in river Mahanadi of Orissa, India and first dam completed in Independent in India. In 1944, A.N. Khosla, Chairman of CWINC made a preliminary survey of the Mahanadi river in Orissa to identify the site for the dam. The preliminary survey would be completed by February 1946, he said, and construction of the first dam commenced by October, 1946. A tentative scheme worked out by the CWINC after the survey with the help of the Government of Orissa and the state comprised.

Thus, the multipurpose river valley projects which were initiated during 1943-46 were on the river Damodar, the Mahanadi, the Sone and Kosi, while substantial work relating to the Damodar Valley Projects was completed during 1943-47, a beginning was made with others and progress in various magnitudes achieved.

Conclusion

The person behind India's water sector development as well introduction of large dam technologies and multipurpose big river valley projects into India was none other than revolutionary B.R. Ambedkar. Here, Rohan Desoza reveals that in the post-independence India romance has wrongly been attributed entirely to Nehru's vision for industrialisation through multipurpose river valley projects. It was B.R. Ambedkar, who, in fact, throughout the mid 1940's as the then member for Labour in the Viceroy's council, played the most central role in introducing large dam technologies in India (D'Souza 2000).

Dr. Ambedkar, however, expected the states to ensure that the benefits of the project should go ultimately right down to the grass roots, i.e. everyone living in the valley and some of those in the vicinity and all had their share in the prosperity which the project should bring. Ambedkar's vision on sustainable infrastructural development is still relevant in today's world. Off course, Babasaheb was emphasised on the proper resettlement and rehabilitation of people who are affected from the development projects. Dr. Ambedkar reminded the provinces of their collective responsibility and need to put their shoulders together to the task and urged upon them.

Thus, Dr. Ambedkar and his Department laid down the foundation for a new water policy on the eve of independence preparing the ground for the prosperity of the emerged nation which is still relevant in the contemporary world. In other words, Babasahib's vision for nation's water resource sector development is still relevant, even after the lapse of six and half decades. Ambedkar was the visionary man and under his knowledge in the area of economics, politics and constitutional law, he helped the central government and his department in the articulation of water and power policy and planning and under the efforts of Ambedkar India has emerged with a new water resource development policy in the post-independence era.

END NOTES

Central Water Commission (2016), Ambedkar's Contribution on Water Resource Development, A research Project by Central Water Commission, Ministry of Water Resources, River Development and Ganga Rejuvenation, Central Water Commission: New Delhi.

D'Souza, Rohan (2000), "Whey Ambedkar Should be Against Large Dams", Seminar 496.

Jadhav, Narendra (2015), *Ambedkar and Economic Extraordinary,* Konarak Publishers Private Limited: New Delhi.

Kamble, G.S. (2014), Dr. B.R. Ambedkar's Contribution in Formulation of Water Policy, *Research Direction*, Vol. 2, 2014.

Thorat, Sukhadeo (1998), *Ambedkar's Role in Economic Planning and Water Policy,* Shipra Publication: Delhi.

12

Identity Construction of the Untouchables by Dr. B.R. Ambedkar Through Buddhist Relics and Ethics

Ruchika Singh

The end of the 19th century, witnessed the epoch of the Globalisation and the cumulative socio-cultural crisis for ages in the form of untouchability in Indian society. This issue of untouchability was addressed in the pragmatic realism by B.R. Ambedkar who with his heartfelt efforts inculcated Buddhism in his philosophies and made world witness radical social transformation in the Indian society. The relics and philosophies of Buddhism changed the destiny of the untouchables/depressed classes by providing them space of acceptance as they are and not as they should be in the eyes of World. This space of acceptance gave them will and hope to resolve their identity crisis and a vision that they can also experience virtues of equality, fraternity and liberty as other sections of the Indian society. This illuminating vision was provided to the depressed classes or untouchables by outstanding efforts of Dr. B.R. Ambedkar who sorted these socio-economic barriers by providing them constitutional rights, securing their position in employment sector through the medium of job reservation, exercising accessibility to land and above all accessibility to education in order to liberate and empower themselves from all odds of life.

The objective of this paper is to dwell in the issues of morality, humanity and welfare state which were constantly sidelined in the era of Globalisation and how the process of Globalisation on serious front was affecting the lives of the untouchables/depressed classes/dalits in Indian context. It was in this pretext the rigorous efforts of social reformer like

B.R. Ambedkar has been over the years remembered and idealised as the saviour of the untouchables.

In order to get definite vision, it's must to refer to the life-sketch of Gautama Buddha, his preaching's, relics and philosophies because it changed every space and discourse with its presence and relevancy. Though his teachings, principles and philosophies changed every time and space differently but the major change was witnessed in the world in the inception of 20th century by B.R. Ambedkar, who changed the fate of untouchables for endless time span and he did it by incorporating the beliefs and philosophies of Buddhism. He had a firm opinion that by accepting Buddhism, the torturous experiences of the untouchables can be removed not only from the memories of untouchables but at the same time will create a hope of liberating their souls from the clutches of segregation and marginalization.

This brought into existence the belief that Ambedkarism was nothing but just extension of Buddhism. It was in this realization, we observe that Why Ambedkar was so much moved and motivated by Buddhism? The answer to this observation lies in its accessible approach and functionality to fit every time and space. Ambedkar believed that Buddha had a far-sighted vision which presented him as one who was capable of visualizing the social conflict which was the creator of the universal struggle for survival and existence, a struggle which was fought for ages between kings, nations, householders, father and Son, Sister and Brother, between companions and so on for ages. This conflict or struggle was not only constant but was perpetual also because it was essential for competency and survival. They all comprise the root of all sorrows and sufferings in the world, [1] these ethics were talked about on a stretch by B.R. Ambedkar who referred them with the issues of social justice and defined that the only possible way to deal them was by following the path of humanitarian convictions. This presents him appear as larger than life experiences and all prepared to carry constitutional reforms which in turn provided untouchables an opportunity to get themselves sanctified by legal ventures.

So, one can witness that because of these principles of Buddha, he had profound impact on him and the reason lies in its relevancy and applicability. The essence of Gautama Buddha's principles and relics lies on four noble truths.[2] These four noble truths were: there is suffering (*dukkha*), it has a cause (*samudaya*), it can be removed (*nirodha*) and last but not the least the way to achieve all this is by following Eight-fold path.[3] They all have inspired Ambedkar a lot and that's why he chose to associate himself with realism and presented these principles and relics as the only possible way to achieve happiness, compassion, security, peace, belongingness, acceptability and harmony in day to day lives. This in turn laid the foundation of universal concepts like liberty, equality and fraternity in Indian society. This he categorically mentions in his speech when he said that "My philosophy has a root in religion and not in political science. I have derived from the teaching of my master, the Buddha, liberty, equality and fraternity."[4]

After brief overview of the four noble truths of the philosophies of Gautama Buddha it's essential to talk about middle-path which has been conceived as path that existed between extreme indulgence and extreme asceticism.[5] The middle path has been perceived as a scientific path which completely denies its relation with (Hindu) Aryan Truths, and propose Dalit Truths to record their encounters in order to fit in the model of modern Buddhism.[6] This middle-path has been considered as the amalgamation of three paths i.e. path of purity, path of righteousness, and path of virtue where Path of purity does not mean purity of caste or class only instead as a path which stood for not harming or injuring, not stealing, speaking truth, deny lust, negate indulgence in intoxication of drinks. Thus, together constitute the platform that promotes standard of living and lays foundation of social code and conduct that has universal acceptance to it and has been rightly addressed in the actions of B.R. Ambedkar who not only imbibed in his philosophies but at the same time tried to bring them in actions, thoughts and above all in the memories. Ambedkar considered them as a path that will prevail egalitarianism and foundation of classless society which in turn will lay down the foundation of social revolution which entails on social justice and equality[7] to the depressed classes and will provide them a platform to accept themselves as they are and not as they should be? And in turn Will provide them vision what they want to attain in their lives? Along with this will float the notion that—to what extent they are prepared to counter exploitative ideologies that have denied them their space and have challenged their identity consciousness for ages?

After talking about middle path, it's the turn to talk about Astangika Marga or eight-fold Path, or the path of Righteousness which has been considered as the threshold of Buddha's ethics and relics always. This path has been accepted by both monks as well as laymen,[8] and it was demarcated under three heads, moral precepts (Sila), mental development (Citta) and knowledge (Panna).[9] These Ashtamarga or eight-fold path has been visualised as the benchmark of the Buddha policy of Dhamma and has been associated with changes in order to fit in the process of modernisation which has been explicitly illustrated in "The Buddha and His Dhamma".[10] The constituents of eight-fold path were-right views, intention, conduct, speech, action, effort, livelihood, recollection and meditation.[11] This gives the viability and visibility to the Dalits or untouchables or depressed classes to reform themselves by making themselves educated, preparing themselves for agitation and be organised to fight against all odds and tyrannies. He believed that depressed classes can liberate themselves consciously only by educating themselves and this only will empower them to prepare for agitation against all that challenges and diminishes their identity and they can achieve it by efficiently organizing themselves.[12] This cites his famous slogan i.e. educate, agitate and organise themselves to fight all odds irrespective of time and discourse. The middle path gave a possible solution to the well-thought queries of the untouchables and this motivation was put in action and practice by Ambedkar while laying down his policy making processes.

Just after brief overview of middle path it becomes essential to have a fair look of the reason and causes that motivated Gautamaa Buddha the most and the answer we trace lies in the laws of causation (Paticca—Samuppada) and through this law he tried to present that existence of everything is conditional and is always dependent on cause.[13] Ambedkar constituted his doctrine of impermanence[14] on three aspects such as composite things, of individual being, the self-nature of conditioned things on the law of causation. He firmly believed that what so ever exists in the world existed because of the combinations of causes and conditions and if these combinations ever challenged and dissolved then it will ultimately lead to destruction. The reason for this lies in the fact that this Universe is Transient (anicca) and has to its sustainability attached to its abiding entity.[15] This shows that Ambedkar knew by heart that the only way Dalits or depressed classes can sustain is by empowering themselves to master all know how's of the laws of causation. So that they can prepare themselves for all agitations that they will undertake while carrying cumulative efforts to organise themselves in order to sustain their identity.

Ambedkar not only focused on the laws of causation but has to his credit questioning the normative religious practices which he shares with Buddhism i.e. rejecting idol worship, existence of God, Existence of soul, Karma. Just like, Gautama Buddha he also rejected these practices because of the superstitions attached with them. He believed that if one wants to have true understanding of nature, one should avoid superstition, demagogue in religion and politics. He believed in the concept of space (akash).[16] Ambedkar then talks about Gautama Buddhas understanding of Dhamma and Dharma where he clearly describes how Dhamma has been considered as a philosophy for all and has its genesis in serving humanity whereas Dharma refers to few. Ambedkar distinguishes Dharma as reflection of Hinduism whereas Dhamma is a way to reach perfection in life and live in Nibbana (following eight-fold path is also part of it).[17] This presents that he knew by heart that the practice of Dhamma means serving humanity and only by this the issues of inequality, untouchability and exploitation can be eradicated from the society for forever. The purpose of Dhamma was to lay foundation for perfect society or kingdom of righteousness.[18] Ambedkar viewed Dhamma policy as the essential feature of Buddhism which he considered as an ideology that can engage all and will effectively dissolve the issues between poor and rich. He knew very well that it's only Buddhism which offers equality to all irrespective of gender and thus serves cherish able momentum for humanity, [19] this in turn will not help depressed classes only but will help everybody universally.

With this insightful observation one sees that Ambedkar too believed in Gautama Buddha's principle of Ahimsa or non-violence. This principle deeply motivated and guided him always and that's why he categorically puts it as a principle to love all.[20] Ambedkar knew that its only through Ahimsa,[21] heart of people can be changed to accept depressed classes as one among them and not someone who are indifferent to them in terms of credentials, competency and above all as human being.

Thus, in retrospect we can say that the principles, teachings and philosophies of Gautama Buddha influenced, inspired a lot Ambedkar and he used it widely to reach the utmost spheres of untouchability. This was the reason why Ambedkar in the passing years gave it a new name, 'Adi Buddhism or Dalit Buddhism' because of its farsighted implications and effects. He believed that if we accept and apply these principles and teaching we will be able to avert man made evil policies and exploitative actions to attain higher levels of humanity. So, we can observe that era of Globalisation though filled with economic and financial trajectories as its contours of relevancies and utilities has simultaneously put a deep silence on social and moral paradigms of ethics, philosophies and conduct in Indian society. This age long silence was broken by ardent efforts of Dr. B.R. Ambedkar who not only gave hope and vision to Dalit community but provided them an platform to develop and empower themselves in the coming years. He provided holistic vision to the dalits/depressed classes/untouchables that they can attain everything by following the philosophies of Buddhism in the era of Globalisation.

END NOTES

1. B.R. Ambedkar, The Buddha and His Dhamma, (Dr. Baba Saheb Ambedkar Writings and Speeches, Vol. 11), Education Department, Government of Maharashtra, Bombay, 1992, pp.57-58.
2. This has been stated in Digha-nikaya-Sutta, 22, H.C. Warren, Buddhism in Translations, Harvard University Press, Harvard, First Print-1992, pp.372-74.
   The abridged form mentioned in A.L. Basham, The wonder that was India, p.271.
3. Upinder Singh, A History of Ancient and Medieval India: From the Stone Age to the 12th century, Dorling Kindersley (India) Pvt. Ltd, Delhi, 2009, pp 304
4. The BBC Radio Talk, Dr. Ambedkar on 3rd October, 1954
5. Upinder Singh, A History of Ancient and Medieval India: From the Stone Age to the 12th century, Dorling Kindersley (India) Pvt. Ltd, Delhi, 2009, pp 304
6. The word Dalits very vivid in its meaning and usage as per social relevancy and denotes here as original and noble. Its stands for positivity and historically referred as indigenous, humble, etc.
7. Mohammad Shabir, "Dr. Ambedkar's Quest for social justice: An Analysis of contemporary scenario," p.37
8. T.W. Rhys Davids, tr. Dialogue of Buddha, London, 1950, pp.62-63

9. H.C. Warren, Samyuktta—Nikaya, op.cit, p.165
10. B.R. Ambedkar, The Buddha and his Dhamma, op.cit, p.123
11. Romila Thapar, Early India: From the origin to AD 1300, Penguin Books India (P) Ltd. Delhi. 2002, p.168
12. Thomas Mathew, Ambedkar: Reform or Revolution, Segment Book Distributors, University of California. 1991, p.67
13. H.C. Warren, Vasuddhimagga, chapter 18, Motilal Banarsidass Publishers, Delhi, 1999, p.168
14. Upinder Singh, A History of Ancient and Medieval India: From the Stone Age to the 12th century, Dorling Kindersley (India) Pvt. Ltd, Delhi, 2009, p.304
15. B.R. Ambedkar, The Buddha and his Dhamma, op.cit, p.261
16. B.R. Ambedkar, The Buddha and his Dhamma, op.cit, p.513
17. Ibid, pp.229-309
18. B.R. Ambedkar, The Buddha and the Future of his Religion, Bhim Patrika Publication, Jalandhar, 1975.
19. D.C. Ahir, Dr. Ambedkar Pilgrimage to Buddhism, Dr. Ambedkar Buddhism and social change, (ed.) A.K. Narain, D.C, Ahir, B.R. Publication, New Delhi, 1994, pp. 10-11
20. The policy of non-violence or Ahimsa of Buddhism has been an eye opener for ages and has to its credit followers like Asoka, the great monarch of Ancient India and so many.
21. Upinder Singh, A history of Ancient and Early Medieval India: From the stone Age to the 12th century, Dorling Kindersley (India) Pvt. Ltd.. Delhi, 2009, p.306

13

Ambedkar and Women's Rights

Shweta Singh

The root of women's empowerment is as old as human civilisation. In ancient Indian scriptures one may find the solid evidences of women emancipation. Since ages it has been established that women emancipation is the barometer of the comprehensive success of any society. However due to gamut of factors these cardinal bedrock of sustainable development had been evaporated from different societies. Western world claims that they have been the harbingers of women movements. The origins of the concept of empowerment go back to the civil rights movement in the USA in the 1960. It has since then been interpreted differently and filled with new meanings and is today used in such different sectors as business, social work, development discourse and by advocates of very different political discourses. The different definitions of empowerment range between defining it as a largely individual process of taking control of and responsibility for one's life and situation, and defining it as a political process of granting human rights and social justice to disadvantaged groups of people. At the former end of the continuum, where empowerment is defined largely as an individual process, empowerment can be used in the conservative political rhetoric of freeing the government of responsibility for injustices and for granting social security. Instead, the argument makes individuals and communities responsible for their own social security and welfare, without providing the necessary support and resources.

The empowerment of women is located within the discourse and agenda of gender equality and is increasingly being taken in the agendas of international development organisations, perhaps more as a means to achieve gender equality than as an end in itself.

At the Social Summit in Copenhagen in 1993 and the International Conference on Population and Development in Cairo 1994 Governments committed themselves to the empowerment of women. This commitment was operationalised and formulated into a clear action plan at the Fourth World Conference on Women in Beijing 1995 where Governments committed themselves to the "empowerment and advancement of women, including the right to freedom of thought, conscience, religion and belief, thus contributing to the moral, ethical, spiritual and intellectual needs of women and men, individually or in community with others and thereby guaranteeing them the possibility of realizing their full potential in society and shaping their lives in accordance with their own aspirations."

In Western world after Second World War, equal franchise to women had been granted. The first woman becoming PM in Britain was in 1980s. France, US and many important countries of the Western enlightened block has no women President or Prime Minister till date. In contrast, South Asia has been a harbinger of women participation in democratic process. Srimao Bhandranaika became Sri Lanka's prime Minister. Benazir Bhutto became maiden female PM of orthodox Pakistan and since 1991, politics of Bangladesh is driven by both leading Begums of Awami and Nationalist party. Indira Gandhi became India's PM in 1966 only. At the state level many women's have become CM. In contemporary India, West Bengal, Tamil Nadu and Rajasthan is led by women CM's. in 2014 general election women representation in Lok Sabha has gone up to over 11 per cent. Five women are in the union cabinet.

Women rights as human rights were not accepted by the Universal Declaration of Human Rights (UDHR). In 1993 Vienna Convention which was convened to discuss about the future discourse of human rights, it was consensually agreed that women rights should be accepted as an integral part of human rights. Since then, it became the bedrock of the international regime of human rights. The end of the cold war gave new grounds for the women rights. With surging media imprint it became global concern to ensure women rights. United Nations has passed gamut of conventions to promote the cause and majority of nations has rectified it.

Western world gave equal voting rights to their women folk around the end of the Second World War. India and many newly emerged independent countries gave equal rights to their women folk just after their independence. But women emancipation is not confined with these selected representations. It has many facets and social, economic and cultural components are crucial for genuine women emancipation. There is classic difference in the emancipation of women in western and eastern world. In western world, women are economically and socially strong but politically weak. In eastern world it is a contrast. In India too, women possesses full political participation but neglected in terms of economic and social emancipation. A community will only achieve holistic development when they possess all aspects of rights.

After our independence, Dr. Ambedkar was the revolutionary crusader for women emancipation. Even before him there has been a long list of social reformer who laid the foundation of women emancipation. In independent India, Ambedkar got the opportunity to formulate the constitution. He gave constitutional protection to women rights right from the first day of its implementation. As first law minister of the country, he laid the foundation of strong legal protection of women rights. He put Hindu women within the framework of 'Hindu Code Bill' and gave them equal rights. Dr Ambedkar brought forward the Hindu Code Bill with an objective to redefine the Hindu society. "...if you want to maintain the Hindu system, the Hindu culture, the Hindu society does not hesitate to repair where repair is necessary. The Bill asks for nothing more than repairing those parts of the Hindu system which have almost become dilapidated".[1] The Bill was introduced to the constituent assembly on 11 April, 1957, to free up personal laws so as to liberate the individual and ensure equality before law. The Bill mainly focused on right to property, order of succession to the property and maintenance, marriage, divorce, adoption, minority and guardianship.

Dr Ambedkar unequivocally supported monogamy and proposed to ban polygamy. "...I must point out the I do not think any member in this house will be able to point out having regard to customary law or having regard to our Shastra that a Hindu husband had all times an unfettered, unqualified right to polygamy. That was never the case. Even today in certain parts of South India there are people who follow this, a section of the Nattukottai Chattiyars—the case has been reported in the Reports of the Privy council itself, I am not depending on mere heresy of evidence—but among the Nattukottai Chettiyars there is a custom that a husband cannot marry a second wife unless he obtains the consent of his first wife. Secondly when consent is obtained, he must allot to her certain property, which in the Tamil language is called 'moppu'. That property becomes her absolute property so that if after her consent the husband marries and ill-treats her, she has a certain amount of economic competence in her own hands to lead an independent life. I cite this as an illustration to show that there has not been an unqualified right for polygamy."[2]

Dr Ambedkar had shown several other examples like one from *Arhashastra* that polygamy was not permitted unconditionally in Hindu society and proposed monogamy as the ultimate rule of life. Other that marriages, Dr Ambedkar also spoke on divorce, adoption, guardianship, inheritance and most importantly on uniform civil code.

He was a passionate advocate for the common civil code for all women irrespective of their religious affiliation. Article 44 of Indian constitution provided its mechanism but unfortunately it has not been implemented till date. Many women groups are claiming that they are intended to emancipate women but kept stony silence over the implementation of Common Civil Code. Supreme Court has given many directives to government of India to implement it but it has even not changed the status quo. Although if implemented it will provide genuine equality to women folk despite their religious affiliations.

Ambedkar was an ardent crusader for women rights. He started many benefits to working women like maternity leave which was only a dream before independence.

In due course of time, many laws were enacted by successive governments to empower women. Although women's reservation bill in Parliament and state legislatures has not been passed till date despite the fact that it was passed by the Rajya Sabha in 2010 only. One of the significant legislation was enacted through 73rd and 74th constitution amendment for 1/3 participation of women in grass root bodies. It was implemented in 1995 and today 1.5 million elected representatives from the grass root level institutions are women. They have brought transformational changes in the governance in these local self-bodies. India has witnessed the world's largest experiment in grassroots local democracy, triggered by the 73rd and 74th Amendments to the Indian Constitution, which created a third tier of governance—Panchayati Raj Institutions (Village Councils) and urban local bodies. These are elected bodies and cannot be dissolved by administrative order.

Women's Emancipation: Ambedkar's Dream and Reality

It is close to reality that the remarkable changes in the position of women in free India have been marked; there is still a great divergence between the constitutional position and stark reality of deprivation and degradation. Whatever whiff of emancipation has blown in Indian society, has been inhaled and enjoyed by the urban women, their population belonging to the rural areas are still totally untouched by the wind of changes. They still have been living in miserable conditions, steeped in poverty, ignorance, superstition and slavery. Even urban skilled and well educated and well placed women's are prone to harassed by their in laws and others and they are so weak that they are not invoking existing stringent laws to protect themselves. The reporting rate to the police is much below the expectation. The pyramid of patriarchy is still intact with a lesser version. Judiciary has been proactive in the protection of women rights but due to delay in the judicial process the progress has not been appropriate. Rural women in the other hand are also prone to gamut of discrimination due to relative prevailing poverty and patriarchal social mindset.

There still exists a wide gulf between the goals enunciated in the Constitution, legislations, policies, plans, programmes and related mechanisms on the one hand and the situational reality on the status of women in India, on the other. The human rights scenario in the country continues to be dismal and depressing. Women are being brutalized, commodified, materialised and subjected to inhumane exploitation and discrimination. Even urban women are discriminated through domestic violence and harassment at the work place. Only limited number of cases appears in the press and reported to law enforcing agencies.

Even in India despite their vast numerical strength, women occupy a marginalised position in society due to several socio-economic constraints. Social evils like dowry deaths, polygamy, child marriage, female infanticide, forced prostitution and crime against women have not been uprooted from our country. This has inhibited the effective participation of women in the political processes and institutional structures of democracy.

Abroad-based political participation of women has been severely limited due to various traditional factors such as caste, religion, feudal attitudes and family status. As a result, women have been left on the periphery of political life.

The increasing gender gap has tended to divide men and women into two different worlds. It is surprising that the much economically developed parts of India have fewer women than their less developed Eastern parts of the country. It seems that even better education has not been able to upgrade the mindset of the people to respect women within developed areas. Today in high tech world women need freedom from—sexual exploitation, economic exploitation, rape, eve-teasing, etc.

The struggle to lift this curtain of unequal relationship and wipe out the unseen tear from the eyes of women is the most formidable challenge of our times. These are prevailing problems of our womenfolk and Ambedkar foresaw all those problems and provided adequate remedies to uplift them at par with their male counterpart.

Empowerment means women must exercise full participation in decision-making process in all relevant walks of life, and full participation with men and fully participating with men in finding equitable and practical solutions to issues in family. Apart from this empowerment includes women right to have control over and decide freely and responsibly on matters related to their sexuality, including sexual and reproductive health, free of coercion, discrimination and violence. Equal relationships between women and men in matters of sexual relations and reproduction including full respect for the integrity of the person, require mutual respect, consent and shared responsibility for sexual behavior and its consequences.

The process of empowerment is multi-dimensional and it enables women to realise their full destiny and powers in all spheres of life. Woman's empowerment begins with consciousness—perceptions about herself and her rights, her capabilities and her potentials, awareness of how gender and socio-cultural and political forces affect her. Political empowerment, economic development and social upliftment of women are necessary and desirable to fight myriad forms of patriarchal domination, and discrimination at every stage. In fact, women's empowerment is central to the achievement of the triple goals of equality, development and social justice.

Twentieth Century has brought a great change in the life of women all over world and 21st Century is the century of women. In 1948, Universal Declaration of Human Rights (UDHR) was pronounced but women rights did not figure as an integral part of human rights. It was only incorporated as human rights within international conventions after 1993 Vienna Summit. With the end of the cold war coincided with the demise of then USSR and prominence of Globalisation it was further facilitated. Woman's attitudes, values, inspirations, ways of feelings, standards of behaviour and acting for effective participation in all walks of life are becoming reality. Rays of hope are becoming brighter and radical changes in and through women's thrust in socio-economic and political process, will be instrumental to healthier, happier and progressive state in near future. As the largest vibrant democracy in the world, India has been continuously experimenting with a number of forms and modes of organisations and structures to achieve gender equality.

Ambedkar's contributions have been enormous to provide structured mechanism to women to fight back against these prevailing socio-economic discriminations. Nation has celebrated 125th birth anniversary of Dr. Ambedkar in 2016. But the real tribute to Ambedkar will be real equality to women in all walks of life. He has given adequate legislation and philosophical grounds for real women emancipation. His contribution for women emancipation therefore has been transformative.

END NOTES

1. Dr Babasaheb Ambedkar: Writing and Speeches, Vol 14, pt.1, Government of Maharashtra, Mumbai, 1955, p.283
2. Ibid, P-268-69.

14

Relevance of Thoughts and Philosophy of Dr. Ambedkar in Nation Building

S.N.Chaudhary

There is a long debate on the concept of Nation and Nation Building. Nation is not only collection of individuals with diverse social and ethnic background, geographical boundary and administrative space. It is a space in social, psychological, economic and political sense where diversities and differences along with unity and integration in different realms of life at individual and collective level are found. If both material and non-material concerns of natives as well as new settlers are equitably addressed by change agents in a successful manner. It leads to the institutionalization of citizenship. Citizenship without the concept of citizen is not possible. One of the pre-conditions for successful growth and expansion of citizenship is sense of longingness, we feeling, trust and reciprocity, irrespective of any birth or worth based attributes. For citizenship special care for those geographical space and social groups is essential who have suffered neglect and marginalization since long.

Broadly speaking there are two types of nationalism. These are Western and Eastern. According to Kohn (1945) the western nationalism emerged in England and France during the period 1600-1800 and the Eastern type of nationalism emerged in later Centuries. In the case of former nation is identified with masses and popular forms of politics.

And in this way it tends to provide a cultural justification for and already existing political structure. In other words, it provides political interpretation of nationalism. In contrary to this, in the Eastern nationalism, there is a justification of creation of nation-states in economically and politically less developed countries in the world. In this case, political boundary is constructed and legal and political space is allotted looking into ethonographic demands. These are the two extreme forms of nationalism. Thoughts and philosophy of Dr. Ambedkar is an attempt to integrate these two diverse interpretations of nationalism.

Ambedkar was of the opinion that spread up nationalism is a pre-condition for nation building. How a person or group who is denied legitimate rights, whose human rights are violated and whose quality of life is low can have the feeling of high level nationalism? To him, for nation building sense of belongingness among individuals, groups and communities is essential. If national concerns and concerns of diverse ethnic groups are properly addressed, it can lead to nation building and the notion of nationalism can become culture.

Besides scholarship of international repute Dr. Ambedkar was also an agent of social change in democratic direction. He spoke in favour of strong nation. To him, strong nation leads to strong internationalism and without strong internationalism with high social and moral order, strong nationalism is not possible. There may be different ways of nation building; he suggested some prescriptions which are full of the philosophy of inclusion. These suggestions are even today relevant. Broadly speaking, he presented four perspectives are logically acceptable and pre-conditions for nation building in India, these are as under:

Perspective on Economic Development and Planning

Ambedkar was basically economist. Therefore, economic issues led crucial role in his prescriptions. Even today, India lives in villages. Villager's sources of livelihood are by and large farming but because of social practice of division of land among brothers along with conversion of agricultural land for non-agricultural purposes, there is fragmentation of land on frequent basis. Fragmented land is not appropriate for proper agricultural production. It is also not economical. If the land is fragmented, it is costly to use it. Therefore, he said that economic development of villagers with intensive spirit is a pre-condition for national development. Hence, he was in favour of consolidation of land, he said that without increasing capital investment in farm work, farmers are forced to have low surplus and therefore, low saving. And under the condition, further sub-division of land becomes unviable which in term leads to poor quality of life. Therefore, he was in favour of increased agricultural production and for which he suggested that investment of all varieties in farm work should be increased. He was in favour of decreasing deployment of labour in agriculture. He also laid in favour of modernization of skill and capability of labour. He suggested that if surplus agricultural labourers become skilled they should be deployed in industrial sector. Ambedkar was in favour of industrialization in the country. He perceived industrialization as a vehicle of economic development and social transformation. Here his views are similar to the views of Jawaharlal Nehru, who was in favour of industrial revolution in the country. Nehru perceived Dams and Industries as temples of modern India. To him, Industrialization can lead to high income, high employment and breaking down of social and cultural barriers in a speedy manner. Karl Marx perceived technology as a wheel of society. To him, whenever there is a change in technology, it is likely to change different elements and components of society. Even a traditional society can become complex and modern because of industrial and technological modernization. Ambedkar endorsed such interpretation. He strongly said that various types of freedom i.e. freedom from hunger, freedom from wants etc; is only possible if villagers dependence on agriculture is reduced and their dependence on secondary and tertiary sector occupations are increased. He said that industrialization will lead to an increase in capital, surplus, productivity of labour and enlargement of holdings. And industrialization with not possible without strong and all weather pucca road, proper electricity, ensured irrigation, effective and functional communication network and so on. To him, if we want progress in the field of health, education, housing, sanitation etc; it requires money, which is not possible if the society is fully dependent on agriculture.

On the one side, he was in favour of industrialization but on the other hand he was against capitalistic model of development. What is capitalistic model of development? This model believes in tickle-down. It believes in top-down model of development. It do not believe in creation of pre-condition of development at the micro level. Therefore, here one see contradiction in his approach. To him, in the democratic set-up capitalistic path is undesirable. This model of development can widen gap between social groups and different geographical regions. Masses are forced to remain in margin in this model. Rather he was in favour of planned economic development. He said that mode and nature of planning can be conditioned in the light of ethnic requirement. Planning is rather mechanical not eternal. Planned development can only lead to economic development with peace and solution of problems relating to housing, clothing, education, health and right to work with dignity. Ambedkar observed that there should be both fair condition of work for labour and also fair condition of life for them. He was also in favour of fair and compulsory education up to the age of 14, medical relief, proper water supply, electricity, fair wages and maternity, sickness and holiday relief to labourers.

Ambedkar had grass-root level practical experience of the sufferings of under privilege segment of society. Therefore, he was in favour of special attention to them. How can a nation can become strong and powerful if its significant number of population is deprived and neglected? Therefore, he suggested a prescription which is popularly known as positive decrimination. In the form of basic amenities, full employment and social security measures for them. According to him, industrialization must be encouraged which will create more wealth which in turn will improve quality of life of common people under the direction of the democratic state, without translation of provisions of protective discrimination. It is difficult to improve quality of life of masses and encourage sense of belongingness among them in favour of nation building.

Perspective on Water/Power and Labour Welfare

He had equal and intensive concern for all these three issues as minister for labour, he inspired central government policy for Central Water Commission and Central Electricity Authority, River Valley projects and Electric Supply by multi purpose approach on Damodar valley Project Calcutta, Mahanadi valley Project at Cuttack and on Electric power Project at Delhi. He was in favour of proper use of water of river sone, Mahanadi and Deccan especially for irrigation, navigation and power production. Dr. Ambedkar perceived water as a wealth. Therefore, when the rivers of Orissa, Bihar and U.P. were over flowing with flood, he wanted to regulate it for purposes mentioned above. He was also in favour of construction of 100's and 1000's of canals and reservoirs. It seems that he was perhaps the first thinker in India who had an idea to manage flooding rivers in India from north to south and from east to west, as it has been already experimented with Mississippi river in America and Thames river in England. To him, no matter whether labourers are working in industrial sector or in informal sector their human rights must be respected. Without their welfare development of the work sector and owners of factories or farms is not possible. Therefore, he formulated an inclusive labour policy. There are three features of labour policy propounded by him. These are:

(a) It provides safeguards and social security measures to workers.
(b) He was in favour of equal opportunity to employers and employees to participate informulative labour policy and form trade unions; and
(c) He was in favour of establishment of machinery for enforcing labour laws effectively and also settle related disputes.

Ambedkar had global experience of exploitation of labourers by employers. Therefore, besides enforcement of above mentioned policy he was strongly in favour of giving right to these labourers to raise voice of protest through satyagraha and strike in favour of their legitimate demand. He also placed Industrial Disputes Bill in Bombay Legislative Assembly in which he recommended that the problem of industrial workers must be dealt with by an assertive committee consisting of industrialists, government representatives and representatives of industrial workers.

Perspective on Caste System, Women and Education

To him, caste system refers to segmental division of Indian society with anti-social elements as its attributes which have historically suppressed possibility of welfare and development of so called untouchable castes.

Referring to his views on caste system Dhananjay Keer, his authentic biographer (1954) rightly said "it has killed public spirit, destroyed sense of public charity and narrowed downed public opinion. It has restricted a man's royalty to his caste, made virtue and morality caste ridden. Caste does not appreciate merits in a man from the other castes (p. 270)." Ambedkar discussed the history of slavery in India and observed that 7 and 13 tribes of slaves have been found in India as described by Manu and Narada respectively. Under the given situation which is undemocratic the formula of one man one vote, one vote one value can bring political equality in a restricted sense. For social and economic equality, besides plethora of welfare measures, there is need to adopt holistic approach through Indian Constitution, state initiatives and societal commitment.

Dr. Ambedkar had strong sense of respect and sympathy for Indian Women. He was not at all satisfied with their low socio-economic status. To him, how can a nation become powerful if its half population is neglected. Therefore, he was in favour of offering various rights to women. He was entrusted to formulate Hindu Code Bill for Common Civil Code. Needless to mention that during those days in 1951 he was law minister of government of India. For this purpose he critically examined the spirit of Mitakshar and Daybhag schools relating to marriage. After going through all the procedures relating to marriage and divorce as prescribed by these two schools, he gave the concept of Hindu Code Bill. The Bill incorporated measures and steps for social, economic and cultural freedom to women. The zist of Hindu Code Bill was revolutionary in the sense that many concessions where proposed for women who were completely denced in the past. J.L. Nehru was Prime Minister of India, inspite of various discussions and Nehru's inclination in favour of the bill, it was not supported in the constituent assembly and it was not passed in reaction to which Dr. Ambedkar resigned from the position of Law Minister in 1951.

Ambedkar had himself tested the fruit of methodical education. He himself was master of seven languages. He perceived education as a liberator. Therefore, he was in favour of popularization of Modern education for liberty, security and equality. Therefore, he supported the concept of Hill theory poularized by John Deway and V. Necholus. According to this concept all the members of the community need not be highly educated and betterly placed in prestigious occupations but if large number of members of any community are highly educated then they accumulate prestige, name and fame and ultimately power and authority. Therefore, he was in favour of popularization of quality ridden methodical education especially among the marginalized groups. To what extent we are following the advice of Dr. Ambedkar while popularizing primary, secondary and higher education among marginalized groups in participation and the entire society in general? Of course, there is mass enrolment today at the primary level but quality of teaching and learning is a distant dream in primary schools specially run by the state where maximum number of dalit and tribal children are enrolled. Can one achieve the message coming out of the phrase "Educate, Unite and Agitate" wind by Dr. Ambedkar while making education, so-called instrumental at the cost of world view and philosophy of education?

Perspective on Infrastructure

Whether infrastructure is a pre-condition for social and economic development in a developing society of social and economic development needs to be followed by infrastructural development or both can go side by side is a debatable issue. But after Second Global War many European countries were engaged in repairing the damaged infrastructure and establishment of new infrastructure. In India which is an agrarian society, the first priority was to construct roads, connect cities with villages and ensure frequent interaction between towns and villages. Therefore, Ambedkar strongly emphasized construction of buildings, expansions of railways, construction of market places, school buildings, factories and hydro and thermal power projects and so on. In short, to him infrastructural development was a pre-condition for economic development which will in turn lead to social transformation in a democratic direction.

Concluding Remarks

Today there is a serious debate on environmental and development. It is assumed that development leads to environmental degradation. There are many empirical studies which support the above conclusion but Ambedkar was in favour of respectful co-existence of environment and development. As a symbolic when he established Milind College at Aurangabad, he developed a beautiful park which was full of trees, plants, gardens, lawns and beautiful landscapes.

Dr. Ambedkar emphasized that today organic linkage between societies are increasing at the global and at the regional level. Therefore, development and change taking place at one place is likely to reach to another place easily. But one has to be serious on the issue of equitable distribution of resources and benefits. Today, many countries specially Latin American countries are experiencing bad taste of foreign direct investments "FDI". Hence, privatization is also dysfunctional. Therefore, Dr. Ambedkar was in favour of strengthening once own capabilities and identities to improve one's bargaining power in the international market. In this context it is worthwhile to mention that he was in favour of public sector enterprises because he perceived it as an engine of growth and the source of employment. But we have opted globalization for change and development. For many globalization is a new Avtar of modernization. In many cases globalization contributes to exclusion and marginalization as it was done by modernization in the past. But the counter argument is that instead of accusing globalization the marginalized groups should avail its benefits by fulfilling its pre-conditions and basic requirements. But how to ensure access to essential requirements of globalization particularly by the marginalized groups? This is a burning question which needs immediate attention by all the stakeholders in the interest of marginalized groups in particular and nation building in general.

REFERENCES

Keer Dhananjay (1954), *Dr. Babasaheb Ambedkar: Life & Mission*, Mumbai: Popular Prakashan (reprint 2016).

Naik C.D. and R.S. Kureel (2013), *Dr Ambedkar's Vision for Nation Building*, Indore: Shree Parasmani Publication.

Murli Manohar Joshi (2016), 'Ambedkar wanted Sanskrit as Nat/l Language", *The Times of India*, April 25, 2016

Rajput, J.S., (2016), 'Realize Babasahib's Dream of Education for the Weak', *The New Indian Express Magazine*, Chennai, March 18, 2016

Pawar, J.V (2015), *Dr. B.R. Ambedkar's Social Revolution*, Bhashya Prakashan, Mumbai.

15

Dr. B.R. Ambedkar on Humanism

Swaraj Basu

In the past and even to-day Dr. B.R. Ambedkar is primarily projected as the messiah of Dalits and in the process his greatness as an intellectual, as reformist and his vision for humanity has failed to get desired recognition. He was a multi-faceted personality in true sense of the term. His ideas on liberation and development had strong humanistic appeal. His criticism of Hinduism is mostly perceived from a very narrow perspective without taking note of his prime concern for the liberation of human being irrespective of their social origin. It is the oppressed humanity and their sufferings which made him to sacrifice his life for their right and dignity. Throughout his life his writings and actions speak volume about his strong humanitarian convictions. In this article I would like to focus on the humanistic concerns in the ideas of Dr. Ambedkar. Dr. Ambedkar's life proves his deep attachment with Indian cultural tradition and at the same time he was a critic of fanaticism and orthodoxy in the name of religion. He was not against religious belief of the people but was against the misuse of religious belief to discriminate and oppress the people.

Humanism in Indian Cultural Tradition

India represents diversity in terms of cultural tradition but at the same time the essence of India's greatness lies in its respect of all traditions without compromising its core value of giving supremacy to humanism. Faith in humanity is at the core of Indian cultural tradition and the Upanishads provide the foundation of humanism. Following successive intellectual movements the meaning of the term humanism has seen various interpretations but essentially humanism emphasises the infinite potential of human beings. Deep concern to the human life and also immense potentiality of human being are at the core of the Upanishadic thought. Great seers and philosophers have drawn our attention at different points of time to the supremacy given to human values in the Upanishads. The Buddhist philosophy also advocated for the importance to be given to the service of man compared to the worship of god. In place of superstition and unreason Buddha prescribed the way to conquer anger through kindness. Humanism is at the core of Buddhist philosophy by advocating strongly for social equality. Importance of human values and strong condemnation of differences in the name of religion, caste and other identities is also very well reflected in the Bhakti movement spanning over centuries, particularly in the middle ages. Ideas of Ramananda, Kabir, Ravidas, Tulasidas, Chokhamela, Tukaram, Sri Chaitanya and many others made us realize that pure devotion is the only way to liberation and devotion is beyond differences created by people only without any rationale. All these saints were great visionaries and they set before the world an idea of love and universal brotherhood. They were opposed to the teachings of religion which did not appeal to the human reason. Kabir particularly showed the hollowness of rituals and orthodoxy and through his teachings he drew our attention to the values of humanism.

'Pandit, look in your heart for knowledge.

Tell me where untouchability came from, since you believe in it.

Mix red juice, white juice and air—a body bakes in a body.

As soon as the eight lotuses are ready, it comes into the world. Then what's Untouchable?

Eighty-four hundred thousand vessels decay into dust, while the potter keeps slapping clay on the wheel, and with a touch cuts each one off.

We eat by touching, we wash By touching, and from a touch The world was born. So who's untouched? Asks Kabir.

Only he Who has no taint of Maya.' (*The Bijak of Kabir*, trans. by Linda Hess and Shukdev Singh, Delhi, 1986, p.55).

Moving to modern times we find the echo of this great cultural tradition of valuing human dignity above religious orthodoxy in great thinkers of Indian Renaissance. Nineteenth century thinker Swami Vivekananda through his life and teachings showed us that priest craft, caste superiority, untouchability, etc. have given birth to social dissension and disharmony. Vivekananda proclaimed, "The basis of all systems social or political rests upon the goodness of man. No nation is great or good because Parliament enacts this or that, but because its men are great and good."

Thus starting from the time of the Upanishads till the days of the Renaissance we find in Indian cultural tradition certain dominant values which direct us towards the realization of the inherent potentialities of human being without any discrimination. We come across the primacy given to the ideas of humanistic thought. Humanism teaches the need for brotherhood and equality of all. In modern times Mahatma Gandhi and Rabindranath Tagore were ardent advocates of human dignity and emphasised on love to remove hatred existing in society in different forms. Service to mankind is the service to god. Hiranmoy Karlekar in an article has very aptly explained Tagore's faith in humanity giving reference to Tagore's address, Shabhyatar Shankat (Crisis of Civilisation), delivered by Tagore to mark his 80th birth anniversary celebration on 8th May 1941.

> "The world was then plunged into the monstrous violence of World War II. Earlier, Hitler had launched his hideous persecution of Jews and Japan had unleashed a reign of unspeakable atrocities in China. The erstwhile Soviet Union was reeling under the impact of Stalin's murderous purges."

Tagore began his address by saying that his early acquaintance with the West was through its uplifting literature which had made him a deep admirer of it. He even hoped like many others that Britain would, in keeping with its libertarian traditions, guide India to freedom. His faith in the West had been shattered by Britain's exploitative and savagely repressive rule and the West's insane propensity to violence. He said he no longer believed in the West's emancipatory role and humankind's new leader would arise in the East. As translated by this writer, one of the most striking passages in the address reads:

> "But it is a sin to lose faith in human beings; I shall protect this faith to the last. I would hope that after the total, all-encompassing destruction, there would perhaps begin a pure self-unfolding of history on the cloudless sky of renunciation on the Eastern horizon where the Sun rises. And one day, unvanquished human beings will surmount all obstacles and advance on a victorious journey to regain their lost status. I consider it a crime to believe that humankind's limitless, unredressable might is the ultimate [reality].
> I will say today before going that the day has come before us to prove that the power-drunk arrogance of even the mightiest is not safe."
> [*Source*: *The Daily Pioneer*, New Delhi, URL: http://newageislam.com/spiritual-meditations/hiranmay-karlekar/the-philosophy-of-harmony/d/7377]

It is in this backdrop of deep rooted value of humanism developed and strengthened, in spite of hindrances and aberrations, in Indian cultural tradition we would explain the importance of Dr. Ambedkar's ideas as a great humanist which is generally overshadowed by limiting his contribution in nation building.

Humanism in Ambedkar's Ideas

To understand Ambedkar's humanism it is essential to situate him in historical context and to comprehend how through his ideas he tried to ensure human dignity cutting across all barriers created by men only. Lack of proper comprehension of our cultural tradition and narrow sectarian interest had given birth to dogmatism and social oppression in the name of cultural tradition. Cutting across classes he raised his voice for equality and justice. He dedicated his life to install a sense of self-respect and pride among different sections of society, particularly those who are oppressed. Being born in a family of Dalit and experiencing social oppression at various stages of his upbringing, Dr. Ambedkar made it his life's mission to dedicate his entire life for the service and cause of the downtrodden people. In his own words he acknowledged that three great Indians who shaped his ideas were Buddha, Kabir and Jyotiba Phule who represent three different historical periods but together they represent great Indian cultural tradition which emphasises respect for humanity and equality of human being. Ideas of Buddha and Kabir in matters of religion give importance more to human concerns and love for all than religious orthodoxy in any form. We find the reflection of this value at the core of Dr. Ambedkar's ideas. Writing on the leadership of Ambedkar Eleanor Zelliot wrote, '...in his student days at Columbia, Ambedkar had written a thesis claiming that Indian culture and the Indian people are basically homogenous, and he never departed from this belief. It may be that his American experience made him wary of a separation based on racial difference. It may be that his father's devout Hinduism, which included membership in the Kabir Panth, and his own interest in the dominant sanskritic culture urged him toward a solution more identified with India's proudest traditions'. (Eleanor Zelliot, *From Untouchable to Dalit: Essays on Ambedkar Movement*, Manohar Publishers, Delhi, 1992, p. 58). This observation of Eleanor Zelliot is very important to understand the essence of Ambedkar's ideology which was very much rooted in India's cultural tradition and at the same he did not hesitate to raise his voice against those discriminatory and orthodox practices which promoted social prejudices and oppression in various forms in the name of our great cultural past. His protest was not against Brahmanical religion but against that orthodoxy in Brahmanism which promoted discrimination and oppression of one section of society by another. He believed in the religion of humanity and not in religion of ritualism. This idea of Dr. Ambedkar is reflected when he said, '...you must give a new doctrinal basis to your Religion—a basis that will be in consonance with Liberty, Equality and Fraternity, in short, with Democracy. I am no authority on the subject. But I am told that for such religious principles as will be in consonance with Liberty, Equality and Fraternity it may not be necessary for you to borrow from foreign sources and that you could draw for such principles on the *Upanishads*.' (Source: *Dr. Babasaheb Ambedkar: Writings and Speeches*, compiled by Vasant Moon, Vol. I, Bombay, 1989, pp.77-78).

Starting with the famous Mahad Satyagraha in 1927 with which his journey as the leader of the socially oppressed people began and till his death in 1956, we find that in his entire public life Dr. Ambedkar tirelessly fought for dignity and self-respect of the oppressed people. Dr. Ambedkar's criticism of caste system, Brahmanical religion and his relentless struggle against upper caste domination need to be understood from the perspective of his concerns for humanism and not merely as a criticism of Brahmanical religion. I would like to refer here Dr. Ambedkar's ideas as expressed in his writings on annihilation of caste. He wrote,

> 'Thirteen millions of people living in the midst of civilisation are still in a savage state and are leading the life of hereditary criminals! But the Hindus have never felt ashamed of it. This is a phenomenon which in my view is quite unparalleled. What is the cause of this shameful state of affairs? Why has no attempt been made to civilize these aborigines and to lead them to take to a more honourable way of making a living? The Hindus will probably seek to account for this savage state of the aborigines by attributing to them congenital stupidity. They will not probably admit that the aborigines have remained savages because they had made no effort to civilize them, to give them medical aid, to reform them, to make them good citizens. But supposing a Hindu wished to do what the Christian missionary is doing for these aborigines, could he have done it? I submit not. Civilizing the aborigines means adopting them as your own, living in their midst, and cultivating fellow-feeling, in short loving them. How is it possible for a Hindu to do this? His whole life is one anxious effort to preserve his caste...Not that a Hindu could not be taught the sense of duty to fallen humanity, but the trouble is that no amount of sense of duty can enable him to overcome his duty to preserve his caste. Caste is, therefore, the real explanation as to why the Hindu has let the savage remain a savage in the midst of his civilisation without blushing or without feeling any sense of remorse or repentance. The Hindu has not realized that these aborigines are a source of potential danger. If these savages remain savages they may not do any harm to the Hindus. But if they are reclaimed by non-Hindus and converted to their faiths they will swell the ranks of the enemies of the Hindus. If this happens the Hindu will have to thank himself and his Caste System'. ((Source: *Dr. Babasaheb Ambedkar: Writings and Speeches*, compiled by Vasant Moon, Vol. I, Bombay, 1989, pp. 52-53).

A close reading of the above passage from Dr. Ambedkar's writings points to the fact that he was very concerned about the consequences of the caste system on humanity. Through his writings he wanted to make the adherents of Hinduism aware that how the caste system was weakening the strength of Hindus by creating divisiveness within. In the interest of Hinduism and also of humanity efforts must be made to bring in social equality. Saving humanity and not the caste system was his prime concern. His exposure to western liberal tradition and his understanding of Indian cultural tradition convinced him that nothing was more important than human dignity. Therefore if we look at his career spanning 1927 to 1956 as a political ideologue, reformer and leader of the oppressed people we find that he wanted to ensure dignity and justice to all who were denied of this. His relentless struggle succeeded in forcing the leadership of India's liberation movement to make him the chief architect of the constitution of independent India. In this responsibility also his prime concern was to ensure the right of equality and human dignity.

In his role as the chairperson of the constitution drafting committee Dr. Ambedkar incorporated the principles of fundamental rights to all citizens in the constitution with the objective of establishing the basic human values in the society. He did not envisage the constitution merely as an instrument of governance, he desired to make the constitution as the guiding spirit to ensure individual freedom, justice and human dignity. The constitution drafted by Dr. Ambedkar provided constitutional guarantees and protections for a wide range of civil liberties like freedom of religion, abolition of untouchability and outlawed all forms of discrimination. Preamble to the constitution ensures justice, social, economic and political, liberty, equality and fraternity. He was equally concerned for the equal rights of women and advocated for social and economic freedom for them. Dr. Ambedkar vociferously advocated for social democracy based on the principles of liberty, equality and fraternity and he argued that without social democracy political democracy becomes meaningless.

We can draw conclusion from the above discussion that Dr. Ambedkar did not represent only a particular section of society rather his major concern was to protect people from any form of tyranny, injustice and exploitation. In short he gave voice to the ignored humanity comprising of workers, small peasants and landless labourers. It is pertinent to mention in this context that how we find the reflection of Swami Vivekananda's vision of New India and concern for the marginalized in Dr. Ambedkar's vision for humanism. Vivekananda had envisioned the dawn of a new India in the following words:

> 'Let new India arise...out of the peasant's cottage grasping the plough; out of the huts of the fishermen, the cobbler and the sweeper. Let her spring from the grocer's shop, from beside the oven of the fritter seller. Let her emanate from the factory, from marts and from markets. Let her emerge from groves and forests, from hills and mountains'. (Swami Vivekananda, *The Complete Works*, Vol. VII, Calcutta, 1979, p. 327).

16

Dr. Ambedkar and His Notion of Education, Unity and Agitation for the Development of Dalits and Democracy

Sudhir Gupta

Dr. B.R. Ambedkar was a product of both tradition and modernity. He was a person who experienced caste based discrimination and suffered violation of his human rights and dignity at different stages of life but at the same time he also gradually availed benefits of forces of modernisation and development. His both childhood and adult socialization is full of contradictions. Many of us experience contradiction but sometimes it becomes difficult to manage it, Ambedkar successfully managed contradictions and challenges in his life. There are different ways to overcome individual and community based contradictions. Democracy is one among these but during his early part there was no democracy in our society in the present sense of the term. India was ruled by British administration for roughly around two hundred years. Over the time, British administration became largely indifferent on social issues because of bad taste during 1857 revolt. Therefore, it became indifferent on social issues like caste, women, untouchability, religion, etc. However, due to some practical purposes it promoted English education. It also diffused some values which were universal in nature. Ambedkar used this opportunity first for his own development and subsequently for the development of marginalized groups as well as the entire nation. Needless to mention that Ambedkar was the champion of seven oriental and foreign languages. Knowledge of Marathi helped him to know views of Marathi Social reformers.

English education helped him not only to read great philosophers and scholars of the world but it also helped him to critically understand religious texts and teachings of Hinduism which were available in English. It helped him to make serious comments on number of Hindu social institutions and cultural practices. Similarly English based methodical education helped him to realize importance of democracy and its three fundamental preambles namely freedom, equality and fraternity. He went to Columbia University (USA) for higher education. Access to education in this university and social contact which he developed there had wonderful impact on his life. Dealing with this his biographer Keer (reprint 2016) said, "Life in America, a foreign land, was a unique and moving experience in life that Ambedkar met with in New York. There, in company with other students and colleagues he could move freely. He could read, he could write, he could walk, he could bathe and he could rest with a status of equality. Meals at regular hours, eating on a table cloth, and napkin! To him life at Columbia University was a revelation. It was a new world. It enlarged his mental horizon. A new kind of existence began. His life gleamed with a new meaning (p. 27)!

This experience brought radical change in his personality which he retained through his life. He became champion of both science and scholarship and democracy. To him democracy is a form of government by which revolutionary changes are bought about in the economic and social life of people without bloodshed. For smooth running of democracy the requisite conditions are: (1) There should no open social inequalities, (2) There is need of one opposition party to find faults with government, (3) Man's equality must be recognised in judiciary and legislature, (4) Moral values must be observed by the Constitution, (5) Moral principle must be observed in society as it is assumed that principle is the foundation of democracy, and (6) Social conscience (p. 23). He said that freedom not simply refers to liberation from various types of exploitation and denial of human rights but also it refers to liberation from blind faith, bad habit, individualism, self-centeredness, cunningness and so on. It refers to openness of mind and thought and formation of inclusive character and tolerant behavior.

So far as the notion of equality is concerned he was in agreement with many scholars that equality in the mechanical sense of the term is not possible. Society is bound to be unequal but relative equality is the need of the hour. The gap between societies, which are the creation of many forces, must be reduced in the wider interest of groups, regions and societies. And for this purpose there is need to store the stage of equality of opportunity. Equality of opportunity does not mean simply removal of inequality but it refers to creation and diffusion of enabling factors at all levels and for all who can contribute to as per their capability and avail benefits as per once requirement. And here we see similarity between Mahatma Gandhi and Dr. B.R. Ambedkar. If societies wish to become strong it has to ensure that all the institutions and methods working in democratic set-up must be directed to promote equality, in the absence of which one cannot actualize the philosophy of "live and let live". And for equality it is essential that at the very outset inhibiting factors must be eliminated and enabling factors must be promoted by both state and society through various methods. Dr. Ambedkar and his vision was directed to these issues throughout his life.

The third dimension of democracy is brotherhood. The concept of brotherhood is more social and cultural than political and legal. It is based on faith, trust and reciprocity. It is based on the notion of "live and let live". For this, faith knowledge and respect for each other's concerns, problems, culture, etc.; is essential. Ambedkar worked throughout the life for the attainment of this philosophy. Critically speaking if the society is segmented on the basis of caste with high amount of rigidity and if resources are disproportionately availed in society, in that situation, inequality and deprivation will flourish which in turn will lead to tension and anxiety. Dr. Ambedkar was very much aware of this situation. Therefore, through his vision as well as action, he attempted his best to address the question of brotherhood. Referring to his concept of democracy and importance of liberty, equality and fraternity Naik and Kureel (2013: 22) rightly said: "If the political democracy is not based on social democracy then, it cannot last long;

for the social democracy recognise liberty, equality and fraternity as principle of life. Liberty, equality and fraternity are an undivided unbroken whole traid. If there be no social equality then the liberty would mean the rule of the handful of persons over the general masses. If the equality were devoid of liberty then it will sap initiative spirit of individual man's life. If there be no fraternity then liberty and equality will not grow naturally. The Indian people must admit one thing that in Indian society two things are wanting. They are social equality and economic equality."

Dr. Ambedkar was not only a product of modern education which enabled him to become thinker of international reputation but writings and speeches of great scholars of Columbia University made him aware to work as a translator of his own philosophy. Dr. Ambedkar was highly influenced by *Jyotiba Phule* and his wife. The couple believed that expansion of modern education is most powerful instrument for liberation and development. *To Phule*, education does not mean simply knowledge but without wisdom education is meaningless. Ambedkar was influenced by Phule in the broader sense of the term therefore, he was in favour of quality education to all, particularly the marginalized population. He supported the concept of ***"Hill Theory"*** popularized by John Deway and V. Necholus. As per this concept it is not possible for everybody to get high level education and high level government job. But if large number of people from any individual caste or community gets high education and prestigious job it will enhance social and economic status of the entire caste or community, Dr. Ambedkar supported this theory and for this purpose in mind as a symbolic effort he established ***Milind College*** at Aurangabad. He said that large number of down-trodden should avail quality ridden methodical education which will enhance their social status and prestige. It will liberate them from caste occupation. It will encourage occupational mobility. It will liberate them from miseries and deprivation. For the expansion of education, particularly among scheduled castes of Presidency of Bombay he and his friends established *'Bashishkrit Hitakarini Sabha'* on July 20, 1924. Following were specific objectives of this organisation:

(a) To promote the spread of education among the Depressed Classes by opening Hostels or by employing such other means as may seem necessary or desirable.

(b) To promote the spread of culture among the Depressed Classes by opening libraries, social centres and classes or study circles.
(c) To advance and improve the economic condition of the Depressed Classes by starting Industrial and Agricultural Schools, and
(d) To represent the grievances of the Depressed Classes.

To him, there are several social functions of education. One among these is to inculcate those values which can bring science and scholarship in once life. The other function of education is to make people assertive and argumentative. It makes us informed and critical citizen. If education makes us argumentative, we can raise voice against forces and conditions responsible for denial of human rights. But education is not sufficient enough to challenge negative part of historical forces. For this, there is need to have unity among masses. Here unity means awareness of negative social processes and common reaction against it. It refers to unity of heart and mind. If people are united nobody can crush them for longer period. Hence, he perceived unity as a liberating force. Unity is not possible if there is no common cause. If education in the broader sense is available and people are united on common concerns then only there is possibility of voice against unjust or what Dr. Ambedkar called agitation against injustice. In other words, for the actualization of social transformation in the democratic direction, he advised underprivileged section of society to follow the "***Philosophy of Educate, Unite and Agitate***". Ambedkar strongly believed that for tenable nation building, it is essential on the part of everybody to respect human rights of all particularly those who have suffered since long. According to Keer (op.cit.) "Untouchability has ruined the Untouchables, the Hindus and ultimately the nation as well. If the Depressed Classes gained their self-respect and freedom, they would contribute not only to their own progress and prosperity but by their industry, intellect and courage would contribute also to the strength and prosperity of the nation. If the tremendous energy the Untouchables are at present required to fritter away in combating the stigma of untouchability had been saved them, it would have been applied by them to the promotion of education and development of economic resources of the nation as a whole (p. 93).

Therefore, he expected that on the one side state should be sensitive and responsive, general society should be active and accountable and marginalized groups should be assertive through the means of phrase mentioned just above. He strongly argued that for strong a nation the feeling of nationalism among its citizen is a necessary condition and the feeling is only possible if the philosophy of equality of opportunity is translated into action in the true sense of the term.

END NOTES

Keer Dhananjay (1954), *Dr. Babasaheb Ambedkar: Life & Mission*, Mumbai: Popular Prakashan (reprint 2016).

Naik C.D. and R.S. Kureel (2013), *Dr Ambedkar's Vision for Nation Building*, Indore: Shree Parasmani Publication.

17

Ambedkar's Contribution Towards Indian Parliament

S. Prabhakar

Dr. B.R. Ambedkar was one of the architects of Indian Constitution. His contribution to the deliberations in the Constituent Assembly was immense. Dr. Ambedkar's contribution is there for everyone to see. He has ensured that adequate safeguards for minorities, backward and tribal areas, and depressed and other backward classes are there in the Constitution.

Replying to the discussion on the Constitution on November 26, 1949, he said: "Without going into the merit of constitution, however good and faultless a constitution may be, but if those who implement it are incompetent and useless, that constitution results in an evil. Similarly however defective a constitution may be, but if its executors are good the same constitution results in the good of the people."[1]

Jawaharlal Nehru, the Prime Minister, declared the 7 Member Cabinet in which Dr. Ambedkar was anointed as the first Law Minister of the Independent India. He started his work within a fortnight by submitted a comprehension report on 29th August 1947 itself suggesting functions of the Constituent Assembly which included continuing and completing the work of Constitution making which commenced on the 9th December, 1946. Being the Chairman of the Constitution Drafting Committee, he had played a crucial role in the drafting. Dr. Ambedkar's contribution is there for everyone to see. One of the eight objectives was to ensure adequate safeguards for minorities, backward and tribal areas, and depressed and other backward classes. His role in the framing of India's Constitution led to his becoming the first Law Minister.

His comments on the eve of the adoption of the Constitution explain the true spirit of the Constitution. "The working of a Constitution does not depend wholly upon the nature of the Constitution.... The factors on which the working of (the) organs of State depends are the people and the political parties they will set up as their instruments to carry out their wishes and their politics." Our Constitution was adopted on 26th November, 1949. His deposition before the Southborough Committee, which drafted the Government of India Act, 1919, is notable as he had argued for creating separate electorate with reservations for Dalits and other religious communities. The voice for reservation never got silenced. His role in launching an active movement against untouchability became a public movement. Its impact is still on. There was a demand by the RSS Chief for a review of constitutionally-guaranteed reservation policy.

Constituent Assembly authorized the Parliament to change the old laws in accordance with the Directive Principles and the Fundamental Rights in order to establish a society based on equality, prosperity and self-reliance. Ambedkar stood for inclusive growth and integration. India had the distinction of being the world's largest economy in the beginning of the Christian era, as it accounted for about 32.9 per cent share of world GDP and about 17 per cent of the goods produced in India had long been exported to far off destinations across the world.[2] Hence, we can say that Globalisation is not a new concept. A grand push has been given to Globalisation, liberalization and privatization in July, 1991. Since then, India had made great strides in every conceivable field of significance.

On 26th January, 1950, while handing over the Constitution to the nation, gave golden word advice to all concerned and to achieve these two equalities also at the earliest.

> "On the 26th of January, 1950, we are going to enter into a life of contradictions. In politics we will have equality and in social and eco. Life we will have inequality. In politics we will be recognizing

> the principle of one man one vote and one vote one value. In our social and eco. Life, we shall, by reason of our social and eco. Structure, continue to deny the principle of one man one value. How long shall be continue to live this life of contradictions? How long shall we continue to deny equality in our social and economic life? If we continue to deny it for long, we will do so only by putting our political democracy in peril. We must remove this contradiction at the earliest possible moment or else those who suffer from inequality will blow up the structure of political Demo. Which this Assembly has so labouriously built up."

To Dr. Ambedkar, the soul of democracy is the doctrine of one man, one value.

In November, 2016, in Lok Sabha, two days were allotted for discussion on commitment to India's Constitution as part of 125th Birth Anniversary celebrations of Dr. B.R. Ambedkar. During the discussions, rich tributes were paid by wide range of political parties. His significant contribution to the drafting of the Constitution, his role in the deliberations of the Constituent Assembly, and his functioning as a Law Minister are dealt in this paper. This paper also brings out whole gamut of issues concerning Ambedkar. It will also go into the contribution of Ambedkar and his relevance in the present political set and Globalisations. It is primarily based on the inputs on these 2 days debate as this gives a clear indication of where we stand today. This was also to pay our homage to the revered memory of Dr. Ambedkar, the Chairman of the Drafting Committee and principal architect of the Constitution.

Ambedkar and Reservation

There is a need to know as to how reservation issue came up for the first time in India. Ambedkar seeing the inequalities in the early 1890s thought of reservation for those who are deprived and who have been historically wronged over the ages. Ambedkar and reservation go hand in hand. Way back in 1891 itself, the demand for reservation of government jobs was made with an agitation in the princely State of Travancore against the recruitment of non-natives into public service overlooking qualified native people. A decade later, Maharaja of Kolhapur in Maharashtra, Chatrapati Sahuji Maharaj introduced reservation in favour of Backward Classes as early as 1902 primarily to eradicate poverty from amongst them and to give them their due share in the State administration.[3] The notification of 1902 created 50 per cent reservation in services for Backward Classes/communities in the State of Kolhapur. This notification is the first Government Order which provided reservation for the welfare of depressed classes in India.[4] There were a few other instances particularly in Tamil Nadu which were aimed at demolishing the wall created by the upper classes between them and the untouchables. It is a known fact that Tamil Nadu has more Ambedkar statues than any of its leaders like Periyar, Anna, MGR, etc. It may be true of the whole country too. It is a testimony of his spearheading the cause of Dalits, Backward Classes, SCs, STs, and oppressed strata of society.

He was one of the very few Indian Statesmen-politicians who actively participated in the discussions on Constitutional matters from the Montagu-Chelmsford Reforms in 1991 to the Cabinet Mission in 1946 proposals.[5] Even in the first session of the Round Table Conference, he let the British government know that the consent of the people be the touchstone of the Constitution.[6] As stated above, though there were instances of providing reservations to Backward Classes and to bring social justice, his fight for social justice is remembered the most because of his stature during our freedom struggle and as Law Minister. His singular thinking that SCs, STs and Dalits have to be brought to the mainstream because of their oppression for centuries faced resistance. His steadfastness in giving reservations to SCs and STs was opposed by many. His uncanny ability and powerful conviction had won the day.

People belonging to Dalits, SCs and STs consider Ambedkar as messiah as because of him only they could get various benefits—be it in admissions in pursuing education, be it Government services or SC and ST Members in Lok Sabha, SC and ST Members of Legislative Assemblies of Parliament, State Legislatures, Parliament. This made people in this category to rub shoulder to shoulder with other upper strata of society. This paved way for them to rise about the ordinary and dream for achieving the insurmountable which since then was not even dreamt of.

Major credit for everything involving reservations to SCs, STs, Dalits and Other Backward Classes, during and after the demise of Ambedkar, should go to the architect of Indian Constitution, Dr. Ambedkar as he had espoused the cause of them way back in 1919 when he deposed before the Southborough Committee, which drafted the Government of India Act, 1919, for creating separate electorate with reservations for Dalits and other religious communities.

Relevance of Ambedkar today is there for everyone to see. His name is referred to whenever Constitution is discussed or any major amendment to our Constitution takes place in Parliament. His contribution in various fields, particularly in providing reservations to the SCs and STs, comes out at regular intervals in the debates and discussions in Parliament. His role in the framing of India's Constitution led to his becoming the first Law Minister.

Ambedkar as Labour Minister

Ambedkar's Parliamentary career started in 1926 when he was nominated as a Member of Bombay Legislative Council. He held the membership till 1934. Later, he also held the post of Opposition Leader in the Bombay Legislative Assembly. His legal acumen, academic excellence, negotiating skills and administrative abilities fetched him the membership of the Defence Advisory Committee in 1941. Afterwards, he was given the Labour portfolio, which he held till July 1946.

As the Labour Member of the Executive Council of the Governor General of India, Dr. Ambedkar succeeded in getting 8 and one-third per cent reservation in appointments for the depressed classes. Thus, we can say that he has the deep understanding of the plight of downtrodden even before the framing of the Constitution. Not only that, as Labour Minister, he was the first to establish employment exchanges. He was instrumental in bringing in several social security measures to promote democracy and harmony in the industrial sphere. For the first time, the tripartite approach was introduced to settle issues between the employers and the employees.[7] His innovative thinking has also paved for the setting up of a Labour Administration to deal with prevention and settlement of industrial disputes, enforcement of labour laws and promotion of labour welfare in industries falling under the Central sphere.

After Independence, when the time had come for the formation of the new Cabinet of Independent India, the Prime Minister Pandit Nehru's choice of Law Minister fell on Dr. Ambedkar. The most important labour legislation that was introduced by Ambedkar during his tenure as Labour Minister was the Minimum Wages Bill. He understood the psyche of the Hindu women and the depressed classes. To ameliorate the lot of the Hindu women, he drafted the Hindu Code Bill and introduced it in Parliament on February 6, 1951 to bring about reforms in the Hindu society and codify certain branches of the Hindu law. This Bill was primarily sought to bring in gender equality. This attempt of his was not successful.

Another landmark legislation brought out by him in the Provisional Parliament was the Representation of the People Bill, 1950 which dealt with varied issues including stipulating qualifications, disqualifications of membership, dealing with corrupt and illegal practices during elections. Ambedkar resigned as Law Minister in 1951 due to differences of opinion with his Cabinet colleagues on many issues including stalling of his draft of the Hindu Code Bill in Parliament. He entered Rajya Sabha in March, 1952. Thus, continued to enrich the proceedings with his views on national issues till his demise. Social justice and combating inequalities are dear to Ambedkar. He fought for these principles all his life.

Parliament and Social Justice

Parliament's role in delivering the social justice is tremendous. The importance of social justice is enshrined in the Constitution of India. Constituent Assembly authorized the Parliament to change the old laws in accordance with the Directive Principles and the Fundamental Rights in order to establish a society based on equality, prosperity and self-reliance.

To understand the social justice in the modern perspective, first we have to know as to what is meant by social justice. According to Wikipedia, the free encyclopedia, *social justice,* refers to the concept of a society in which justice is achieved in every aspect of society, rather than merely the administration of law.... It can also refer to the distribution of advantages and disadvantages within a society.[8]

It is stated that—In India 90 per cent of social legislations pertain to the realm of human rights and thus 'social justice' found active support at the hands of human rights champions and one such ardent supporter is the 'media' such as press, TV and other instruments of the media.[9] With over 70 per cent of the population still living in the rural areas, the task of the Government to dispense social justice has increased manifold, as people still lack in many areas, for example, enjoying the basic necessities of life, deprived of basic legal rights to take up their causes in the courts.

After the Constitution came into being on 26th January, 1950, Parliament has enacted a number of laws to initiate the process of social justice, which in turn helped the Government agencies to make the laws not only effective but also to implement them in letter and spirit. For example, Parliament had enacted laws in connection with marriage, divorce, reservation, untouchability, labour, children, women, factories, atrocities, agriculture et al which had undoubtedly hastened the social justice to percolate deep into the weakest and vulnerable strata of society. It would not be an exaggeration to say that Parliament, along with State Assemblies contribute in bringing about social justice in multifarious fields.

It is stated that Legislature is an agency which determines the nature and aims of social justice. To deliver social justice to the people, first and foremost requisite is, people should be identified. Second comes the interests, needs and the problems of those who are in need of social justice. It is widely believed and accepted that law is an instrument of social justice. It is also believed that social justice must flow from the legal system as otherwise 'rule or law' will break down.[10] Social justice includes welfare, and empowerment of disadvantaged and marginalized sections of the society, namely, Scheduled Castes, Aged persons, Persons with Disabilities, Backward Classes, Victims of Drug Abuse, etc.

Parliament should generate public awareness about its role, powers and functioning, particularly matters concerning social justice. Parliament wields enormous power in the governance of the country. The actions of government can be questioned and scrutinized by Parliament in its functioning. This advantage should be taken seriously by bringing more and more issues concerning social justice.

Articles 15,16,17 of the Fundamental Rights and Articles 38, 39, 39A,

41, 43, 43A and 46 of the Directive Principles, related to the various social, economic and political justice, getting inspiration from the protective umbrella of Article 31(C) and thus, contributing to the process of transformation in the society. It is not an exaggeration to state that 'social justice' and 'rule of law' are interdependent. Both have to go together in order to achieve justice, equality and freedom.

Our Constitution provides for abolition of untouchability, prohibition of discrimination on grounds of religion, race, caste, sex or place of birth, equality of opportunity in matters of public employment, promotion of educational and economic interests of SCs, STs and other weaker sections, reservation of seats for SCs and STs in the House of the People, and Legislative Assemblies of the States, Panchayats and Municipalities.

Our Constitution contains various provisions for the development of such marginalized groups, for instance, Article 341 for SCs, Article 342 for STs, Article 340 for OBCs, Article 30 which provides the right to minorities to establish and administer educational institutions, and so on.[11]

Constitution in Securing Social Justice and Equality

To understand the social justice in the modern perspective, first we have to know as to what is meant by social justice. According to Wikipedia, the free encyclopedia, *social justice,* refers to the concept of a society in which justice is achieved in every aspect of society, rather than merely the administration of law.... It can also refer to the distribution of advantages and disadvantages within a society.[12]

Let me go back to the situation prevailing at the time of India attained Independence, Constituent Assembly took the arduous and painstaking task of framing a new Constitution for India. This precisely is considered as a milestone in the history of social justice.[13]

It is widely believed and accepted that law is an instrument of social justice. It is also believed that social justice must flow from the legal system as otherwise 'rule or law' will break down.[14] As such, 'Social Justice as stated above, includes welfare, and empowerment of disadvantaged and marginalized sections of the society, namely, Scheduled Castes, Aged persons, Persons with Disabilities, Backward Classes, Victims of Drug Abuse, etc.

After the Constitution came into being on 26th January, 1950, Parliament has enacted a number of laws to initiate the process of social justice, which in turn helped the Government agencies to make the laws not only effective but also to implement them in letter and spirit. For example, Parliament had enacted laws in connection with marriage, divorce, reservation, untouchability, labour, children, women, factories, atrocities, agriculture et al which had undoubtedly hastened the social justice to percolate deep into the weakest and vulnerable strata of society. It would not be an exaggeration to say that Parliament, along with State Assemblies, contribute in bringing about social justice in multifarious fields.

It is stated that Legislature is an agency which determines the nature and aims of social justice. To deliver social justice to the people, first and foremost requisite is, people should be identified. Second comes the interests, needs and the problems of those people who are in need of social justice.

It is stated that in India 90 per cent of social legislations pertain to the realm of human rights and thus 'social justice' found active support at the hands of human rights champions and one such ardent supporter is the 'media' such as press, TV and other instruments of the media. With over 70 per cent of the population still living in the rural areas, the task of the Government to dispense social justice has increased manifold, as people still lack in many areas, for example, enjoying the basic necessities of life, deprived of basic legal rights to take up their causes in the courts.

It is stated that Legislature is an agency which determines the nature and aims of social justice. To deliver social justice to the people, first and foremost requisite is, people should be identified. Second comes the interests, needs and the problems of those people who are in need of social justice.

It is widely believed and accepted that law is an instrument of social justice. It is also believed that social justice must flow from the legal system as otherwise 'rule or law' will break down.[15] Social justice includes welfare, and empowerment of disadvantaged and marginalized sections of the society, namely, Scheduled Castes, Aged persons, Persons with Disabilities, Backward Classes, Victims of Drug Abuse, etc.

Parliamentary Initiatives on Social Justice

Parliament and Acts

Various Acts have been passed in Parliament which aimed at extending reservation opportunities to certain classes to promote equality in the society or imparting social justice in different strata of society. For example, Protection of Civil Rights Act, 1955 and the Scheduled Castes and the Scheduled Tribes (Prevention of Atrocities) Act, 1989; The Rehabilitation Council of India Act, 1992 (34 of 1992); The National Commission for Backward Classes Act, 1993; The Persons with Disabilities (Equal Opportunities, Protection of Rights and Full Participation) Act, 1995 (01 of 1996); the National Trust for Welfare of Persons with Autism, Cerebral Palsy, Mental Retardation and Multiple Disabilities Act, 1999 (44 of 1999); and the Maintenance and Welfare of Parents and Senior Citizens Act, 2007. Responsibility of implementing these Acts lie with the Ministry of Social Justice and Empowerment.

Professor Hiren Mukerjee's Memorial Parliamentary Lecture

On 11th August, 2008, another important initiative was taken by Lok Sabha with the Inaugural Professor Hiren Mukerjee Memorial Parliamentary Lecture delivered by Prof. Amartya Sen. It would not be out of place to mention the theme of the First Lecture. It was 'The Demands of Social Justice'. In his speech, Prof. Sen reminded of the speech of Hiren Mukerjee about the need for a social commitment to help produce a society that "enables all people to rise to the full stature of their being."

The then Speaker, Somnath Chatterjee introduced this Lecture Series with a view to help bring in some of the issues of great concern to the common people of our country and of contemporary relevance to the centre-stage of our socio-political discourse. He thought it right to think that it is only appropriate that the Parliament, being the highest representative body of the people, should initiate that process. In his welcome address, he stated, "we have to go a long way in building a progressive and prosperous India that our Founding Fathers had visualised for the country at the dawn of Independence. Providing social and economic justice to the vast segments of the masses who have been kept out of the mainstream of our socio-political life should be among the core concerns of our country today....." He is sure that this Lecture would stimulate a national debate on the need to create conditions for all our citizens, regardless of their caste and creed; to enjoy justice and equality; and other democratic rights for a dignified existence.

16th Lok Sabha and Ambedkar

Debate in the 16th Lok Sabha on commitment to India's Constitution as part of 125th Birth Anniversary Celebration of Dr. B.R. Ambedkar took place on 26th and 27th November, 2015. Special sittings to commemorate 125th birth anniversary celebration of Dr. B.R. Ambedkar took place on 26th and 27th November, 2015. The 26th November is significant because the Constituent Assembly adopted the final draft of the Constitution and this happened to be the last meeting of the Constituent Assembly.

On the first day, the 26th November, 2015, the debate started with the remarks of the Speaker, Lok Sabha, Sumitra Mahajan. She paid homage to the revered memory of Dr. B.R. Ambedkar, the Chairman of the Drafting Committee and the principal architect of the Constitution and other members of the Constituency Assembly. She said that on this day, on 26th November, 1949, 66 years before, the Constituent Assembly had adopted the Constitution of India. While highlighting many achievements, including smooth transition of power and change of governments eight times, and 16 bloodless Lok Sabha elections, she informed the House that Baba Saheb Ambedkar was of the firm belief that a vibrant and stable democracy can be found only on the basis of social harmony.[16] She further said, this debate was also to discuss our 'commitment to India's Constitution'. The basic or fundamental features of our Constitution are Parliamentary system of government, fundamental rights, directive principles, secularism, and protection of minority rights, federalism, republicanism, and people as masters of our destiny, independence of judiciary and the power of judicial review. She remarked that in our Parliamentary democracy, it is endeavoured to ensure peaceful coexistence and progress of all communities irrespective of caste, creed, religion and language. We have put in place great institutions like Election Commission, National Human Rights Commission, Union Public Service Commission, Comptroller & Auditor General, etc. which are very crucial element in democratic governance. She said that Ambedkar made significant contribution to workers welfare and development of agriculture and irrigational facilities, Reserve Bank of India, Finance Commission.

Rajnath Singh, Home Minister of the country highlighted how his government is following the path of Ambedkar on ensuring women empowerment and providing equal rights to men and women. He said that Ambedkar's every word in the Constitution aimed at giving justice to each and every section of our society. In this context, he referred to Article 17 which provides for total abolition of untouchability thereby treating every individual with honour and dignity.[17] Sonia Gandhi highlighted our Constitution which imbibed secular values which has made our democracy and governance more accountable. Many other leaders of political parties who spoke on the occasion highlighted the contribution made by Ambedkar to the Constitution and to the country.

Thawar Chand Gehlot, Minister of Social Justice and Empowerment highlighted as to what his government is doing to remove economic disparity and to bring social harmony in the country with a view to strengthen the unit of integrity of the country as envisaged in the Constitution of India by Ambedkar. He stated that his government is making all the places related to Ambedkar to be developed as monuments. A magnificent national monument of Dr. Ambedkar is coming up at a cost of Rs.100 crore in New Delhi.[18] He stated that his ministry has increased the allocation to the tune of 7.5 to 8 per cent in SCs sub-plan; issued a Stamp on Ambedkar; sending 100 students to foreign countries where Dr. Ambedkar had gone in pursuit of his studies; showcased a tableu of Dr. Ambedkar on 26th January, 2015, etc.[19]

On the second day, the 27th November, 2015, Venkaiah Naidu, minister of Parliamentary affairs and urban development highlighted his contribution in setting up the Reserve Bank of India and Employment Exchanges. He said that Ambedkar will always be remembered as a leader who worked in letter and spirit to bring social equality and harmony in practice through social transformation. Jyotiraditya Scindia of Congress said that if we want to pay a true homage to Ambedkar, we need to give statutory approval to SCs/STs Sub-Plan, and to pass SCs/STs Atrocities Act and to maintain freedom of religion, freedom of expression and our diversity.[20] Bhartruhari

Mahtab of Biju Janata Dal said that Ambedkar was an illustrious leader, a nationalist, a jurist, a philosopher, a thinker, a historian, a great orator, a prolific writer, an economist, a scholar and a social reformer. He said that Ambedkar everyone is given an opportunity to excel and lack of opportunity has actually put large sections of our society in backwardness.[21] Tathaghat Satpathy of Biju Janata Dal is of the opinion that we have to go a very long way to give justice to every single individual Indian.

Mehbooba Mufti, leader of Jammu & Kashmir Peoples Democratic Party said that Ambedkar framed the Constitution keeping in mind future generations. Nishikant Dubey of Bharatiya Janata Party stated that every person must have the right of safe drinking water and of an environment that is not harmful to one's health or well-being are some of the recommendations of the National Commission to Review the working of the Constitution which submitted its report in 2002.[22] Smriti Zubin Irani, minister of human resource development said that Ambedkar established an education society to bring about intellectual, moral and social democracy. She also stated that Ambedkar wanted free and compulsory education to be a fundamental right of every child in the country. She remembered the House that it was Ambedkar in September, 1949 who sponsored an amendment to make Sanskrit the official language of the Indian Union.

Prime Minister, Narendra Modi highlighted the important role played by Ambedkar in framing the Constitution which fulfilled the dream of dignity of India, unity and integrity of India. He stated that our Constitution could not have been a social document without the involvement of Ambedkar.[23] He lauded Ambedkar thoughts on economic issues.[24] He ended by saying that his government is leaving no stone unturned to fulfill Ambedkar's vision and for an inclusive India.[25] In the end, a Resolution was proposed and passed. It states:

RESOLUTION

"We, the Members of Lok Sabha, in this Special Sittings of the Lok Sabha on 26th and 27th November, 2015 for celebrating the "Constitution Day" as a part of the One Hundred and Twenty-Fifth Birth Anniversary Celebration of Dr. B.R. Ambedkar.

Having remembered with gratitude, the commitment of Father of the Nation, Mahatma Gandhi; pioneering and monumental role played by Pandit Jawaharlal Nehru, Dr. Rajendra Prasad, Sardar Vallabhbhai Patel, Maulana Azad and other founding fathers of our Constitution and their contribution in enabling us to give to ourselves the Constitution on the 26th November, 1949; and having enacted it on the 26th January, 1950; and

Having recalled with appreciation, the invaluable services rendered by Dr. B.R. Ambedkar as the Chairman of the Drafting Committee of the Constituent Assembly and all its Members in the framing of the Constitution of India;

Do hereby solemnly affirm our commitment to the principles and ideals of the Constitution, and resolve to:

(a) uphold and maintain the sanctity and supremacy of the Constitution;
(b) respect the constitutional institutions, their freedom and authority;
(c) protect the sovereignty, unity and integrity of our country and its democratic, socialist and secular character;
(d) maintain transparency, probity and accountability in public life; and
(e) dedicate ourselves to equality and social justice and contribute to the task of building a strong republic."

The Resolution was unanimously adopted."[26]

While delivering the valedictory address of the winter session of Lok Sabha on 23.12.2015, Speaker Lok Sabha stated that during the special sittings of two days on 26th and 27 November 2015 to commemorate the 125th Birth Anniversary of Dr. B.R. Ambedkar, the debate lasted for 13 hours and 53 minutes wherein as many as 147 members participated.

Press and Ambedkar

The role of the Press in bringing more issues relating to rendering social justice before the people would create a conducive atmosphere. Parliament can be made more vibrant by bringing before it more issues. Coverage of Parliament and the issues concerning people, rendering social justice, combating inequalities should be increased in press to a very great extent. Press should also keep in mind the efforts of Parliament and its initiatives concerning social justice. At present, it is not so. Miniscule portion of the debates are highlighted in the print and electronic media. This trend should be corrected forthwith.

While addressing on the 60th Anniversary of India's Independence, on August 15, 2007, PM, Dr. Manmohan Singh quoted: "As Babasaheb Ambedkar said in the last session of the Constituent Assembly, our Constitution has given us not just a political democracy but also a social democracy guaranteeing equality of all and empowerment of the weak and the marginalized. Ambedkar vociferously advocated for Parliamentary democracy.

On the occasion to mark 60th Anniversary of Independence on 15th August, 2007, Somnath Chatterjee Speaker of 14th Lok Sabha, while stating that Pandit Nehru had visualised and to enrich our political democracy, stated that Dr. Ambedkar had contemplated such visualisation and enrichment of our political democracy. This clearly shows the vision of Ambedkar behind our Constitution.

Ambedkar's portrait was unveiled in the Central Hall of Parliament House by then Prime Minister, V.P. Singh on April 12, 1990. His Excellency L.M. Singhvi, High Commissioner of India in UK paid a glorious tribute and home to Dr. B.R. Ambedkar at Dr. Ambedkar Centenary Celebration functions held at the House of Commons on 14 April, 1992 by reciting a poem on Ambedkar:

Babasaheb, Jewel of India, diamond bright
Your message a beacon in the world's sight
A dazzling torch of justice and light
You taught us that might is not right.

Controversy over a cartoon on Ambedkar erupted Parliament on May 21, 2012. Members of Parliament cutting across parties reacted with rare unanimity and an unwarranted sense of outrage to the cartoon of Nehru and Ambedkar included in a textbook published by the NCERT.

Amartya Sen while addressing a special event at the London School of Economics (LSE) to mark the 125th birth anniversary of Dalit rights activist Babasaheb Bhimrao Ramji Ambedkar said, "One issue that keeps coming up in India is people being branded as 'anti-national' for not toeing a certain line.[27] He referred to Ambedkar as a great social revolutionary and an intellectual powerhouse. He further added, "it is through education we can truly bring about change in the world. That is the vision which Babasaheb Ambedkar gave us for a united nation.[28]

Every year, on the occasion of 'Mahaparinirvan Diwas' at Parliament House Laws in New Delhi, political leadership led by Prime Minister pays tribute to Bhim Rao Ambedkar. Narendra Modi while releasing two commemorative coins of Rs.125 and Rs.10 denomination as part of the 125th birth anniversary celebrations, said Ambedkar was a visionary and a profound thinker whose economic thought and vision is still not fully developed and needs to be appreciated, even though his contribution towards social justice has been recognised.[29]

While participating in the discussion in the Lok Sabha on the commitment to the Constitution as part of the 125th birth anniversary celebrations of Ambedkar, Sonia Gandhi also stated that Constitution's ideals are under threat today.[30] She further stated that Ambedkar had observed that howsoever good a Constitution may be, if those implementing it were bad people, then the ultimate effect would also be bad.[31]

India had inked a deal on 28th August, 2015 with the 'exchange of contract' between the Maharashtra government and the owner of the three-storey bungalow in London where B.R. Ambedkar had lived as a student in the 1920s.[32] An Exhibition—Making of the Constitution by the Constituent Assembly—was inaugurated by the Prime Minister on 26th November, 2015 in the Parliament Library building, New Delhi which focused on the process of drafting of Constitution.[33]

A panel discussion was organised on 'Combating inequalities for the achievement of Sustainable Development Goals (SDGs)' to commemorate the 125th birth anniversary of Ambedkar on April 13, 2016 by the Permanent Mission of India to the United Nations. This was the first time the United Nations observed the birth anniversary of Ambedkar.[34] These news reports show that our country is alive to the issues of inequalities, social justice, etc. Once Ambedkar defining ways and methods of Buddhism to reform the society stated that world cannot be reformed except by the reformation of the mind of the man, and the mind of the world.

Conclusion (Influence of Ambedkar) not Needed

He died on December 6, 1956. His contribution was lauded by everyone. Paying rich tributes to Dr. Ambedkar, the then Speaker of Lok Sabha, Ananthasayanam Ayyangar, said: "Dr. Ambedkar was a great and dynamic personality. He rose from humble beginnings and became a leader of the Scheduled Castes. He was a great scholar and writer and more than all, he was a powerful speaker. He piloted our Constitution. In the field of social reform, he initiated many wholesome measures. In his death, India has lost one of her great sons."

Mahatma Gandhi had described Dr. Ambedkar as a "patriot of sterling worth". Nehru in his condolence speech remarked, "There is no doubt that no one took greater care and trouble over Constitution making than Dr. Ambedkar...." On his death, Dr. Rajendra Prasad, President of the Indian Republic said, "Ambedkar was the architect of our Constitution and his services in various capacities, particularly for the upliftment of the depressed classes, could not be exaggerated. Prominent leader and educationist, Prof. K.V. Rao stated that the Constitution was in almost a literal sense "Ambedkar's child". He not only prepared its draft but also 'piloted' it. He explained its provisions, suggested changes, and accepted amendments.

In recognition of his distinguished services, Dr. Ambedkar was conferred posthumously nation's highest award, the Bharat Ratna, in 1990 and commemorated the centenary year of his birth in 1990-91 as the Year of Social Justice.[35]

Ambedkar's fight to bring in social justice is not over yet. It takes years ahead to achieve justice to the deprived, socially, educationally and politically. The dreams of Ambedkar would only get fulfilled the day each one belonging to the oppressed strata of society unshackles himself and join the national mainstream in every conceivable sphere and contribute to the development of the country.

Ambedkar all his life fought for a way of life which recognises liberty, equality and fraternity as the principles of life. All his life he fought for the disadvantaged people. He fought against the system. He was rightly called a compassionate rebel by the late President K.R. Narayanan. Through Parliamentary initiatives we can fulfill his dream of bringing about social democracy.

This is the apt time to introspect after 69 years of Independence as to what we have achieved. We have 172 millions living below the poverty line as of 2016. Have we fulfilled the dreams echoed at the time of Independence? Have we got rid of unemployment, poverty? Are we guilty of not doing enough for the people who had high hopes when we attained Independence? Have we taken care of the downtrodden and the disadvantaged sections of society? The list goes on and there is no stopping. The answers to all these questions is known to everyone and anyone can see if one takes a pause and reflect on the reality we are faced with now.

Though India has come up great institutions like the Supreme Court, Judiciary, CBI, UGC, UPSC, NHRC, CAG, the Election Commission, etc. many issues still plague our country even after 69 years of Independence. The latest Annual Status of Education Report (ASER) gives a dismal picture about our educational status. For example, only 25 per cent read simple English in Class 5. The Ministry of Human Resource Budget is hardly Rs.8,000 crore for 2016-17, which is too low an allocation considering the status of education in our country. So also budgetary allocations of Health & Family Welfare Ministry (Rs.5,000 crore); and Environment, Forests & Climate Change Ministry (Rs.3,000 crore). Kaushik Basu, Chief Economic Advisor to the World Bank recently remarked about erosion of jobs. He stated that erosion of jobs is like climate change; it happens slowly but its impact is devastating.

Though India has achieved maximum economic growth in the last 22 years between 1991 and 2013 as per the UNDP Report, the ground reality is something different. We could see inequality in society. Malnutrition is growing. We see Judiciary-Executive tussle. Article 356 has repeatedly been misused over the last six decades, as visualised by Ambedkar.

As per the Oxfam International Study, wealth of richest 62 persons risen by 44 per cent in 2010. In 2010, the 388 richest people owned the same wealth as the poorest 50 per cent. This dropped to 80 in 2014 before falling again in 2015 to 62.[36] This is the outcome of global economy. Global economy has simply failed when so many have so little and so few have so much, the Democratic Candidate, Bernie Sanders during his primary campaign in the USA remarked. Disparity between rich and poor is increasing as stated above.

There is an urgent need to concentrate on education and health, and to provide employment. Regular special recruitment drives to fill up vacant posts to OBCs, SCs, and STs in government jobs should be taken seriously. Reservation Cells and Liaison Officers to take care of the welfare of SCs, STs, and OBCs in Government ministries and departments should be rejuvenated.

I am of firm conviction that Indian Parliament is making all out efforts to fulfil the commitment made by the founding fathers of Indian Constitution, including Ambedkar, in fulfilling the hopes and aspirations of people, through its multifaceted initiatives. One cannot overlook the stupendous contribution being made by the Committee System in further Parliamentary democracy and ensuring good governance to the people of our country. Hence, I would say with authority that Parliament is contributing to the national interest in its own way.

Discussions in Parliament, without any iota of doubt, helped in finding out solutions. There is a need to relook at everything we are pursuing. Efforts should be made to change the system and mindset through Parliamentary initiatives. Efforts should also be made to make Parliamentary debates and interventions more effective. As enumerated in detail, Parliament through its many initiatives over the last six decades has invariably served the national interests, which includes ensuring social justice to disadvantageous sections of society but also in combating inequalities.

END NOTES

1. *Ambedkar and Constitution* by Dharam C. Vyas, pp. 236. Chapter 7 – Dr. Ambedkar and the Constitution (Cyber Tech Publications: New Delhi: 2014)
2. http://en.wikipedia.org/wiki/Globalisation_in_India, Retrieved on 8.7.2016.
3. http://en.wikipedia.org/wiki/Reservation_in_India, accessed on 3.18.2010
4. Ibid.
5. http://www.legalservicesIndia.com/article/article/dr-b-r-ambedkar-the-father-of-Indian-constitution-1609-1.html 5.7.2016.
6. Ibid.
7. Profile of Dr. Bhimrao Ramji Ambedkar by Lok Sabha Secretariat.
8. http://en.wikipedia.org/wiki/Social_Justice, Accessed on 3.5.2009.
9. Jatava, D.R., *Social Justice (In Indian Perspective)* p.208.
10. Jatava, D.R., *Social Justice (In Indian Perspective)* p.207.
11. Eleventh Five Year Plan (2007-12) – Inclusive Growth, Vol. 1, Chapter VI – Social Justice.
12. http://en.wikipedia.org/wiki/Social_Justice, Accessed on 3.5.2009.

13. Jatava, D.R., *Social Justice (In Indian Perspective)* p.122.
14. Ibid. p.207.
15. Jatava, D.R., *Social Justice (In Indian Perspective)* p.207.
16. http://164.100.47.132/Synop/16/VI/Sup+Synopsis-26-11-2015.pdf Retrieved on 8.7.2016.
17. http://164.100.47.132/Synop/16/VI/Sup+Synopsis-26-11-2015.pdf Retrieved on 8.7.2016.
18. http://164.100.47.132/Synop/16/VI/Sup+Synopsis-26-11-2015.pdf, Retrieved on 8.7.2016.
19. http://164.100.47.132/Synop/16/VI/Sup+Synopsis-26-11-2015.pdf, Retrieved on 8.7.2016.
20. http://164.100.47.132/Synop/16/VI/3Sup+2Sup+Sup+Synopsis-27-11-2015.pdf, Retrieved on 8.7.2016.
21. Ibid.
22. http://164.100.47.132/Synop/16/VI/3Sup+2Sup+Sup+Synopsis-27-11-2015.pdf, Retrieved on 8.7.2016
23. http://164.100.47.132/Synop/16/VI/3Sup+2Sup+Sup+Synopsis-27-11-2015.pdf, Retrieved on 8.7.2016
24. *The Pioneer,* 7.12.2015.
25. *The Indian Express,* 7.12.2015.
26. http://164.100.47.132/Synop/16/VI/3Sup+2Sup+Sup+Synopsis-27-11-2015.pdf, Retrieved on 8.7.2016.
27. *The Millennium Post,* dated 17.6.2016.
28. *The Millennium Post,* dated 17.6.2016.
29. 'PM Vows to fulfil Ambedkar's Vision' in *The Pioneer,* 7.12.2015.
30. *The Pioneer, 27.11.2015.*
31. Ibid.
32. *Tribune,* 28.8.2015.
33. *The Economic times,* 27.11.2015.
34. *The Indian Express,* April 9, 2016.
35. Profile of Dr. Bhimrao Ramji Ambedkar by the Lok Sabha Secretariat.
36. https://www.theguardian.com/business/2016/jan/18/richest-62-billionaires-wealthy-half-world-population-combined, Retrieved on 8.7.2016.

18

Globalisation and Human Rights in a Welfare State: Some Reflections on Ambedkar's Perspective

Suresh R

A welfare state is a government that completely looks after the welfare of its citizens. Such a government provides for its citizens' physical, material and social needs rather than the people providing for their own needs. The purpose of the welfare state is to create greater economic equality or to ensure at least a certain minimum standard of living for all citizens. However as a result of Globalisation the state has been compelled to withdraw from welfare activities. Thus Globalisation is one of the great challenges for the politics and economics of the welfare states.

In a developing country the prevailing social and economic inequality further get augmented with the accelerated pace of Globalisation which in turn causes unrest in the society. In the realm of human rights the Globalisation process helps the protection and promotion of civil and political rights. However the social and economic rights get neglected as a result of withdrawal of the state from initiating welfare as well as corrective measures towards economic equality. In this context the apprehension raised by the Chairman of the Constitution drafting committee on the eve of adoption of the Indian

Constitution about the incongruence between the gross social and economic inequality on the one hand and political equality on the other is still valid. This paper is an attempt to examine Globalisation and human rights in a welfare state through Ambedkar perspective.

Globalisation and its Political Dimension

No single universally agreed definition of Globalisation exists. However, Globalisation may be defined as the expansion of economic activities across political boundaries of nation state. It refers to as a process of increasing economic integration and growing economic interdependence between countries in the world economy. It is associated with not only increasing cross border movement of goods and services, capital, technology, information and people but with an organisation of economic activities, which saddles national boundaries. It is also defined as a process of integrating domestic economy with global economy.

When we look into the political dimension of Globalisation, it appears as a process through which sovereign nation states are crisscrossed and undermined by transnational actors with varying prospects of power, orientation, identities and network. The sovereign nation states today appear to share the stage of world politics with other actors. A system of overlapping authority and multiple loyalties seem to exist at the global politics. It appears that nation states have come to share their authority over their citizens and their ability to command their loyalties on the one hand with regional and world authority, and on the other hand with sub national authorities to such an extent that the concept of sovereignty cease to exist.

There is divergent perception about Globalisation. [1] This can be well represented in a table.

	Globalist	Critics of Globalist
Concepts	One world	Internationalisation not Globalisation Regionalism
Power	Erosion of state Sovereignty Decline of nation states Rise of multilateralism	The nation state rules Inter-governmentalism
Culture	Emergence of global popular culture Erosion of fixed Political Identities	Resurgence of nationalism and national identity

	Globalist	Critics of Globalist
Economy	Global informational Capitalism The transnational economy A new global division of labour	Development of regional blocs New Imperialism
Order	Multi layered global governance Global Civil Society Global Polity Cosmopolitanism	International society of states Political conflict between states Persists International governance and geopolitics

Globalisation: A Reality

Whether we like it or not Globalisation process has become a reality today. In this circumstances it would be interesting to look into the role of state in the Globalisation process, welfare state and Globalisation process, how a state transform from planned system to open market economy.

On the question of role of state in the Globalisation process one can certainly point to examples where Globalisation constraints on national policy choices. State has only minimal role in the Globalisation process, especially in developing countries. The developing countries, in order to cope with the changes, which are taking place at the global level, in the socio-economic and political fields, accelerate the process of Globalisation, as they have limited options before them. In the long run the developed world stand benefit from the Globalisation process as they acquire new markets in the developing countries with their superior technology and capital for investment. Their investment is mainly in the production of consumer durables, which in turn siphon out the resources of the developing world. Further, when the process of liberalization and privatization, gain momentum because of Globalisation, the role of state declines.

Globalisation and Human Rights

The Globalisation process has brought about some important consequences for the enjoyment of human rights. We can broadly classify human rights as civil and political rights, and economic, social and cultural rights. The civil and political rights have greatly strengthened in many countries. As a consequence of the Globalisation process the contemporary phenomenon such as privatization, deregulation, structural adjustment programme and related pressures from international financial institution and developed countries have adverse effects on the enjoyment of economic and social rights of the citizens of the developing countries.

During the cold war period the interdependence of civil and political rights on the one hand and the economic, social and cultural rights on the other was a constant bone of contention both between East and West and between North and South. All governments continued to pay lip service to the notion that two sets of rights are interdependent, indivisible, and interrelated. The UN human rights organs have regularly endorsed the proposition.[2]

Just as carefully targeted policies and eternal vigilance are necessary to ensure respect for civil and political rights, so too is it essential that specific policies, programmes be devised and implemented by any government which aim to ensure the respect of economic, social, and cultural rights to its citizens.[3] Now the question is how far the state could play a leading role in ensuring the economic, social and cultural rights of its citizen, as Globalisation put some constraints on national policy choices.

Further it appears that a genuine democratic system and generation of relatively high level of per capita income are sufficient evidence of comprehensive respect for human rights, is fallacious. The world conference on human rights (1993) in its report shows that in many countries the basic economic, social and cultural rights of large number of their citizens were denied. High infant mortality rates a significant incidence of hunger or malnutrition, mass unemployment, large scale homelessness, and high dropout rates from educational institution are all indication of violation of economic, social and cultural rights and hence human rights.[4]

When market goes too far in dominating social and political outcomes, the opportunities and rewards of Globalisation spread unequally and inequitably, concentrating power and wealth in a selected group of people, nation and corporation by marginalizing others, the respect for human rights is sacrificed. Inequality between countries has increased the income gap between the fifth of the world's people living in the richest countries and the fifth in the poorest was 30 to 1 in 1960, 60 to 1 in 1990 and 74 to 1 in 1997. [5]

By the late 1990's the fifth of the world's people living in the highest income countries had 86 per cent of the world GDP (Gross Domestic Product) the bottom fifth just 1 per cent; 82 per cent world export market the bottom fifth just 1 percent; 68 per cent of direct investment the fifth just 1 per cent. Again, the OECD (Organisation for Economic Cooperation and Development) countries with 1 per cent of the global population have 71 per cent of the global trade in goods and services; 58 per cent of foreign direct investment and 91 per cent of all internet users.[6] The gross economic inequality prevalent at the global level is also well reflected in a developing welfare state like India.

Welfare State and Social, Economic Equality

A welfare state is a government that completely looks after the welfare of its citizens. Such a government provides for its citizens' physical, material and social needs rather than the people providing for their own needs. The purpose of the welfare state is to create greater economic equality or to ensure at least a certain minimum standard of living for all citizens. A welfare state provides education, housing, sustenance and healthcare for its citizens. It also provides benefits such as pensions and unemployment insurance, and it provides equal wages through price and wage controls. This type of government provides public transportation, childcare, social amenities such as public transport and libraries as well as many other goods and services. Some of these things are paid for through government insurance programs, and others are paid for by taxes. Moreover, acceptance of welfare state is recognition of social rights of everyone to have a fair share of the fruits of growth in society and an incentive to develop a sense of solidarity with the rest of the society.

If we look into the economic situation of a welfare state like India it is demonstrated that it has achieved an annual growth rate of eight per cent in GDP however poverty, illiteracy malnutrition still exist in the society. Though India is a welfare state the disparity between rich and poor is widening in an alarming rate. According to government of India's estimation nearly thirty per cent of the population still lives below poverty line. The development based displacement of people from their native land, and denial of land for cultivation are violations of human rights. Mainly the corporate sector is involved in activities which are detrimental to the smooth conduct of society in a welfare state. At times the activities of the corporate sector adversely affect the enjoyment of human rights of the underprivileged section in the society.

Caste System in India and Social Inequality

Even before India got its independence, Mahatma Gandhi launched his political career through Satyagraha or truthful struggle, against racist policies in South Africa. In 1946, India was the first country to raise its voice against apartheid at the UN, and played a leading role in its abolition. The Indian Constitution prohibits discrimination on grounds of religion, race, caste, sex or place of birth, and affirms the right to equality, including equality before law, and equality of opportunity in matters of employment as fundamental rights. The Indian Criminal Code and the Indian Penal Code contain provisions which prohibit racial discrimination and dissemination of ideas which promote disharmony on various grounds including race.

In the international area India played an active part in the drafting of the International Convention on the Elimination of all forms of Racial Discrimination and was among its early signatories. India considers that besides theories of racial superiority, that are a legacy of the colonial period, the other sources and causes of racism and racial discrimination must be addressed.

Caste System in India—Is it Apartheid?

Although India championed the cause of apartheid in all international forums apartheid like social stigma, caste system is still prevalent in India. Although the caste system has been abolished in India formally, it is practiced in the Indian society informally still. In the prevailing social hierarchy in India, the lower castes are treated inferior. The slow pace of social mobility in the Indian social system shows that caste determines one's social status in the society. The effects of caste system and the practice of apartheid policy are same. The only difference is that while apartheid policy had the official support, caste system has only the informal or societal support. Thus, with regard to the effects caste system in Indian society, and the apartheid or racial discrimination practiced by the Whites in South Africa, there is much similarity between these two social evils. The existing apartheid like caste system in the Indian society is one of the major hurdles to accomplish social equality in India and the protection and promotion of human rights of the backward classes.

Conclusion

Globalisation is especially one of the great challenges for the politics and economics of the welfare states. When the economy is opened for free trade a specific social group will be adversely affected. Every change in domestic policy of nations produces winners and losers in the society. Again, the privileged strata produced by the welfare state become powerful defendants of status quo. They oppose any move towards Globalisation. The deeper social policy structure are embedded in interest groups and the more political parties have internalized the welfare state ambition of the privileged strata the higher are the hurdles for Globalisation in a welfare state. Again the transition from planned system to open market economy becomes more difficult in a democratic country. This is mainly because in a democratic country the privileged majority always resists any major change in the economy and no political party can ignore the privileged majority. Further, the economic reforms in a developing country would be a difficult task. For in the developed west the economic revolution preceded the political revolution whereas in the developing world the political revolution preceded the economic one. The economic reforms in a democratic country with an unstable economy would be difficult compared to economic reforms in a democratic country with a relatively stable economy. Thus the welfare states in the developing world are in a vicious circle. The more they move towards the process of economic reforms, the more political instability which in turn further worsen their economy.

The Globalisation process has brought about some important consequences for the enjoyment of human rights. The civil and political rights have greatly strengthened in many countries. As a consequence of the Globalisation process the contemporary phenomenon such as privatization, deregulation, structural adjustment programme and related pressures from international financial institution have had adverse effects on the enjoyment of economic and social rights of the citizens of the developing countries. The welfare states in the developing economy are thus in a vicious circle. The more they move towards accelerated pace of Globalisation, the more economic instability, and the more economic instability, the more political instability and *vice versa*.

It appears that the apprehensions raised by B.R. Ambedkar on the eve of the adoption of the Indian Constitution regarding the social and economic inequality are still relevant. He said "On the 26th of January 1950, we are going to enter into a life of contradictions. In politics we will have equality and in social and economic life we will have inequality. In politics we will be recognizing the principle of one man one vote and one vote one value. In our social and economic life, we shall, by reason of our social and economic structure, continue to deny the principle of one man one value. How long shall we continue to live this life of contradictions? How long shall we continue to deny equality in our social and economic life? If we continue to deny it for long, we will do so only by putting our political democracy in peril. We must remove this contradiction at the earliest possible moment or else those who suffer from inequality will blow up the structure of political democracy which this Assembly has to laboriously built up."

END NOTES

1. Suresh. R, The Political Dimension of Globalisation: A Human Rights Perspective, in Dr Mohanakumar (Ed.) Globalisation, State and Democracy in India, Serials Publications, New Delhi, April 2016 ISBN: 9788183873550, pp 103-12.
2. Suresh R. Human Security in India: Problems and Policy Options, International Journal of South Asian Studies Vol. 5 No. 2 July-Dec 2012 ISSN 0974 – 2514
3. Suresh R. Foreign Policy and Human Rights: An Indian Perspective, Madhav Books, Gurgaon, 2009 ISBN 978-81-907891-1-0
4. UN Doc.E1993/22
5. UNDP Report 1999
6. Ibid.

19

Ambedkar and Gandhi's Revolt against Hindu Social Order and Depressed Class: A Comparative Analysis

Tridib Chakaborti and Pratyay Dutta

The influence of Babasaheb Ambedkar and Gandhi's on nationalist India are well-known. They all through their entire life wanted total freedom and upliftment of the Indian masses, i.e., their material and moral advancement. In the pre and post-independence period, Ambedkar divided Indians into two classes, the rich-the upper class and the poor-the lower class. The former constituted the overwhelming majority of our people and he referred to them as the 'masses'. Ambedkar was never tired of drawing the attention of the youth of our country towards the urgent need to work for the betterment of their condition. He also laid down a positive programme for this work. Besides this, both Ambedkar and Gandhi wanted a radical cure for the chronic distress of our people. They were not for keeping up the status quo of the Indian society, but at the same time, wanted a complete overhaul of the whole thing.

In the history of modern Indian political thought, Bhimrao Ramji Ambedkar and Mohandas Karamchand Gandhi, more commonly known as 'Mahatma' (meaning 'Great Soul') were leading front runner of Indian politics and the builders of modern India with a contemporary eye. Their continuous struggle for the cause of humanity was indeed measured not in terms of the 20th century but will remain forever in the chronicles of history. Both were an original thinker, a unique leader and above all a true rebel and played an important part in the awakening of modern India. They were not ivory tower philosophers, rather political scientists in modern sense of the term. Both were essentially a man of people and action. To them, the greatest fact in the history of mankind is not what the common people achieves materially but the growth of their soul from age to age in its true search for the moral truth and wisdom. They also thought that, those who takes part in the adventure of the soul-searching process gradually secures an ever-lasting place in the annals of world history and movement. In the archives of world history, the greatness of Gandhi and Ambedkar exist not only in their heroic struggle for India's freedom, but also for their total insistence on the creative power of the soul. Although, Gandhi and Ambedkar were mainly responsible for the overall mighty upheaval of Indian nation which broke its old chains of tyranny on the basis of relentless national movements within the country, at the same time, their way of thinking process and method of ethical and social revolution were palpably unique. Ambedkar, while discovering his own social philosophy never called himself a Marxist and he did not proclaim himself as an anti-Marxist either. In the course of time, he however, made a deep study of the ideas of Karl Marx and other the then socialist thinkers in Europe and America. In fact, Ambedkar came in close touch with Gandhi and in his way of action, was deeply influenced by Gandhi's ideals, ethics, values and methods, etc. Ambedkar considered Gandhi's ideas of civil resistance and non-cooperation method as an original creation of the 20th century. As long as Gandhi was alive, Ambedkar hoped for an overall socialistic transformation of the Indian National Congress (INC). Later on, after Gandhi's sudden assassination, he despaired of the then Congress party which at that time transformed it totally on the basis of ideological differences cropped up within the party. Therefore, as a symbol of protest, Ambedkar agreed to leave the then Congress party in order to build up a progressive and dynamic alternative to it within the country. During these crucial hours, Ambedkar thought that Congress gradually had become a *status quo* Party and to him, only a progressive alternative of it could bring about a thorough radical change in the then Indian society. While Ambedkar laid great stress on resistance to evil, at the same breathe, he felt the sole importance of constructive activity under Gandhian influence. Moreover, he knew very well that politics is inseparable from power hunger and that the question of mere power cannot be evaded easily. At the same pace, he was very much clear in his mind that no fundamental transformation is possible unless state power is overtly controlled, guided and above all tamed by people's power. In this case his idea was quite similar with Jayaprakash Narayan, who always believed in the people's power and mass action towards nation building process. The purpose of the article is to highlight a comparative analysis between Ambedkar and Gandhi, against the backdrop of the Indian value system, which influenced and moulded their style of leadership in the movements against untouchability and caste system within Indian society. This article also briefly undertakes to review their voices against these chronic evils inherent in the then Indian society and therefore an attempt has been made for a better way to overcome these planted social ills.

As a true enlightener, Ambedkar and Gandhi both were an ardent champion of the basic education of the common people and wholeheartedly demanded that the colonialists with all their orthodox spiritual education should be kept away from the sphere of public education. Besides this, they fervently criticised religious fanaticism and regarded it as an obstacle in the way of vital human progress. Characterising Ambedkar's ideas of enlightenment, it must be specially stressed here that his decisive features towards his whole socio-political philosophy, were a steadfast faith in people for their great constructive powers, and an ardent love for the working masses, sympathy for their wants and sufferings, and above all a passionate urge in order to free them from colonial and social oppression, etc. Dividing the Indian society into two categories of classes i.e. the higher, that is the rich, and the lower, that is the working people—Ambedkar always worked for total resurrection of Indian people pinned all his hopes on the latter. As a social reformer, both stood for liberty, equality and free thinking and most importantly criticised educated Indians for not devoting their much needed time and energy in order to uplift the poor and ignorant of India. It is not a matter of doubt that, Ambedkar as well as Gandhi had a profound faith on the idea of nation building in India. It is a fact that, Vivekananda preceded Ambedkar in being vocal about caste discrimination and was clairvoyant about its remedies as well as the pitfalls which may arise for those who want to cure it. Subsequently, Vivekananda's discussion on caste discrimination predated Ambedkar to tread the same path and in this case, their views were almost the same, with the crucial difference that Vivekananda wanted to make the modification from within by the change of inner being, while Ambedkar wanted to make the change by rejecting entirely by the then Indian socio-political system. Moreover, Ambedkar and Gandhi entirely desired a thorough modernisation of India along with the removal of abject poverty and degradation of the Indian people. Their theories of social change, that is why were mostly grounded on the Indian perception of history and simultaneously, were a true champion of Indian nationalism. In the quest for socio-political doctrines of Ambedkar and Gandhi, the resurrection and emancipation of Indian people were attuned with the awakening of Shudras and Workers-peasants within the fold of political power. Therefore, they were opposed to exploitation of all kinds prevailing in India during that time and denounced the Indian class character of civilisation process. They finally wanted to uplift the Indian masses and wished to witness in them the fountain of hope in order to strengthen future India. In the 20th century, it was a New India they wanted to build up on the basis of equality, fraternity, respect, solidarity, etc.

Ambedkar and Gandhi both were firm believers in the search for economic equality, not absolute equality but the maximum possible attainable equality and pleaded for the equalitarian drive of modern civilisation. At the same time, they fervently disliked the exploitative aspect of world capitalism. While building his own socio-political philosophy, Ambedkar was not unappreciative of what the Communist societies really did to certify the minimum consumption needs and social security guarantees for the common people of this land. Subsequently, he detested the over centralisation, violence and suppression of mind couched in the so called Communist system. Ambedkar's major criticism of both the systems was that these ideologies subscribed to the self-centred ideals of an ever-increasing material standard of living within the frontiers of Euro-American-Communist national states and not to the notion of a decent standard of living for all mankind. In this context, Ambedkar as well as Gandhi was a formidable champion of social equality. Ambedkar held that the caste system and the hierarchical order based on birth, etc. were the single most central factor for the decline of this great nation and its repeated subjection to external aggression and foreign rule. So, Ambedkar launched a 'destroy caste' movement throughout the country. In a traditionally unequal society like India, he felt that equality cannot be established by merely providing some equal opportunities to all. In the post-independence scenario, he pleaded that the backward classes, women, harijans, adivasis and the retarded among the minorities should have to be given special opportunities to bring them up on the social ladder as compare to the level of the advanced within Indian society. Like Rammanohar Lohia, Ambedkar was totally opposed to the propagation of a feudalistic language as a medium of instruction and administration. Moreover, he was also opposed to any feudal forms of dress and lavish residential buildings across India and held that the existence of these privileges was only the other side of the dire misery and poverty of the common people. In fact, apart from Gandhi, no other leader has put so much intonation and effort on man-woman equality within the country. After India achieved its independence, Ambedkar always encouraged women to play an active role not only in politics but in every walk of life. In this case to upgrade their standard of living, he had deep sympathy for their entire cause. In 1952, in one of his public speech, he highlighted the terrible problems of village women who fetch water from long distances, and have to make all the household chores without proper sanitation and smoke-free fuel. Ambedkar maintained that as long as there remains massive injustice along with unequal relation between the white one-third and the coloured two-thirds of the world, neither can armaments be abolished nor permanent peace be established over this small earth. Later on, he emphasised that after the invention of lethal nuclear weapons, a saturation point has been reached towards the development of world history and thereby the method of armed revolution had become gradually irrelevant. Under Gandhian influence, Ambedkar considered civil disobedience and non-violent resistance as the sovereign remedy of the 20th century. In the history of the Indian nationalist movement, both Gandhi and Ambedkar were well aware that a vast majority of our people live in countryside. So, to bolster the national movement throughout the country, the vast majority of our common people could become an active symbol of aspirations of the poor peasants, the landless people and agricultural labourers, etc. Like a true nationalist, both Gandhi and Ambedkar, who not only advocated the primary need for a fundamental recording of the then social relations based on an equalitarian drive but also provided an instant ideological basis for this revolutionary transformation within the purview of Indian society. In fact, in due course of time, they also wanted the speedy consummation of the anti-imperialist and anti-colonial revolution-struggle around the globe and during the post-independence years, both had their true support towards the anti-imperialist movements of Asia, Africa and Latin American countries, etc.

In the annals of social movements of India, among those who vastly contributed towards the social advancement of the Harijans, Gandhi and Ambedkar were the most prime leaders of their time. In this context, the former came from a caste of *Vaishya* status, while the later was born into an untouchable caste; the former approached the problem from the standpoint of an upper caste Hindu who wanted to rot out untouchability from the fabric of society, while the latter identified himself with the struggle against the exploitation which the untouchables had suffered under the upper caste Hindus over the centuries. Gandhi, as a believer in Hinduism, felt that the system badly needed to be reformed of the excrescence of untouchability. Ambedkar, on the contrary, was convinced that the problem was a part of Hinduism which was enshrined in its sacred scriptures. It is our own hypothesis that the ideological differences between Gandhi and Ambedkar were not merely from personal approaches. In this context, even today, they continue to be debated within the purview of Indian society. Both Ambedkar as well as Gandhi was totally dedicated to the broad ideals of social and economic equality and at the same time, they were firm opponent of statism. Like J.S. Mill, they valued privacy and freedom of an individual in a liberalised society and detested the pretension of the state to control over every aspect of national life. In this case, Ambedkar held that freedom of dissent and freedom of expression was an undividable aspect of the humanitarian struggle. He was greatly moved by the misuse of Sections 107-109 of the Criminal Procedure Code as designed by the British Government and later continued by the then Indian Government against the poor and helpless of India. Afterwards, he exposed the racket of fulfillment of fixed quotas for arrests under these sections and he raised his voice against these draconian sections the MISA of the poor people. This resulted in that he tirelessly continued to fight for civil liberties in the courts as well as outside for the depressed and oppressed people of India and he sued a case against these injustices. Finally, the Supreme Court of India gave two decisions in his favour which undoubtedly constituted an important landmark in the struggle for human freedom.

In the history of freedom struggle directory of India, both Ambedkar and Gandhi remained the great patriot and also possessed a world mind. Ambedkar wanted to raise his country from the endless squalor and misery; and thereby sought to establish permanent friendship with other sections of the human race around the globe. Ambedkar's fraternal feeling was devoid of any dross of the so-called cosmopolitanism. The basic foundation of Ambedkar's as well as Gandhi's concept of the unity of the human race was their abiding love for *Bharatmata* and they subscribed to the novel concept of the citizenship of the mind, citizenship of ideals without the mere restrictiveness of nationality or race, etc. In the cause of the people's movement of India, Ambedkar and Gandhi had a spiritual bond with the poor, those who were the neglected-dejected and the exploited. On the eve of the freedom movement of India, they became the source of inspiration to the countless young turkeys of our country. They always encouraged the young people to forge ahead and to show their mettle braving all the prevailing odds. Therefore, in a nutshell, Ambedkar and Gandhi shared this endearing quality with other socialist veterans like Narendra Deva and Jayaprakash Narayan respectively. In the pages of the modern Indian socio-political thinkers of our times, such as M.K. Gandhi, M.N. Roy, B.R. Ambedkar, Sri Aurobindo, and above all Narendra Deva, who belonged to that period of nationalist struggle when the efforts for liberation struggle of India had reached into its pinnacle? During that time, the Indian national struggle had passed through its moderate period and later on, gradually entered towards the decisive-extremist stage of 'do' or 'die' for the attainment of *swaraj* (self-rule). During that era, the freedom movement, with all its varying degrees of pressures, wanted to throw off its old shackles and trying to lay the rudimentary foundations of self-governance within the country. At that time, among the host of Indian political leaders who were fighting for the cause of independence struggle, it is important to mention a few, though the sacrifices of numerous others can neither be denied nor ignored. These few were—Sri Aurobindo Ghosh, Gandhi, B.R. Ambedkar and M.N. Roy, et al—because not only they fought for the country's liberation struggle but also established their socio-political doctrines for the betterment of the common masses.

Ambedkar and Gandhi were the redeemer of the depressed, weak and the backward sections of our society and simultaneously unfolded the main virtues i.e., honesty, sobriety, justice, equality and freedom applicable for an Indian socio-political scenario. In their entire life, Ambedkar as well as Gandhi always stood for people's total freedom, equality and fraternity in the social order and at the same time, they acquired an immense knowledge and ability to combat against all the prevalent orthodox forces within the Indian society. Subsequently, in the post-independence years, Ambedkar was the sole creator of constitutional rights for those who were repellently deprived, and to ascertain these rights for Indian people, he unstintingly led many agitations to establish civic rights for the untouchables. In 1952, in a public lecture, the latter demanded their legitimate representation in the legislature, executive and judiciary sector respectively. In the study of modern Indian political thought, both Ambedkar as well as Gandhi was not a policy-maker in the Machiavellian sense, but they did what their knowledge taught them for the time being and always put logic and temper in the history of mankind. Ambedkar used the term 'social justice' to denote that the organisation of society would be thoroughly based on the principles of equality, liberty and justice, and also for the preferential treatment for the weaker sections of Indian society. According to Ambedkar, such classes must be needed to prevent discrimination among them and in this process they must be provided with the basic constitutional rights. In the making for the constitutional rights of the poor, Ambedkar played a great role, especially in regards to the provisions relating to the Fundamental Rights and the Directive Principles of State policy. In this case, Gandhi's reforms were basically confined to make people enough burly with the power of soul-force and also to let them aware of their own rights and duties, and finally, to launch non-violent Satyagraha movement against prevailing unjust laws and policies within the country. Besides, throughout his life Gandhi believed that ultimately truth and non-violence would have to be the guiding principles not only for individuals but also for thorough institutional changes and policy implementation of the country. Subsequently, at the institutional and policy levels of India, Gandhi unquestionably suggested democratic ethics-values and constructive-welfare programmes so as to make the Indian society as dynamic as possible. In this context, under the influence of *Bhagvad Gita*, Gandhi's reforms were to be worked for three levels: *individual*, *institutional* and *policy*. It is a fact that Gandhi's whole political philosophy was a corollary to his own religious, social and moral philosophy and during his long political career, he attempted to apply this moral and ethical truth on the question of social and political life of the country. Gandhi also stressed that participation in politics was like an unavoidable evil, and yet he tried to introduce religion-spirituality into the ambit of modern Indian politics. As a true spiritual enlightener of the country, he was not only a saint but also a revolutionary in true sense, saint in so far as he stood for overall spiritualization of individual life, and a revolutionary in so far as he worked through *satya* and non-violence. While formulating his whole social-political ideas, Gandhi was always for a well-knit society with unity made up from diversities around the globe and in the application of using his methods; Gandhi employed the techniques such as *Satyagraha* and *Ahimsa* of mass action as a means. The philosophical foundation of Ambedkar's patriotism started with the upliftment of the downtrodden and the poor of our country. He fought for their fair share of equality and constitutional rights. His idea about patriotism was not only confined to the overall abolition of colonialism around the globe, but time and again he addressed the issue of freedom everywhere for every individual. For him, freedom without equality along with democracy and equality without freedom could lead to an absolute dictatorship all over the world. At the same time, Ambedkar and Gandhi both remained a great champion of democracy. For them, democracy was more than a form of Government and above all it was form of social organisation. Consequently, they believed that in a democracy, revolutionary changes in the economic and social life of the people to be brought about without total bloodshed. In this context, Gandhi and Ambedkar argued for giving justice to all, especially to those who have been denied justice for centuries and to them, right done for those wrongs, is justice. This was the true spirit behind Ambedkar and Gandhi's concept of justice. Their concept of social justice thoroughly advocated for a social system which was entirely based on true relation between man and man; i.e., caste and caste as well as class and class.

A Blend of Religion and Politics: An Equalitarian

The whole narratives of Ambedkar and Gandhi's life were a continuous evolution, or a journey, from slavery to freedom, inequality to equality and above all, injustice to justice. The main theme of Ambedkar as well as Gandhi's social and political thought and action was centered on the paradox of identity and inclusiveness, and how personal identities, which were necessarily plural, merged in an inclusive community growth for the purpose of common good.[1] In this case, while building the human force in social movements, they both found the resolution of this paradox in universally shared values of love and compassion all through the globe. The search for identity that was inclusive and not decisive remained the starting point of their overall social and political endeavours. In this reference, their political goals were quite similar in pattern, if not identical to each other. In the theory building process, they both proclaimed, it would be conflict-free, inclusive community where love and morality should prevail in Indian society.[2] The socio-political context of their sole action and thought was different, although they were contemporaries who lived in the same country. In the quest for political freedom of India, Ambedkar always placed India's freedom in the larger context towards the destiny of the human race and he used to maintain that India has to be free in any kind of subjection in order to play its role for the emancipation of the human race. Here, we can say that with regard to individual's freedom, Gandhi always advocated for spiritual freedom.[3] Gandhi was a nationwide leader because he made the Congress movement as the nationalist movement and simultaneously, turned the national movement of India into a constructive mass movement. In this context, Ambedkar's foremost endeavour was social emancipation of depressed classes from their so called exploiters in India. In as much as social and political issues impact to each other are that here, one finds Gandhi, the political leader, involved in social reforms, and Ambedkar, the social activist-crusader, engaged in the politics of the then Indian Governance. However, the primacy of their distinct commitments was the establishment of an inclusive community within India which would be governed by the universal values of love, and compassion where both were influenced by the teachings of Buddhist ideology.[4]

As a social crusader, both Ambedkar and Gandhi always aimed at engaging the mind of the Indian people and subsequently, to understand the mindset of the depressed people in order to replace of their motive of thoughts and old behaviour patterns. At the same time, they wanted to lift their sight high in the direction of unity to liberate them through the power of education and spirituality. In the study of modern Indian political thought, Ambedkar was not simply satisfied with just having a new objective of his social philosophy and he wanted it to be the operating and controlling device in the overall development of an individual's social life to see the massive growth of mental faculties of man.[5] Besides this, he was truly a practical man and dedicated his entire life to the service and emancipation of the downtrodden and the weaker sections of the Indian society. Interestingly enough, Ambedkar as well as Gandhi was a liberator of the downtrodden. Subsequently, their socio-politic views with regard to social justice stemmed from their total understanding of the then Indian society which was entirely based on hierarchical caste system, ultimately leading to the enormous plight of the Dalits. Later on, whatever he fought for, co-operated with, revolted against and contributed to, his was the only theme i.e., the service of suffering humanity in its totality. In this context, his valuable teachings were quite similar with Lord Buddha. Alongside, the philosophies of Gandhi and Ambedkar were directly related to secular humanistic outlook which was closely linked with liberal education system and religious inspiration of non-theistic nature.[6]

In his socio-political ideas, Gandhi wholeheartedly advocated for a morally-based and ethics-oriented politics, an overall decentralised polity starting from individual onward to a duty-based scheme of rights and finally, a state with minimum functions. While building his own economic ideas for the country, he initiated the idea of *trusteeship*, *swadeshi*, and above all an indigenised socialism where the basic needs of human beings are to be taken care of, and lastly, a decentralized economy which is far more self-reliant with its sole direction towards an all-inclusive community growth. At the same breathe, Gandhi thought that religion-oriented politics served humanity in its true form and such a politics helped men to lead a better life and emphasises that the more purified a political activity, the more it would serve the people and the nation.[7] Gandhi as well as Ambedkar espoused this philosophy of inclusiveness and thereby abhorred the politics of divisiveness. Their idea of philosophical inclusiveness was one, where the individual and society should be regarded as reflective to each other. In this context, their ideas were quite analogous to each other when they uttered that an individual's self-image, his goals and aspirations is to be reflected in society and vice-versa. In 1955, in one of his public statements where Ambedkar said that, what is good for the individual is also good for the society, and vice-versa. During that crucial juncture, Buddhism, as interpreted by Ambedkar, and Hinduism by Gandhi, clearly deciphered the above mentioned views of inclusiveness.[8] Both Ambedkar and Gandhi deeply studied the history of human relationship under Marxian bend within the purview of Indian society and pragmatically realised the deformation of religion which plagued the nation during that time.[9]

Ambedkar and Gandhi's View on the Origin of Caste System

Ambedkar was of the opinion that the Caste system of the Hindu society which ultimately led to inequality. Caste system breeds inequality and inequality leads to the exploitation of the shudras. Emerging from the *Varna* system and from the Hindu scripts—the *Manusmriti*, the Bhagvad Gita, the *Ramayana*, the *Mahabharata*, the caste system created the caste ladder, indulged in high-handedness towards the shudras, and forced them to live as untouchables and outcastes. Subsequently, Ambedkar's patriotism started with the upliftment of the downtrodden and the poor. He fought for their equality and rights. His ideas about patriotism was not only confined to the abolition of colonialism, but also addressed the issue of freedom for every individual. For him freedom without equality as well as democracy and equality without freedom could lead to absolute dictatorship. Dr. Ambedkar works, among others, includes *Annihilation of Caste* (1935); *Federation vs. Freedom* (1939), *Mr. Gandhi and the Emancipation of the Untouchables* (1942), *Ranade, Gandhi and Jinnah* (1943), *What Congress and Gandhi have done to the Untouchables* (1945), *Who were the Shudras?* (1945), *the Untouchables* (1948), *Buddha and His Dhamma* (1957). Broadly speaking, both Ambedkar and Gandhi were a saviour of the downtrodden. Their views with regard to social justice stem from their understanding of the Indian society based on caste system leading to the plight of the Dalits. They felt that the end of *Varna* system would only help reform the Indian society. It is a fact that they both were unbending to end the stigma of caste system from the roots of Indian society. While emphasizing the impact of caste system in Indian society in the weekly titled *Harijan*, Mahatma Gandhi wrote: "Dr. Ambedkar is bitter. He has every reason to feel so. He has received a liberal education. He has more than the talents of the average educated Indian. Outside India he is received with honour and affection, but, in India, among Hindus, at every step he is reminded that he is one of the out-castes of Hindu society. It is nothing to his shame, for; he has done no wrong to Hindu Society."[10] However, this same piece illustrated one of the fundamental differences between Ambedkar's approach to the caste issue and that of Gandhi. While Ambedkar advocated the complete removal of the very notion of caste, Gandhi focused exclusively on the issue of "untouchability" and argued that caste distinctions themselves didn't need to be removed. Gandhi in another writing clearly mentioned: "It is as wrong to destroy caste because of the out-caste, as it would be to destroy a body because of an ugly growth in it, or of a crop because of the weeds. The outcaste, in the sense we understand it, has, therefore, to be destroyed altogether. It is an excess to be removed, if the whole system is not to perish. Untouchability is the product, therefore, not of the caste system, but of the distinction of high and low that has crept into Hinduism and is corroding it. The attack on untouchability is thus an attack upon this high-and-lowness. The moment untouchability goes, the caste system itself will be purified, that is to say, according to my dream, it will resolve itself into the true *Varnadharma*, the four divisions of society, each complementary of the other and none inferior or superior to any other, each as necessary for the whole body of Hinduism as any other."[11]

Movement Against *Chaturvarnyas* and Caste System

In the 19th century, a great crusader of social equality was Mahatma Jyotiba Phooley who unequivocally carried the movement for social equality in the then Maharashtra and thereby, in 1873, founded *Satyashodak Samaj* (Society of Seekers of Truth).[12] During those crucial hours, Phooley staged a mass revolt against the then tyrannical caste system prevalent in India. Following this, Ambedkar under the profound teaching and inspiration of Phooley, cherished these ideals of society which was entirely based on equality, liberty and fraternity, etc. At the same time, Hindu culture was based on high ideals of non-violence, tolerance, love and above all humanitarian service, though the social life suffered by its inherent contradictions embedded in the then Indian society.[13] According to Gandhi and Ambedkar, the basic ideals of freedom, equality and justice could not be realised practically without the presence of active social life. While finding an answer of this gross disparity inherent in Indian society, Ambedkar prescribed that the gap between theoretical ideals and practical life in the then Hindu society was the main cause of its inexorable weakness and consequent subjugation for centuries,[14] whereas Gandhi envisioned that the Hindu society never remained as an organised system of individuals without a common purpose. There always prevailed dissonance in the name of castes with different rights and purposes within Indian societal periphery. While reiterating this same viewpoint, Ambedkar said, "Hindu society as such does not exist. It is a collection of castes, each caste is conscious of its existence. It is not even a federation."[15]

Gandhi as well as Ambedkar stood for overall equality, justice and freedom to all, regardless of any caste, creed and sex in Indian society. Consequently, they left a permanent inkling on socio-political field of our country and at the same coin, expressed their indelible faith over the existence of our democratic process. Like Earnest Barker, they emphasised that the behavioural patterns of an individual must be governed by the supple principles of liberty, equality and fraternity as a whole. For them, the ideal of fraternity was primarily indispensable in order to unite the people together within the fold of a nation. Ambedkar and Gandhi felt that the Hindu social order did not recognise the principle of equality in its entirety and it also denied fundamental individual freedom. In this reference, according to them, for centuries long the Hindu society was entirely based on graded inequality and the principle of fixity of occupation, regardless of a person's ability and fair quality. Subsequently, in his book *The Movement of Untouchables*, published in 1982, where Ambedkar wrote: "class composition of society is quite based on economic and social consideration and it is a common feature-disease in all societies of the world." [16] In this respect, they believed that, towards the nation building process, political democracy could not be succeeded without proper social and economic democracy. Interestingly enough, in 1951, while attending a political talk-show in America named 'Voice of America' where Ambedkar argued that, "Democracy could not be equated with either republic or Parliamentary form of Government. The roots of democracy lay not in the form of government, Parliamentary or otherwise. A democracy is a model of associated living. The roots of democracy are to be searched in social relationship, in terms of the associated life between the people who form the society."[17] In this context, he clearly reiterated that, in case of gross inequalities prevailing in the Indian society, the state intervention is a must. Moreover, in this talk show in America, therein he also affirmed that, Right to Treatment as an equal, must precede the Right to Equal Treatment as a state policy. At the same coin, he was also aware that, equality of opportunity was definitely a misleading term. Instead of this, he used the term; there should be 'abundant opportunity for equality'. Broadly speaking, Ambedkar and Gandhi, both emphasised on the excessive need for liberty of movement, liberty of speech, liberty of action, and above all, the free need of political liberty in order to choose an individual's government for securing "unalienable rights such as life, liberty and pursuit for happiness."[18] While discovering the impact of Political liberty on Indian society, Ambedkar observed: "Political liberty is really a deduction from the principle of human personality and equality."[19] Subsequently, they admired that, liberty and equality must exist together within Indian society and one without the other was completely absurd. Ambedkar wrote: "As long as you do not achieve social liberty, whatever freedom is provided by the law is of no avail to you."[20]

Critique of Hindu Society and Stride against Atrocities on Untouchables

Ambedkar and Gandhi were of the view that the prevailing caste system in the Hindu society ultimately led to absurd inequality. While reiterating this viewpoint in 1953, in one of his public lecture Ambedkar said: "Caste system breeds inequality and inequality ultimately leads to the total exploitation of the *Shudras*."[21] Ambedkar was opposed to all this processes which ultimately perpetuated caste system in an underdeveloped society like India. During that time, he strongly felt that the end of the *Varna* system would only help to reform and rebuild the then Indian society. In this context, in 1927, at Mahad, while delivering a public lecture, therein he condemned the *Manu Smriti*, for its exaggerated interpretation of Hindu society on the basis of caste hierarchy.[22] In the same event, he opposed the caste system and pointed out its evils in the chronicles of social history of India on the basis of following points:

1. It has been responsible for the decline and downfall of the Hindu society;
2. The *Varna* system, dividing the Hindu society into four classes, he led them into four castes with the Brahman's exploding all the other classes;
3. Inequality, based on the division of society into four separate and rigid sections, is unscientific and illogical;
4. The worst oppression falls on the *Shudras*, denying those benefits of education and life chances by the upper classes;
5. Inequality, based on caste system, opposes all principles of liberty, justice and brotherhood.[23]

However, in his book *Social Philosophy*, published in 1965, where Ambedkar wrote: "The caste difference has destroyed the Hindu Vansha. It drew out the Hindu society into deep darkness, and it has made the society powerless and weak one."[24] Gandhi and Ambedkar both abhorred the prevailing caste prejudices and the built-in inequalities in the then societal system of Indian society. In this context, Gandhi's views on caste system written in *Harijan* published in 1931 were quite dissimilar from the viewpoint of Ambedkar. Following this, in September 1932, under the patronage of Gandhi an All India Anti-Untouchability League was formed in India which was later on renamed as *Harijan Sevak Sangh*. During that time, under Gandhi's leadership, due to its exclusion of leaders of depressed classes on the Governing Body and on account of its weak programmes, Ambedkar was not profoundly impressed by that movement of the then Congress Party. For the overall development of depressed classes all over India, in 1934, he suggested that the League must concentrate on economic, social and educational improvement of depressed classes in India and unfortunately his proposal was rejected by the then Congress Party. In the pre-independence period, Gandhi, as an upper-caste Hindu, recognised it 'a crisis of conscience.'[25] For Ambedkar, a depressed class victim of higher-caste exploitation and denegation, it was like 'a crisis of identity.'[26] During those whirlwind hours of Indian freedom movement, Gandhi felt enormously proud of his Hindu identity and for that, he did not want to discard *varnashrama* in principle. Later on, in his book *Young India*, published in 1942, where Gandhi wrote: "*Varnashrama* as it is at present understood and practised is a monstrous parody of the original; but in order to demolish this distortion let us not seek to demolish the original."[27] Like an egalitarian and a socialist, during that time, he wanted to embark on a social mission in order to remove the old oppressive system in-built in Indian society. According to Ambedkar, a victim of prevailing inequalities inherent in Indian condition, it was not the crisis of conscience but lack of identity, which finally led him to renounce Hinduism, as his sole religion rather than to reform it. In this context, a special case to be mentioned here that, in March, 1927, Ambedkar led a movement with approximately 500 untouchables to use the water of Chawdar tank in Mahad village, Maharashtra. Following this, on August 8, 1930, as President of the First All India Depressed Classes Association (AIDCA), Ambedkar tenaciously demanded safeguards for the downtrodden untouchables within the purview of the Constitution of India. Moreover, in 1931, Ambedkar was not impressed over Gandhi's replacement of the word Harijan instead of Untouchables.[28] In the passage of time, on the eve of the Second Session of the Round Table Conference, held in March, 1931, Ambedkar met with stiff opposition from Gandhi, on the question of political rights for depressed classes of India. Consequently, an important event took place in the ambit of national domain that was, on September 24, 1932; Ambedkar signed the well-known Poona Pact on behalf of the depressed classes of India and also to ensure separate seats for them. Interestingly enough, the pact was later embodied in the Government of India Act, 1935.[29]

Ambedkar and Gandhi's Outlook on the Origin of *Shudras*

By his close scrutiny of Hindu scriptures and evolution of Hindu society, Ambedkar discovered that Brahmins did everything to strengthen the caste system for their vested interest. They added new dimensions of perversion to the original division of Hindu society into classes. For example, in *Rigveda* there is no mention of *shudras*. It mentions only three *varnas* as *Brahmins, Kshatriyas* and *Vaishyas. Satapatha Brahmana* also does not mention shudra as a separate *varna.* In this context, Ambedkar tried to prove that shudras were one of the Aryan communities and therefore formed a part of the *Kshatriyas* in the Indo-Aryan society. *Brahma Purna* mentions *shudras* as a tribe living above the Vindhyas. Ambedkar has referred to a story of the *Chandogya Upanishad* to show that *shudras* were entitled to the study of Vedas.[30] However, there was a continuous feud between *Shudra* kings and Brahmins in which Brahmins were subjected to many indignities and tyranny. So, it was quite natural that Brahmins developed hatred *shudras* who were *kshatriyas.* According to Ambedkar, first, there was change of connotation of the word *shudra.* It lost the name of the particular community or class and it became a general name for a low class people without civilisation, culture, respect, and position. Secondly, the meaning of the word shudra further widened with the passage of time and innocent people were subjected to strict code of Brahmins. Thirdly, as all social rights were linked with the performance of sanskaras, shudras were gradually denied all rights in the society and were looked as inferior by three castes. As a proof of it Ambedkar gave the instance of Shivaji's coronation ceremony. No Brahmin priest was ready to perform the coronation ceremony until Shivaji's Rajput connection was established.[31] Ambedkar took upon himself the task of fighting for the rights of aboriginal tribes (adivasis). He felt restoration of civic rights to untouchables and giving them equal rights with others was the only way to bring about a social revolution in the then Hindu society. Ambedkar therefore launched a powerful movement to bring such a revolution. Whereas like Buddha and Mahavira Gandhi accepted an integrated view of life and as such he condemned the division of religion and politics. He regarded religion and politics as two different sides of the same coin and was a devoted worshipper of the Soul and, by that relation, of God and His humanity. Although Gandhi was mainly responsible for the mighty upheaval of Indian nation who broke its old chains, his way of thinking and method of revolution were unique.

Ambedkar felt that just as individual liberty is necessary for the richness and variety of national development, so self-government is necessary for its completeness and the full deployment of national strength. Like Gandhi, Ambedkar held that if certain classes are dominant and others depressed, the result is that the potential strength of the depressed classes is so much valuable force lost to the sum of national strength. The dominant classes may undoubtedly show a splendid development and may make the nation great and famous in history, but when all is said the strength of the nation is then only the sum of the strength of a few privileged classes. While penetrating the root causes behind India's wretchedness and slumber, Ambedkar ruled that the great weakness of India in the past has been the political depression and the nullifying of the mass of the population. The two great men of India always placed India's freedom in the larger context of the destiny of the human race and said: "A step in evolution which would raise man to a higher and larger consciousness and begin the solution of the problems which have perplexed him since he first started to think and to dream of individual perfection and a perfect society."[32] Ambedkar once mentioned about Gandhi that "His greatest strength in politics was his power to convince others, especially his opponents. No other person was as friendly with the adversaries as he was, no other person could win his enemies as easily as he could. With his weapons of non-violence and within his objectives of truth, he fought the mighty British Empire."[33]

Ambedkar had total disagreement with the status and origin of *shudras* in Indian society with reference to what Gandhi believed about it. In this context, Ambedkar maintained that the caste system completely ruined the essence of the then Hindu society and reorganisation of Hindu society on the basis of *varna* system was not possible because it was very likely to degenerate into a caste system without proper legal control. Moreover, Ambedkar also felt reorganisation of Hindus on the basis of four *varnas* could prove harmful as it would have degrading effect on the mass by denying them opportunity to acquire knowledge. Hindu society must be reorganised to recognise the principles of liberty, equality and fraternity. He expressed that religious sanctions behind caste and *varna* had to be destroyed. Ambedkar said: "A society based on *varna* or caste is a society which is based on a wrong relationship. I had hoped that Mahatma would attempt to demolish my argument but instead of doing that he has merely reiterated his belief in *Chaturvarnya* without disclosing the ground on which it is based."[34]

The Road of Ideological Convergences and Divergences between Gandhi and Ambedkar

Ambedkar and Gandhi, as a defender of the downtrodden, stood and fought for overall social equality all through their entire life and in order to achieve this goal, they kept themselves engaged in the then Indian politics of social struggle. Moreover, as a social humanist, they were a staunch aficionado and supporter of democratic set-up where each and every citizen could rise to the highest position in any society. Besides this, both firmly believed that the spiritual transformation of man was the only cure from prevailing social and political evils within Indian society. It is a fact that Ambedkar and Gandhi, while striving to battle their individual causes did not propound any specific definition or theory of 'social justice' with an academic psyche. In this context, the five basic principles, from the writings and speeches of Ambedkar, through which justice can be fortified in the Indian society and they are as follows:

1. Establishing a society where individual becomes the means of all social purposes;
2. Establishing a society based on equality, liberty and fraternity;
3. Establishing democracy-political, economic and social;
4. Establishing democracy through constitutional measures and
5. Establishing democracy by breaking monopoly of upper strata on political power.[35]

In the quest for Ambedkar and Gandhi's theory of social justice, they were of the opinion that, social justice can be formulated in a free social order through which an individual is an end in itself. As a Marxist, they witnessed that the term of associated life between members of society, must be regarded by considerations based on liberty, equality and fraternity.[36] In a way these above mentioned principles of social justice of Gandhi and Ambedkar, suited for Indian society, were much similar with the principles of social justice as propounded by John Rawls in his 'Theory of Justice'. While formulating his socio-political ideas, Ambedkar entirely stood for social, economic and political equality and also for social, economic and political justice for the people of Third World countries. Later on, in a speech delivered at the All India Trade Union Workers Camp at Delhi, on September 17, 1943, where Ambedkar said: "Justice has always evoked ideas of equality, of proportion, of compensation. Equity signifies equality. Rules and regulations, right and righteousness are concerned with equality in value. If all men are equal, then all men of the same essence and the common essence entitle them to the same fundamental rights and equal liberty....In short, justice is another name of liberty, equality and fraternity.[37] At the same breathe; he wanted rights for Indian women, especially for the overall protection of their sole individual rights. In the same conference, he also reiterated that, "Democracy is not a form of government, but is a form of social organisation...Democracy is primarily a mode of associated living..."[38] While addressing in the Constituent Assembly on December 17, 1946, he said: "Democracy becomes incompatible and inconsistent with isolation and exclusiveness resulting in the distinction between the privileged and unprivileged within the country. So, true freedom was not a mere political freedom, but it has to be social, economic, and intellectual and spiritual in its favour."[39] Besides this, in his thesis entitled *The Problem of the Rupee-its Origin and its Solution* submitted to the London School of Economics where he candidly enumerated: 'the strength of a society depends upon the presence of points of contacts, possibilities of interaction between different groups that exist in it'.[40]

Ambedkar as well as Gandhi's concept of social justice was primarily related to religion i.e., religion of their own thinking and in this way they did not have any strong faith over any particular community as a whole. In the quest of their different political journeys, as a Universalist, they only believed in the religion of humanity. Subsequently, Gandhi in his book *Hind Swaraj*, published in 1941, where he wrote: "I like the religion that teaches liberty, equality and fraternity".[41] Interestingly enough, while following the above mentioned view of Gandhi, Ambedkar emphasised this humanitarian approach of Gandhi by uttering that, 'I tell you, religion is for man and not man for religion. If you want to organise, consolidate, and be successful in the world, change this religion. The religion that does not recognise you as a human being, give you water to drink, or allow you to enter in temples, is not worthy to be called a religion.'[42] After the attainment of India's political independence, in order to provide social justice to the common people, Ambedkar envisioned the operationalization of principle of equality, liberty and fraternity, etc. in the wake of an emerging democracy towards a hierarchically diverse society like India. In the post-independence period, he considered this must be the cardinal principle of any democratic form of government. For the healthy future of the emerging Indian democracy, under Marxian contour, he wanted to strengthen social and economic equality along with political consciousness. According to Ambedkar, "one of the ways to deliver social justice to the individual was like breaking the monopoly of upper strata."[43] On the basis of his extensive study and insightful knowledge for the evolution of human society and social institutions all over the globe, Ambedkar was convinced that democracy was the only form of government which could ensure liberty and equality in a just society. Ambedkar as well as Gandhi, as the prime mover and promoter of social justice and the creator of human rights in the world history, ethically stressed the need for improving the conditions of Indian labour classes in order to provide them with adequate wages, health care, compulsory insurance or social security and above all the educational opportunities to their children. In a nutshell, they were in favour of trade unions provided these institutions must work honestly within the country and as a true humanist, they always stood for the interests of all those who suffered at the hands of elite classes and exploiters in the then Indian society.

Gandhi experienced social discrimination for the first time when he was in South Africa where he engaged himself against the discriminatory attitude of the South African Government against Indians. The problems were akin to that of untouchability as migrants were treated as inferior to the local population which enjoyed numerous basic rights legally not available to Indians. It was then that Gandhi realized the extent of the impact of social discrimination on the underprivileged sections of the society including untouchables. He thought it was necessary to reconstruct the life of the nation. This was only possible through alleviating the social status of untouchables. He always considered untouchability as a cruel and inhuman institution. It violated human dignity. He did not believe that the imperial ambitions of Britain were alone responsible for our slavery but it was the negligence of our national duty which was primarily responsible for it. As he always thought untouchability an evil in Hinduism, he had no hesitation in Hinduism itself Removal of untouchability was the responsibility of the caste-Hindus towards Hinduism. Gandhi called upon the Harijans to magnify their own faults so that they looked as big as mountains and they make regular attempts to overcome them. He said to untouchables, "Never believe that since others have the same faults we need not mind our own. No matter what others do, it is your dharma to overcome the feelings which you find in yourselves." In the process of regeneration of the nation, Gandhi waged an incessant war. He said, "If we are children of the same God how can there be any rank among us." According to him, there was only one Varna, in India, the *Sudras*. He desired that all the Hindus voluntarily call themselves *Sudras*. He criticised those who would claim superiority over fellowmen. He thought there was no such thing as inherited superiority. He was happy and felt satisfied to call himself a scavenger, a spinner, a weaver, and a laborer. He was troubled to see the appalling plight of untouchables in different regions of the country. Its eradication greatly agitated his mind and he devised ways and means from time to time, through his speeches and writings. Gandhi called Harijans as men of God and felt that all the religions of the world consider God pre-eminently as the Friend of the Friendless, Help of the Helpless, and Protector of the Weak. He questioned that in India who could be mare friendless, helpless, or weaker than the 40 million or more Hindus of India who were classified as "untouchables." Therefore, if there were people who could be fitly described as men of God, they were surely these helpless, friendless, and despised people. He said that if India became free with untouchability intact, the untouchables would become worse under that *Swaraj* than they were before the freedom for the simple reason that the weakness and failings would then be buttressed up by the accession of power. Mahatma Gandhi used newspapers including Harijan and Young India to propagate his anti-untouchability views. In his writings he stressed the problem of untouchability and its removal from its roots. He felt that Hinduism, in reality, did not permit untouchability. The *Bhagavad Gita* never taught that an untouchable was in any way inferior to a Brahman. A Brahman was no more a Brahman, once he became insolvent and considered himself, a superior being. Gandhi felt that untouchability would not be removed by the force of even law. It could only be removed, when the majority of Hindus felt that it was a crime against God and man and were ashamed of it. The aid of law had to be invoked when it came in the way of reform, i.e., opening of a temple. He described the social position of untouchables as follows: "Socially they are lepers. Economically they are worse than slaves. Religiously they are denied entrance to places we miscall 'houses of God." Gandhiji never stopped fighting against untouchability. He considered it a blot on Hinduism. He said that a religion that established the worship of the cow could not in all probability countenance or warrants a cruel and inhuman boycott of human beings. Hindus would never deserve freedom, nor get it if they allowed their noble religion to be disgraced by the retention of the taint of untouchability. He found Harijan Sevak Sangh in 1932. G.D. Birla was its president and Thakkar Bapa its Secretary. He always preached among the Harijans, the importance of cleanliness, abstention from carrion-eating and intoxicating drinks and drugs, requirement of taking education themselves and giving it to their children, also abstention from eating the leavings from caste Hindus' plates. Gandhi, therefore, worked very hard and sincerely for their upliftment. The fact that he had many other tasks on hand did not stop him from taking up their cause and he devoted considerable time and energy to bring an end to untouchability.

Ambedkar felt that Hinduism was once a missionary religion but it ceased to be so with the advent of caste system among the Hindus. Caste is inconsistent with conversion. Hindu society is a collection of castes and each caste a close corporation which has no place for a conversion. Indian tribes are backward solely because of reluctance on part of the caste-Hindus to "adopt" them. The caste-Hindus deliberately try to prevent the lower caste, within Hinduism from rising to the cultural level of the higher castes. Caste system breeds anti-social spirit, because of the division of the population into various castes. It has killed public spirit, damaged the sense of public charity, and made public opinion impossible.

Ambedkar traced the origin of "untouchability" to "contempt of the Buddhist and beef-eating by untouchable communities." Ambedkar reiterated that the "Broken men" of the past are the untouchables and they were Buddhists. They never respected Brahmins and considered them impure. Brahmins did not respect the Buddhists either. Brahmins preached against Buddhists and as a result the broken men came to be regarded as untouchables. According to Ambedkar, meat of cows forms a part of the food of untouchable communities of the country. On the other hand, he said no Hindu community however low, excepting untouchables, touches cow meat. He tries to trace the origin of untouchability to the "beef-eating" habit of untouchables. He felt initially all including Brahmins, ate meat including that of cow. Brahmins stopped eating beef to keep themselves apart from the beef-eating people, including the Buddhists. Ambedkar categorically mentioned that if beef-eating had remained a secular affair and not a religious one, a mere matter of individual taste, untouchability would not have arisen. Subsequently, in 1927, at Mahad, he led a 10,000-strong crowd to protest against the Caste-Hindus' decision not to let the untouchables draw water from the public wells. Ambedkar, with 10,000 people, marched to Chowkdar Tank and exercised their civic rights to use the water. This showed untouchables that their strength lay in their very numbers. It was the first of many similar actions which later followed. It also drew attention to the nature of the untouchables' complaints regarding their civil rights. The protest caused great concern to many orthodox Hindus. Afterwards, in 1929, he began temple-entry campaign and many temples were closed down rather than allow in untouchables. Untouchables, 15,000 in numbers, tried to gain entry to the Shree Rama temple at Nasik. They were not allowed inside the temple and riots broke out when they persisted in their attempts to enter the temple. Although the temple entry campaign did not produce sweeping reforms for untouchables, it had important effects in India and the outside world. Ambedkar became the undisputed leader of untouchables and the untouchables realized that they needed to come together to face the common problems they were facing. The latter became increasingly involved in the numerous political problems of untouchables during that time, which he believed were crucial. In the chronology of historical developments of India, when the Simon Commission came to India in 1928 to examine and report on the government system, the then Congress Party boycotted it. Ambedkar, however, used the occasion to explain the grievances of the Dalits and suggested some ways to improve their position. Besides, Ambedkar went on to represent the untouchables at the First Round Table Conference in London (1930).

The Congress Party boycotted the Conference and most of the Indian representatives during that time strongly demanded 'Dominion Status' for their country. Ambedkar used the conference as an opportunity to influence public opinion. He also attended the Second Round Table Conference in 1931 at which he demanded separate electorates for untouchables to which Gandhi opposed. In 1932, the Communal Award was announced in which the Dalits were awarded two votes—one to elect their representatives to separate seats in the Provincial Assemblies and the other to vote with Hindus in general constituencies. Other minorities were given separate electorates. Gandhi was opposed to this award and he started fast-unto-death. He was against dividing the Hindus into untouchables and non-untouchables. Gandhiji believed that untouchability was more of a moral problem and not one that could be dealt with Constitutional principles. In the post-Gandhian era, constant fear of Gandhi's death made Ambedkar to conclude an agreement with the then Congress representatives, which later came to be known as the Poona Pact. As per the Pact, more seats were reserved for the Dalits, but the candidates had to be chosen by joint electorates of both Hindus and untouchables. In 1935, Ambedkar decided to leave Hinduism and thought of embracing Sikhism. He also called upon his cadres to give up the temple entry movement, because it was unlikely to succeed and a change of religion made it irrelevant. He penned a book titled *Annihilation of Caste* in which he elaborated the reasons why he had rejected Hinduism. He said that the caste system was based on religious principles and the caste system can only be abolished if the religious principles on which it is based are destroyed. In the late 1930s, consequently, he formed the Independent Labor Party. However, in 1937 election for Provincial Councils, it did well though the Congress won most seats. Ambedkar was elected and used his position to fight for the Dalits. In the coming years, Ambedkar founded the All India Scheduled Castes Federation, a political body for the Dalits in 1942. In 1945 elections, it failed to win a single seat. The Scheduled Castes Federation fought for better representation for Dalits in the Cabinet. As a result, the untouchable representation soon doubled. As a result, in 1947, the Constituent Assembly abolished untouchability. This constitutional clause had failed to abolish untouchability completely from the womb of the then Indian society. In 1947, he became Law Minister in the Congress Government. He cooperated with Congress as much as he could and simultaneously he was the Drafting Committee Chairman which was given the responsibility to draft the Constitution for the country. However, Ambedkar resigned from the Cabinet with the complaint that the Government was not doing enough for Dalits. He spent rest of his life for laying foundations for the future of the Dalits and strove for the redistribution of surplus and wasteland to untouchables. He founded Ambedkar's People's Education Society, under which he established many colleges and schools and did the groundwork for the setting up of Republican Party of India. In those whirlwind days, he along with half a million embraced Buddhism, and propagated the message among untouchables to embrace Buddhism as it does not have caste system in it.

Dalit Movement as a Vehicle for Humanitarian Struggle in India

Ambedkar and Gandhi, both time and again, explained in their writings and speeches, the origin and mechanism of caste system, along with the multiple types of culture, rituals and manners as its allied institutions in Indian society. During that time, they were both very critical of the *Varnashram Dharma* as interpreted by Manu, and according to them, it was exclusively responsible for the social diseases that immensely afflicted the Shudras and the untouchables more than any other social groups. Besides this, Gandhi and Ambedkar had a deep understanding and knowledge of India's the then societal process particularly on Hindu society. Moreover, they also had a sound understanding about the then social, economic and political evils of the country. That is why, they by and large emphasised the singular need for social action based on drastic social change to strengthen the inner roots of democracy, socialism and humanism in India. In this context, Ambedkar and Gandhi both were a serious Indian sociologist and most importantly social philosopher who time and again explained the impact of social values in a notable and radical way which was highly indigenous in nature. In the post-independence years, they both developed a humanistic sociological outlook and economics of their own. What is more, in the whole social analysis that one finds in Ambedkar and Gandhi's writings and speeches was basically their understanding of democratic and social humanism suited for the modern global scenario. In short, Ambedkar as a Dalit leader of India in the pre and post-independence years, idealized with the common man as the main theme of his entire socio-political philosophy. In fact, they were completely unique, radical and revolutionary in their overall approach towards the interpretation of human situation and its intermittent improvement in Indian society. Likewise, Ambedkar and Gandhi's movement of conversion, was, in no way, motivated by any mere material gain either for themselves or for the people whom they guided throughout their entire life. In this context, undeniably Ambedkar and Gandhi were a social emancipator within the country, for all those hapless people who have been deprived repeatedly from human dignity for a long period of time and above all from respectful social existence. In this context, while concluding his observation about Gandhi and Ambedkar collectively, Dr. D.R. Jatav has rightly described Ambedkar and Gandhi as a social humanist of India in the 20th century.[44] Therefore, in a nutshell, in the pre and post-independence years, they unrelentingly waged a struggle against the then hierarchical Hindu social system in order to rebuild a new just social order based on freedom, equality and justice, etc.

Conclusion

Leadership is something that nobody gets on demand instead it comes inherently with leaders as rewards. For instance, Sir Aurobindo, Swami Vivekananda and Lokmanya Tilak were the few leaders till 1920s who stirred India with their deeds and powered equally with the words. After the death of Tilak, the mantle of leadership came naturally to Gandhi, who during that time already had lead few nationalist movements such as Champaran and then Khilafat to motivate the masses to take part in India's battle for freedom. India at that time needed the same kind of leaders such as Ambedkar and Gandhi who could stir the nation for a radical change towards nation building with the help of their erstwhile leadership. In this article an attempt has been made to discuss some themes of social justice based on Indian soil and in this connection, it also highlighted the importance of Ambedkar and Gandhi's theory of social justice as a whole with a contemporary outlook. As a prime mover of Indian national struggle, Ambedkar and Gandhi's life were full of ventures and challenges, which stemmed from the pains and plights of the downtrodden. Therefore, they always stressed: the highest good for man was to realise the basic importance of being a 'real human being.'[45] So, in that sense Ambedkar as well as Gandhi was a great optimist of their time. Simultaneously, as a true moralist, they had immense faith over man's total capacity to distinguish between true and false, right and wrong and that is why, on the eve of

India's independence, Ambedkar adopted a realistic and moderate outlook when he felt that the British were about to withdraw from India. Furthermore, in 1946, in order to safeguard the rights of the depressed classes of India, he gradually accepted the membership of the Constituent Assembly and decided to cooperate with the then Congress Party. Ambedkar and Gandhi tried to apply their own logic to politics, religion and social philosophy of India. Like Gandhi, Ambedkar was as a pure idealist, who always believed in the overall purification of means to achieve ends. Interestingly enough, as a Gandhiate, Ambedkar thought that only good means could bring good and lasting results within the Indian society and though ideologically he had great differences with Gandhi regarding many the then issues starting from caste movement to harijan development for India. In the post-independence scenario, Ambedkar became a constitutional liberal and a moderate in outlook and firmly believed that constitutionalism could bring more faithful results in the then Indian society for the overall development of the lower strata and though in this field of action he had uncountable ideological differences with Gandhi. According to them, social changes could be brought about in the then Indian society by various means of which the most important one was mobile and consolidated ideas for rapid socio-developmental process. On the eve of India's independence, they initiated to form a particular forum within Indian society so that the masses or those interested in bringing about a thorough social change could express their solidarity till the achievement of the purpose. Both had an eye on the rampant poverty and were very much struck by pitiable conditions of half-nourished people of India with miserably low living standard. In the pre-independence period, they entered into mainstream politics to promote the cause of social service and in this case their special focus always was the total development of people's power in India. That is why they followed the demands of contemporary history and politics and moved accordingly. In fact, they were the chief spokesmen of their time and were not a political ideologue in a true academic sense and their political ideas can be re-collected from their writings, speeches and multiple national activities. They were by nature a true emancipator of a just cause, democrat, secular, nationalist, internationalist, liberal, idealist and above all a patriot and social revolutionary in their overall socio-political outlook and would remain forever in the pages of world history.

END NOTES

1. W.N. Kuber, *Ambedkar: A Critical Study*, Shivlal Agarwal Compnay, New Delhi, 1977, p.101.
2. B.R. Ambedkar, *Who Were Sudras*, Saroj Publications, Hyderabad, 1990, p.11.
3. B.R. Ambedkar, *Dr. Babasaheb Ambedkar Writings and Speeches*, Vol.3, Mumbai Education Department, Government of Maharashtra, 1987, p.13
4. B.R. Ambedkar, *Babasaheb Ambedkar Writings and Speeches,* Vol.1, Mumbai Education Department, Government of Maharashtra, 1982, p.101.
5. B.R. Ambedkar, *The Untouchable*, Bheem Patrika Publication, Jalandhar, 1952, p.17.
6. B.R. Ambedkar, *Communal Deadlock and a Way to Solve it,* S.Chand and Company, New Delhi, 1948, p.11.
7. B.R. Ambedkar, *What Congress and Gandhi have done to Untouchables*, L.N. Agarwal, Agra, 1946, p.17.
8. B.R. Ambedkar, *Mr. Gandhi and the Emancipations of the Untouchables,* Indian Printing Works, Lahore, 1943, p.30.
9. Ahluwalia Shashi (ed.), *B.R. Ambedkar and Human Rights,* N.P.H, Ahmedabad, 1981, p.21.
10. Source Material on *Gandhi and the Movement of Hindu Society*, Vol. 1, Govt. of Maharashtra, Bombay, 1982, pp.37-61.
11. *Ibid.*, pp.62-64.
12. B.N. Serbhamani, *Mahatma Gandhi and Ambedkar: Crusader against Untouchability*, Cambridge Book University Press, New Delhi, 1997, p.11.
13. N.K. Bose, *Selections from Gandhi,* Motilal Banarasidas, Ahmedabad, 1948, p.21.
14. Niranjan Dhar, *Ambedkar, Gandhi and Roy*, Minerva Associates Publications, Bombay, 1996, p.45.
15. D.M. Dutta, *The Philosophy of Mahatma Gandhi*, Bharatiya Vidya Bhawan, Bombay, 1957, p.19.
16. Sankar Ghosh, *Political Ideas and Caste Movements in India,* Oxford University Press, Delhi, 1982, p.101.
17. D.R. Jatava, *Dynamics of Ambedkar Ideology*, Orient Longman, Bombay, 2001, p.3.
18. D.R. Jatava, B.R. Ambedkar: *A Vision of Man and Morals*, The Perennial Press, Bombay, 1999, p.101.
19. D.R. Jatava, *The Critics of Dr. Ambedkar*, Chetna Publications, New Delhi, 1997, p.23.
20. Kasiprasad Jaiswal, *Hindu Polity*, The Bangalore Printing Company Ltd., Bangalore, 1955, p.29.
21. W. Renneth Jones, *Socio-Religious Movement in British India,* Cambridge Book University Press, New Delhi, 1997, p.34.
22. Robin Jeanette, *Dr. Ambedkar and His Movement,* Dr. Ambedkar Publication Society, Hyderabad, 1964, p.45.
23. K.N. Kadam, *Dr. Babasaheb Ambedkar and Significant,* Dr. Ambedkar Publication Society, Hyderabad, 1989, p.39.
24. W.N. Kuber, *Ambedkar A Critical Study*, n.1, p.101.
25. G.S. Lokhande, *Bhim Rao Ramji Ambedkar: A Study in Social Democracy*, Sterling Publication, New Delhi, 1987, p.57.
26. P.K. Mohapatra, *Social Justice: A Philosophical Perspective*, D.K. Printers, New Delhi, 1999, p.34.
27. K.M. Panikar, *Caste and Democracy*, Hagarh Press London, 1993, p.56.
28. V.T. Patil (ed.), *Studies on Gandhi and Ambedkar*, Shivlal Agarwal Company, Delhi, 1971, p.67.

29. Ganesh Prasad, *Gandhi and Ambedkar: A Study in Colonial Liberalism*, Ajanta Publications, Delhi, 1962, p.55.
30. For a detailed understanding of Ambedkar's detail classification of the depressed class in India see, story of Shudra Janasruti Vedas by Raikva—*Babasaheb Ambedkar: Writings and Speeches*, Vol.VII, p.108.
31. *Ibid.*, pp.111-112.
32. Babasaheb Ambedkar: *Writings and Speeches*, Vol. V, Mumbai Education Department, Govt. of Maharashtra, 1988, pp.123-124.
33. *Ibid.*, pp.77-79.
34. *Ibid.*, pp.87-88.
35. B.K. Roy, *Socio-Political Views of Gandhi and Ambedkar*, Rajkamal Prakashan, Delhi, 1981, p.11.
36. S. Radhakrishnan (ed.), *Ambedkar and Mahatma Gandhi: Essays and Reflections*, George Allen and Unwin, London, 1949, p.34.
37. B.G. Roy, *Contemporary Indian Philosophers*, Kiitabistan, Allahabad, 1947, p.6.
38. Sushbhan Chandra Sarkar (ed.), *Gandhi and Ambedkar on Indian Economy*, Popular Book Depot, Bombay, 1981, p.77.
39. J.D. Sethi, *Ambedkar and Gandhi: A Symposium*, Vikas Publishing House, New Delhi, 1978, p.101.
40. Iqbal Singh, *Gandhi and Ambedkar: Life, Writings and Speeches*, Asia Publishing House, New Delhi, 1963, p.67.
41. A.K. Sen, *Gandhi and Ambedkar: The Representative Man*, Asia Publishing House, New Delhi, 1956, p.89.
42. B.S. Sharma, *Ambedkar as a Political Thinker*, Indian Press, Allahabad, 1956, p.90.
43. A.R. Wadia (ed.), *History and Philosophy of Social Work in India*, Allied Publishers, Delhi, 1961, p.89.
44. Shushma Yadav, *Social Justice: Ambedkar and Gandhi's Vision*, Dr. Ambedkar Studies Centre Lecture Series-no.2., Department of Sociology, Jammu, 2006, p.89.
45. *Ibid.*, p.90.

Bibliography

Primary Sources

Ambedkar said this during his speech delivered as Chairman of the Constitution Drafting Committee in the Constituent Assembly on 4 November 1948, CAD.

B.R. Ambedkar, "Writing and Speeches", Vol. I, 1979, p.353.

B.R. Ambedkar, The Buddha and His Dhamma, (Dr. Baba Saheb Ambedkar Writings and Speeches, Vol. 11), Education Department, Government of Maharashtra, Bombay, 1992.

Babasaheb Ambedkar Writing and Speeches, Government of Maharashtra, Vol. 3.

Central Water Commission (2016), Ambedkar's Contribution on Water Resource Development, A research Project by Central Water Commission, Ministry of Water Resources, River Development and Ganga Rejuvenation, Central Water Commission: New Delhi.

Constituent Assembly Debate, Vol. V, p. 788.

Constituent Assembly Debates, Vol. XI, Lok Sabha Secretariat, , p.973.

Educational Statistics at a Glance (2014), Government of India, Ministry of Human Resource Development, Bureau of Planning, Monitoring and Statistics, New Delhi.

Elementary Education in India Trends 2005 to 2014, Sarva Shiksha Abhiyan (SSA), Published by National University of Educational Planning and Administration, New Delhi, India.

Eleventh Five Year Plan (2007-12), Inclusive Growth, Vol. 1, Chapter VI, Social Justice.

Raising Agricultural Productivity and Making Farming Remunerative for Farmers, An Occasional Paper of NITI Aayog, Government of India, 16 December 2015.

Secondary Education India, State Report Cards (2013), Rashtrya Madhyamik Shikha Abhiyan, (RMSA) U-Dise, Published by National University of Educational Planning and Aministration, New Delhi, India.

State Report Cards 2013-14 (2013), U-DISE 2013-14, National University of Educational Planning and Administration 17-B, Sri Aurobindo Marg, New Delhi.

The BBC Radio Talk, Dr. Ambedkar on 3rd October, 1954.

Secondary Sources

Articles

B.R. Ambedkar, Small Holdings in India and Their Remedies, Published in *Journal of the Indian Economic Society*, Vol. I. 1918.

Balakrishnan Chandrasekaran, B.R. Ambedkar, The Greatest Free Market Economist of India, in *Economics*, January 22, 2014.

Barnwal, Bijay K., "Dr. B.R. Ambedkar's Quest for Gender Equality: Its Relevance in Contemporary Feminist Discourse", Online International Interdisciplinary Research Journal, (Bi Monthly),

Bhalchandra Mungerkar, "Annihilating Caste", *Frontline*, Vol. 28, Issue 15, Jul.16-29, 2011.

Bharati, T., "Ambedkar and Uplift of Women," published in an edited book Ambedkar and Social Justice, Volume II, 1992.

Bharti Chhibber, Globalisation and its Impact on Women: *A Critical Assessment, Mainstream*, Vol. XLVII, No. 21, May 9, 2009.

Bhimrao Ambedkar, Small Holdings in India and Their Remedies, *Journal of the Indian Economic Society*, Vol. I, 1918.

Brij Kishore Sharma, "A Product of Joint Efforts", *Organiser*, November 24, 2015.

Cohen, Stephen P. (May 1969), "The Untouchable Soldier: Caste, Politics, and the Indian Army", *The Journal of Asian Studies*, 28 (3).

D'Souza, Rohan (2000), "Whey Ambedkar Should be Against Large Dams", Seminar 496.

Dhanvijay, Ms. Vaishali, "DR. Babasaheb Ambedkar's efforts for women empowerment and present status of Women in Society," *Electronic International Interdisciplinary Research Journal* (*EIIRJ*), Vol. I, Issue II, April 2012.

Dr. Vijay G., "Dr. B.R. Ambedkar's Contribution for Women's Rights", *Variorum, Multi Disciplinary e Research Journal*, Vol. 2, Issue I, August 2011.

Gurnam Chand, "Dr. Ambedkar: Architect of the Indian Constitution", *Mainstream Weekly*, Vol. XLIX, No. 17, April 16, 2011.

Jafferlot Christopher: 'Which Ambedkar', *The Indian Express*, 26.12.2015.

Kamble, G.S. (2014), "Dr. B.R. Ambedkar's Contribution in Formulation of Water Policy," *Research Direction*, Vol. 2, 2014.

Kotzee B. (2013), "Introduction: Education, Social Epistomology and Virtue Epistomology", *Journal of Philosophy of Education*, Vol. 47, No. 2.

Krishna Gopal, "BR Ambedkar's Ideas on Economy Need to be Studied," *Economic Times*, June 22, 2015.

Mukherji. N. (2002), "Academic Philosophy in India", *Economic and Political Weekly*, Vol. XXXVII, No. 10

Omvedt, Gail (2012), "A Part That Parted", *Outlook*, August 20, New Delhi.

Prof. Upendra Baxi: "How not to recall an icon", *The Indian Express*, 18.04.2016.

R.G. Kadapatti and S.T. Bagalkoti, "Small Farms and Agricultural Productivity A Macro Analysis," *International Journal of Social Science Studies*, Vol. 2, No. 3 July 2014.

S. Mahendra Dev, "Small Farmers in India: Challenges and Opportunities," *Indira Gandhi Institute of Development Research*, Mumbai, June 2012.

Shashi, S.S. (ed), "Ambedkar and Social Justice", Volume II, Director Publications Division, Ministry of Information and Broadcasting, Government of India, Patiala House, New Delhi, 1992.

Shweta Wankhede, Impact of Dr. Ambedkar's Thoughts on Indian Economy, *Dr. Babasaheb Ambedkar International Association for Education, Japan.*

Shyam Chand, "Dr. Ambedkar on Democracy", *Mainstream*, Vol. XLV-51, 2007.

Sirswal. R.D. (2011). "Dr. Ambedkar's Ideas on Education and Social Change," *Weslyan Journal of Research*. Vol. 4, No. 1.

Venkatesh Atherya, "A New Resonance," *Frontline*, Vol. 19, Issue 15, July 20 to August 02, 2002.

Books

A.K. Sen, *Gandhi and Ambedkar: The Representative Man*, Asia Publishing House, New Delhi, 1956.

A.R. Wadia (ed.), *History and Philosophy of Social Work in India*, Allied Publishers, Delhi, 1961.

Achary Kautilya: 'Arthshastra', Rajpal and Sons, Delhi, 2000.

Ahir, D.C. (1990), *The Legacy of Dr. Ambedkar*, B.R. Publishing Corporation, New Delhi.

Ahluwalia Shashi (ed.), *B.R. Ambedkar and Human Rights*, N.P.H, Ahmedabad, 1981.

Ambedkar, B.R. (1946), "*Who Were Shudras?*" Bombay, Thacker and Company, pp.16-17.

Ambedkar, Bhimrao Ramji (1946), "Chapter X: Social Stagnation". *Pakistan and the Partition of India*, Bombay: Thackers Publishers.

Arun Shourie, *Worshiping False God*, Rupa & Co, New Delhi, 1997, Romila Thapar, 'Interpreting Early India', Oxford University Press, New Delhi, 1992.

B.G. Roy, *Contemporary Indian Philosophers*, Kiitabistan, Allahabad, 1947.

B.K. Roy, *Socio-Political Views of Gandhi and Ambedkar*, Rajkamal Prakashan, Delhi, 1981.

B.N. Serbhamani, *Mahatma Gandhi and Ambedkar: Crusader against Untouchability*, Cambridge Book University Press, New Delhi, 1997.

B.R. Ambedkar, *Communal Deadlock and a Way to Solve it*, S. Chand & Co., New Delhi, 1948.

B.R. Ambedkar, *Dr. Babasaheb Ambedkar Writings and Speeches*, Vol. 3, Mumbai Education Department, Government of Maharashtra, 1987.

B.R. Ambedkar, *Mr. Gandhi and the Emancipations of the Untouchables*, Indian Printing Works, Lahore, 1943.

B.R. Ambedkar, *The Buddha and the Future of his Religion*, Bhim Patrika Publication, Jalandhar, 1975.

B.R. Ambedkar, *What Congress and Gandhi have done to Untouchables*, L.N. Agarwal, Agra, 1946.

B.R. Ambedkar, *Who Were Sudras*, Saroj Publications, Hyderabad, 1990.

B.R. Ambedkar: *What Congress and Gandhi have done to the Untouchables*, Thacker & Company Ltd., Bombay, 1945.

B.S. Sharma, *Ambedkar as a Political Thinker*, Indian Press, Allahabad, 1956.

Baisantry, D.K., *Ambedkar The Total Revolutionary*, Segment Book Distributors: New Delhi.

Chalam, K.S. (1993), *The Relevance of Ambedkarism in India*, Rawat Publications, Jaipur and New Delhi.

Chalam, K.S. (2008), *Modernisation and Dalit Education: Ambedkar's Vision*, Rawat Publications New Delhi.

D.C. Ahir, Dr. Ambedkar Pilgrimage to Buddhism, Dr. Ambedkar Buddhism and Social Change, (ed.) A.K. Narain, D.C, Ahir, B.R. Publication, New Delhi, 1994.

D.M. Dutta, *The Philosophy of Mahatma Gandhi*, Bharatiya Vidya Bhawan, Bombay, 1957.

D.R. Jatava, B.R. Ambedkar: *A Vision of Man and Morals*, The Perennial Press, Bombay, 1999.

D.R. Jatava, *Dynamics of Ambedkar Ideology*, Orient Longman, Bombay, 2001.

D.R. Jatava, *The Critics of Dr. Ambedkar*, Chetna Publications, New Delhi, 1997.

Debjani Ganguly, *Caste and Dalit Life Worlds: Postcolonial Perspectives*, Orient Longman Private Limited (South Asian Edition), New Delhi, 2008.

Dr. Babasaheb Ambedkar: Writings and Speeches.

G.S. Lokhande, *Bhim Rao Ramji Ambedkar: A Study in Social Democracy*, Sterling Publication, New Delhi, 1987.

Gail Omvedt, *Ambedkar: Towards an Enlightened India*, Penguin Books India, Delhi, 2004,

Ganesh Prasad, *Gandhi and Ambedkar: A Study in Colonial Liberalism*, Ajanta Publications, Delhi, 1962.

Ganguly, Debjani and Docker, John (eds.) (2007), *Rethinking Gandhi and Nonviolent Relationality: Global Perspectives*, Routledge studies in the modern history of Asia, London: Routledge.

Gopal Guru (2002), Ambedkar's Idea of Social Justice in Ghanshyam Shah (ed), *Dalits and the State*, Concept Publishing Company, New Delhi.

Granville Austin (1999), *The Indian Constitution: Cornerstone of a Nation*, Oxford University Press, New Delhi.

H.C. Warren, *Vasuddhimagga*, chapter 18, Motilal Banarsidass Publishers, Delhi, 1999.

Iqbal Singh, *Gandhi and Ambedkar: Life, Writings and Speeches,* Asia Publishing House, New Delhi, 1963.

J.D. Sethi, *Ambedkar and Gandhi: A Symposium,* Vikas Publishing House, New Delhi, 1978.

Jadhav, Narendra (2015), *Ambedkar and Economic Extraordinary,* Konarak Publishers Private Limited: New Delhi.

Jadhav, Narendra, *Ambedkar Speaks* Vol. 1: Konark Publishers: New Delhi: 2013.

Jatava, B.R. (2008), *Ambedkar in Modern World,* ABD Publishers, Jaipur.

Jatava, D.R. (2001), *Sociological Thoughts of B.R. Ambedkar,* ABD Publishers, India.

Jatava, D.R. (1999), *B.R. Ambedkar A Vision of Man and Morals,* ABD Publishers, India.

K.M. Panikar, *Caste and Democracy,* Hagarh Press London, 1993.

K.N. Kadam, *Dr. Babasaheb Ambedkar and Significant,* Dr. Ambedkar Publication Society, Hyderabad, 1989.

Kasiprasad Jaiswal, *Hindu Polity,* The Bangalore Printing Company Ltd., Bangalore, 1955.

Keer Dhananjay (1954), *Dr. Babasaheb Ambedkar: Life & Mission,* Mumbai: Popular Prakashan (reprint 2016).

M.V. Kamath's Book Review of a Book by Sheshrao Chavan, "The Constitutionof India: Role of Dr. B.R. Ambedkar," Atlantic Publishers, 2014.

M.V. Paylee, *Constitutional Government in India,* Bombay: Asia Publishing House, 1960, Constituent Assembly Debates, November 26, 1949, Vol. XI, p.994.

Mahatma Gandhi, *India of My Dreams,* Rajpal & Sons, New Delhi 2008.

N.K. Bose, *Selections from Gandhi,* Motilal Banarasidas, Ahmedabad, 1948.

Naik C.D. and R.S. Kureel (2013), *Dr Ambedkar's Vision for Nation Building,* Indore: Shree Parasmani Publication, *Ambedkar and Constitution* by Dharam C. Vyas.

Naik. C.D. (2003), *Thoughts and Philosophy of Dr. B.R. Ambedkar,* Sarup and Sons Publisher, New Delhi.

Niranjan Dhar, *Ambedkar, Gandhi and Roy,* Minerva Associates Publications, Bombay, 1996.

P.K. Mohapatra, *Social Justice: A Philosophical Perspective,* D.K. Printers, New Delhi, 1999.

P.N. Krishna Mani, "Dr. B.R. Ambedkar: His Role in the Constituent Assembly", in *Dr. B.R. Ambedkar: The man and His Message*, New Delhi: Prentice Hall of India, 1991.

P.T. Borale, *Dr. Ambedkar and the Constitution of India*, Chapter Eleven, *Political Idea and Leadership of Dr. B.R. Ambedkar*, Pune: Vishwanil Publications, 1989.

Quack, Johannes (2011), *Disenchanting India: Organised Rationalism and Criticism of Religion in India*, Oxford University Press.

Rafaqi M. (2013), Dalit Education and Government Policies, *Research Journal of Humanities and Social Sciences*, Vol. 3, Issue 3.

Raut, Nitin, and Ambedkar on Population Policy contemporary Relevance, Shipra Publications: New Delhi: 2014.

Robin Jeanette, *Dr. Ambedkar and His Movement*, Dr. Ambedkar Publication Society, Hyderabad, 1964.

Romila Thapar, *Ancient Indian Social History Some Interpretations*, Orient Longman Private Limited, 1979, New Delhi, 1978.

Romila Thapar, Early India: From the origin to AD 1300, Penguin Books India (P) Ltd., Delhi. 2002.

Romila Thapar, *Interpreting Early India*, Oxford University Press, New Delhi, 1992.

S. Radhakrishnan (ed.), *Ambedkar and Mahatma Gandhi: Essays and Reflections*, George Allen and Unwin, London, 1949.

Sangharakshita (2006), "Milestone on the Road to conversion", *Ambedkar and Buddhism* (1st South Asian edn.). New Delhi: Motilal Banarsidass Publishers.

Sankar Ghosh, *Political Ideas and Caste Movements in India*, Oxford University Press, Delhi, 1982.

Suresh Mane, *Some Reflections on the Constitutional Philosophy of Ambedkar*, Chapter Five, "Studies in Ambedkar" (Delhi: 1995).

Suresh R., *Foreign Policy and Human Rights: An Indian Perspective*, Madhav Books, Gurgaon, 2009.

Suresh R., "Human Security in India: Problems and Policy Options," *International Journal of South Asian Studies*, Vol. 5, No. 2, July-Dec 2012.

Suresh. R., *The Political Dimension of Globalisation: A Human Rights Perspective*, in Dr Mohanakumar (Ed.) Globalisation, State and Democracy in India, Serials Publications, New Delhi, 2016.

Sushbhan Chandra Sarkar (ed.), *Gandhi and Ambedkar on Indian Economy*, Popular Book Depot, Bombay, 1981.

Swami Vekananda, *The complete works of Swami Vivekananda*, Advait Ashram (Publication Dept.), Calcutta, 1986.

Swami Vivekananda, *The Complete Works*, Vol. VII, Calcutta, 1979.

T.K. Oommen, *Nation, Civil Society and Social Movements*, Sage Publications, New Delhi,

T.W. Rhys Davids, tr. *Dialogue of Buddha*, London, 1950.

Thomas Mathew, *Ambedkar: Reform or Revolution*, Segment Book Distributors, University of California. 1991.

Thomas Mathew, *Constitution Making*, Chapter 13, "Ambedkar: Reform or Revolution (New Delhi: Segment Books, 1991)

Upinder Singh, *A History of Ancient and Medieval India: From the Stone Age to the 12th Century*, Dorling Kindersley (India) Pvt. Ltd, Delhi, 2009.

V.T. Patil (ed.), *Studies on Gandhi and Ambedkar*, Shivlal Agarwal Company, Delhi, 1971.

Valeskar, P. (2012), *Education for Liberation: Ambedkar's Thoughts and Dalit Women's Perspective*, Sage.

W. Renneth Jones, *Socio-Religious Movement in British India*, Cambridge Book University Press, New Delhi, 1997.

W.N. Kuber, *Ambedkar: A Critical Study*, Shivlal Agarwal Compnay, New Delhi, 1977.

Index